ANDREW MAR...
non-fiction books...
way theme, and h...
Stringer' series, set on the railways of early 20th Century
Britain. The most recent Stringer novel is *Powder Smoke*. His
most recent non-railway novels are *Soot*, *The Martian Girl* and
The Winker. He also writes and records songs under the name
Brunswick Green. Martin's website is jimstringernovels.com.

Praise for *Yorkshire*

'Very funny and touching ... Martin is a journalist
and novelist with splendid observational skills and a warm,
comic touch, and he spots regional characteristics others
have missed ... Delightful and unexpected facts abound:
who knew that the London Tube map was allegedly
inspired by York's medieval street pattern?'
Daily Mail

'Martin guides up through the geography of "God's
Own Country", but also writes amusingly about the blunt
pithiness associated with a place that shows 'the merest
glimmer of humour, like a small spark struck from a flint"
TLS

'A genuinely funny writer ... also a daring one'
The Times

'He can stop you in your tracks with a well-turned phrase'
Sunday Times

'There is no one else who is writing like Andrew Martin
today ... unique and important'
Guardian

'Iconoclastic, entertaining and often devastatingly witty'
Independent

Andrew Martin

Yorkshire

There and Back

corsair

CORSAIR

First published in the United Kingdom in 2022 by Corsair
This paperback edition published in 2023

1 3 5 7 9 10 8 6 4 2

A CIP catalogue record for this book
is available from the British Library.

ISBN: 978-1-4721-5487-3

Printed and bound in Great Britain by Clays Ltd, Elcograf S.p.A.

Papers used by Corsair are from well-managed forests
and other responsible sources.

MIX
Supporting
responsible forestry
FSC® C104740

Corsair
An imprint of
Little, Brown Book Group
Carmelite House
50 Victoria Embankment
London EC4Y 0DZ

An Hachette UK Company
www.hachette.co.uk

www.littlebrown.co.uk

Contents

Pike Hills

Pike Hills Golf Club, just outside York, used to be a railway golf club, in that it was established by York Railway Institute and subsidised by the Welfare Section of British Rail. Non-railway members could become associate members, but they paid higher subscriptions. As a boy in the 1970s, I was enrolled as a junior member by my dad, who was a railway employee. He used to say, 'I can't think of a better life than that of a professional golfer,' and he'd enrolled me on the off chance I might be eligible for that career. Having watched me play golf for a few weeks, he modified his statement: 'If you can't be a professional golfer, the life of a greenkeeper on a golf course wouldn't be at all bad.'

In his late teens, Dad had played football professionally for York City, albeit only for a couple of games. York City naturally required him to work Saturday afternoons, as did his employer, British Railways. In the 1940s, the question of whether to be a professional footballer or a booking clerk in York Station was finely balanced, and Dad chose BR. His sporting skills did not extend to golf; he just liked golf courses, especially Pike Hills, which was next to a mysterious, ancient wood called – in my day – Askham Bog. It was believed that if you went into Askham Bog and came out again you could consider yourself lucky. Like much of York, Askham Bog has been gentrified, so it's now 'Askham Nature Reserve', and by the same token (to my mind) Pike Hill is no longer a railway course, just as the Railway Institute is no longer a railway institution even though it remains right next to the railway station. It's officially called RI, which stands for anything you want.

On visits to York from my home in London, I sometimes play a round at Pike Hills, usually with my boyhood friend Paul, who grew up in the same York suburban street as me. On a grey, drizzly afternoon a couple of years ago, I was on the first tee with Paul. I hit my drive, which was feeble and sliced.

'Shot!' said Paul, who's a nice chap. He hit his drive, which was not much better, and hooked.

'Shot!' I reciprocated.

'What are you up to on the writing front?' said Paul, as we set off along the fairway.

'Well,' I said, 'I'm thinking of writing a book about Yorkshire. Of course, there's a problem.'

'Oh, yes?' Paul lightly replied.

'The problem being,' I said, 'that I don't live in Yorkshire any more; I just come back to it a lot.'

Paul was puffing on his vaping device while gauging the distance between his ball and the green, as if it made any difference. 'I wouldn't worry too much about that,' he said, which came as a relief but fell short of full reassurance. Paul himself had moved away from York, but he'd moved north – Sunderland way – and insofar as the virtue of Yorkshireness lies partly in its Northern-ness he could not be accused of the same betrayal as somebody who'd moved south.

After about another 250 shots between the two of us,

we were on the tee of the seventeenth green, which is elevated, giving a good view of the clubhouse and – for the more high-minded – York Minster in the far distance. I hit my drive, which was sliced to the extent that Paul's usual endorsement – 'Shot!' – was simply not on; it would have come over as sarcastic. So Paul said something else instead: 'The thing is to be honest about having moved to London. If you're honest about it, people won't mind,' which is why this book about Yorkshire is going to start in London – at King's Cross Station, to be precise.

NORTH–SOUTH

York Road

I think of King's Cross, terminus of the East Coast Main Line, as *the* London station for Yorkshire. St Pancras is also a station for Yorkshire, so you can, to quote Philip Larkin, be 'going up England by a different line', but it would surely be the wrong line, less pure. Yes, St Pancras serves Sheffield and Leeds, but it does so via what is called the *Midland* Main Line, which – as originally defined – drifted into Lancashire, and St Pancras is now formally known as St Pancras International, subscribing to the globalisation that has helped diminish the cultural importance of Yorkshire and the North.

Even King's Cross – 'the Cross' to us sons of railwaymen – used to be more directly connected to Yorkshire and the North than it is today. Up until the 1970s, a couple of dozen coal trains every day rolled into the King's Cross Goods Yard – very useful to ghastly Professor Marcus in *The Ladykillers* (1955). He would drop dead bodies into them from the backyard of Mrs Wilberforce's house, apparently located directly above the mouth of Copenhagen Tunnel (the second one as you head north from King's Cross), where no real house ever *was* located. Much of that coal came from the Yorkshire coalfield, and until 1904 some of it was used to generate gas at the Cross, so it was if Yorkshire had courteously lit London's pilot light, signifying a geopolitical balance.

I thought of King's Cross as being an outpost of Yorkshire in London, and the local nomenclature seemed to support this. There was once a York Road platform, serving the smoky 'Widened Lines' that burrowed through London. To the east of King's Cross is York Way, which was York Road until 1938, and on which there used to be a pub called the Duke of York. There was another pub of that name in the station itself, on platform 10 – the main departure platform as was. Placards on the station urged, 'Take the Yorkshire Post with You', as though by doing so you might get acclimatised for what was to come.

It's true that the most famous train to serve the Cross, the Flying Scotsman, bypassed York. It's also true that the East Coast Main Line only becomes beautiful after York, when it begins to skirt the coast, so that if you get off at York, you're like someone leaving a party at 8 p.m. But to my mind, the ECML took aim specifically at York. In York stands the neo-Georgian building that was the headquarters of the North Eastern Railway, which controlled the northerly stretch of the ECML. Dad worked in that building when it had become the headquarters of the British Rail North Eastern Region. York Station is the first you come to on the ECML with a splendour to match King's Cross. When it opened in 1887, it was the largest station in the world, just as King's Cross had been when it opened in 1852. So I felt York Station to be on a par with the Cross, and from an early age I was as familiar with King's Cross as with York Station. Dad's job entitled us as a family to 'Privilege Tickets', enabling free train travel, and when he was promoted in about 1975, that free travel was in First Class. We also had Privilege Tickets for London Underground, and if there'd been a First Class on that, we'd have been in it.[*]

I would go to London with Dad and my sister half a dozen times a year. (My mother died in 1971, when I was nine, and I have no memory of being in London with her. In fact, I have no memory of my mother ever being outside Yorkshire.) Among those early visits to the Cross were two trips to watch the Rugby League Challenge Cup Final at Wembley. Rugby league, founded in the George Hotel, Huddersfield in 1895, was born out of a north–south divide. League was set up so that players could be paid, which wasn't allowed under the code of Union, which assumed participants were sufficiently well-off not to need to be paid.

In 1970s York, you played league at school if you'd failed your Eleven Plus, union if you passed. I failed and, in my second year at Ashfield Secondary Modern, York, was put into the rugby league team as a punishment for messing about in a games lesson. Rugby league is a 'full contact' sport, but not the way I played it, and I managed to avoid contact with the ball or any other player during the entire first half. Despite this, we were a long way ahead at half-time. As we sucked on quartered oranges, with everybody except me clarted in mud (my kit not only clean, but still pressed), the games teacher-coach congratulated us on a good, fighting performance. But when we trotted back onto the field, he called, 'Martin, I'm taking you off, lad,' and I'm not sure he bothered replacing me. He thought it better the team should play with twelve members rather than thirteen if I was going to be the thirteenth. I never played for any school team again, but in my subsequent years at that school

---

[*]   Despite the connotation of elitism, the term 'Privilege Ticket' is still in use in the railway industry.

I got a 'B' for sport on my reports, rather than the 'C' I deserved, together with the admiring remark, 'Has played rugby for the school.'

A trip south to see the Rugby League Challenge Cup Final was such a classic pilgrimage that in 1975 Alan Plater wrote a BBC2 series called *The Trinity Tales*, an updated version of *The Canterbury Tales,* about a group of Wakefield Trinity supporters going to Wembley to watch the game. Dad would have been about forty when I accompanied him and his mates to Wembley. Even though they were all First Class 'Priv' ticket men, they were quite raucous on the train, thanks to a couple of crates of Long Life lager.

I tried to feign enthusiasm and was flattered to be invited along on such a grown-up jaunt, but I was no more interested in watching rugby league than I was in playing it, and I spent the finals I attended doodling on the programme or furtively reading a book. The excitement of the day lay in the train journeys, and the visit, after the game, to 'the dogs' at White City, which I remember for the white glare of fluorescent lights against the night sky, a delicious cup of instant soup, and the atmosphere of criminality with confident rat-like men wearing coats on their shoulders like Del Boy.

Later, I went to London under my own steam, but never *by* steam train; I was too late for that. Sometimes the engine was one of those haughty-looking diesels called Deltics that could top 100mph. The carriages hauled by a Deltic had compartment rolling stock so that, if in First Class, you'd be travelling in a small room with seats for six. Once, while heading North, Leon Brittain MP, who represented a North Yorkshire seat, got into the compartment I was occupying. Never having been at such close quarters with a famous person, I panicked and feigned sleep, and I remained in pretend sleep until York, not knowing how to feign waking up in any convincing way.

If bored in the school holidays in York, I'd set off for London.

I had my own First Class Privilege Ticket as long as I remained a dependent of my father, and what with university followed by postgraduate law study, I managed to remain a dependent until I was twenty-six. As I headed off on my bike to York Station Dad, instead of saying goodbye, would say, 'Don't lose your Priv!' He'd told me he would be sacked if that ever happened, and one day in 1980, when I was eighteen, I did lose it. By then I had a bank account and a bank card, so I was able to withdraw the money to get home (albeit slumming it in Second Class) from the Lloyd's Bank cashpoint near King's Cross. I anticipated trouble on two fronts. First, would Dad be sacked? Secondly, there was the delicate matter of where I thought I'd dropped the Priv.

The threat of a sacking turned out to be bluff. Dad simply said that, if I gave him a passport photo, he'd put in for another Priv for me, but that turned out not to be necessary, because some stranger posted the original back to us. It was addressed to my father, since I was down on the Priv (which carried our address) as his dependent. The body of the letter was bland, something to the effect of 'I found this in the street, and thought you'd want it back, since it looks an important document.' But in the postscript the sender proved himself treacherous: 'PS, I found it in Old Compton Street, Soho.'

Back in 1979, Soho was almost wall-to-wall sex shops. I used to tell myself that this fascinated me much as I would be fascinated if it were full of fishmongers; that it was the intensity rather than the type of retail that was the draw. Soho certainly was a draw, partly because it was the part

of London most different from York. The idea of a district
of licensed, official decadence ... York wasn't grown-up
enough for that. (Dad, incidentally, never mentioned that
postscript.)

About ten years ago, I wrote a piece about the regeneration of King's Cross. I interviewed a press officer for the
area east of the station, newly designated Regent Quarter
(a name somehow much more irritating than 'Regent's
Quarter' would have been); he told me: 'Nobody's nostalgic for the old King's Cross.' Well, they might be if it was
integral to their formative years. I never tangled with the
real decadence of King's Cross – the drugs and prostitu-
tion, as rather operatically depicted in the film *Mona Lisa*.
But I liked the crepuscular mood of the place when it was
whatever is the opposite of the 'creative hub' it is today.
The goods yard was in the process of being abandoned. The
tracks were hidden by weeds, and there were piles of broken
planks everywhere, so it always seemed like the night
before Bonfire Night. I frequented the above-mentioned
Duke of York pub on York Way while waiting for trains.
I was always there in the evening, but it was impossible to
imagine York Way in daylight back then, what with the
crumbling railway wharves and the closed-down Gothic
Victorian school (you'd have grown up fast if you went to
school there, I bet), its bricks soot-blackened, as opposed to
bright pink, which they are now that the building houses
luxury flats. The York Way Tube station had also recently
closed, since the average King's Cross resident of the time
couldn't *afford* the Tube. (The building survives, an access
point for subterranean graffiti artists.) The air was full of
diesel fumes, courtesy of the locomotives in the station and
the Routemasters lumbering up and down the 'Way'. The
Duke of York (today a stylishly low-lit and 'dog-friendly'

pub called The Fellow) had a foggy black-and-white TV well into the 1990s, and it was always full of railwaymen, with their box-like riveted shoulder bags.

To my mind, the rackety, Dickensian appeal of King's Cross was not too different from that of late-Seventies London as a whole. The population of the capital was falling, and the Tube was being 'managed for decline'. I remember some of the tiles spelling out 'Covent Garden' in that station were missing. In my teens, I washed my hair once a fortnight.* But when I came back from London Tube rides, I always had to wash it, no matter where I was in that cycle. I associated London with vandalism – the glass on the public street maps had always been surgically smashed to obscure 'You are here,' apparently to prevent orientation by out-of-towners. Or perhaps it was just arbitrary vandalism. I did not really believe that London had enough sense of itself to formulate any grievance against non-Londoners. London was complacent and amorphous; it just absorbed people like a great, shapeless sponge. There's a bench in the park near my home in north London bearing a plaque commemorating a man who 'loved London', and that seems odd to me. In 1888, Thomas Hardy wrote that 'London appears not to *see itself.* Each individual is conscious of *himself,* but nobody conscious of themselves collectively.' In this sense, London did not really exist as a place, and you could never say that about Yorkshire.

Or could you?

A leading light of the Yorkshire Society told me, 'It is quite wrong to refer to Yorkshire as a county, despite the cricket club.' (And also, presumably, despite the Yorkshire

---

* Whether it needed it or not. (I supply this familiar joke knowing that some readers would feel short-changed without it.)

Society.) 'It was historically three counties,' he continued, referring to the three Ridings, an Old Norse term meaning third part, the three being North, West and East. There was never a South Riding, except in the title of a novel by Winifred Holtby.[*]

So here was a member of the Yorkshire Society saying that Yorkshire did not exist, and there was me – not a member of the Yorkshire Society – saying it possibly did, because the Ridings were notional subdivisions of *something*, namely the Kingdom of York, which was based on the Danish Kingdom of Jórvik that was decisively killed off by William the Conqueror. The former Kingdom began to be referred to as the shire of York or the county of Yorkshire. There was a further subdivision of the Ridings into wapentakes, and these were the basis of administration of what I'm calling Yorkshire. York itself was aloof from the Ridings, which is typical of my rather un-Yorkshire birthplace. York arbitrated between the Ridings, each one being represented at a Parliament held in York. From 1396, York was a County Corporate, or a 'County of Itself', and between 1449 and 1836 it controlled a former wapentake called Ainsty that was also not in a Riding. This was a territory just to the west of York, and I grew up on a new housing estate located within what had been its borders. There was, and is, a pub near my former home called the Ainsty, and I never knew why.

The Ridings were an old concept that experienced a revival in the nineteenth century, first because the Reform Act of 1832 replaced the parliamentary constituency of Yorkshire (so there's another instance of Yorkshire existing) with constituencies for each Riding. The Local Government Act of 1888 then made the Ridings the basis

---

[*]   That's set in the East Riding, but Holtby was coy about saying so explicitly.

of Yorkshire administration. They became administrative counties – counties within a county – and the Act recognised that the county they were within was Yorkshire. So here again, Yorkshire was acknowledged to exist, albeit as a shell.

It is arguable that the reviled Local Government Act of 1972 treated some places worse than Yorkshire. When the Act came into effect – April Fool's Day, 1974 – Rutland disappeared entirely, being absorbed by Leicestershire. Westmorland and Cumberland became Cumbria. Lancashire lost Liverpool to a new entity called Merseyside. But Yorkshire was badly mauled, and in no other county is the 1974 Act *so* reviled as in Yorkshire. (Yorkshire Day – of which more shortly –was created to rebuff the Act's assault on Yorkshire identity.) By the Act, the Ridings ceased to be administrative units, and Humberside was born, to accommodate Hull and most of the old East Riding. Middlesbrough was put into Cleveland, and other parts of Yorkshire fell into the clutches of wounded Lancashire.

In 1996, Humberside and Cleveland – never popular notions – were abolished. Humberside was replaced by the nostalgically named East Riding of Yorkshire, and this was given the new-fangled designation: unitary authority.

This 'unitary authority' is also a 'ceremonial county' – that is, 'a county for the purposes of lieutenancies', and what, we may wonder, are those? The post of Lord-Lieutenant of a county is an honorary appointment, whose origin dates back to Henry VIII. Lord-lieutenants are the monarch's representative in their lieutenancy. They seek to uphold 'the dignity of the Crown'; to promote voluntary and benevolent organisations; to encourage the business and social life of their counties. You are most likely to see them presenting medals and awards.

The ceremonial counties are sometimes referred to as 'geographical counties', as opposed to administrative counties; they are cultural counties, so to speak. These parallel or shadow counties long predate the administrative meddling of the late-twentieth century, but they have become significant in the wake of that meddling as touchstones of former identities – and the good news is that there are also ceremonial counties called North Yorkshire, West Yorkshire and South Yorkshire, and today Middlesbrough is back in the Yorkshire fold in that it is within the ceremonial county of North Yorkshire. It is in fact a unitary authority within that county, as is York.

We have one further chewy mouthful to digest. The 1974 Act established metropolitan and non-metropolitan counties. There is a non-metropolitan county called North Yorkshire, which excludes the unitary authorities of York and Middlesbrough. So the non-metropolitan county of North Yorkshire has a smaller population than the ceremonial county of North Yorkshire. There are also *metropolitan* counties called South Yorkshire and West Yorkshire, and these are coterminous with the ceremonial counties bearing those names.

People who write about Yorkshire – including me – turn their backs on all this ludicrous gerrymandering. Instead, they address themselves to the Historic County of Yorkshire, and any educated person has a rough idea of its boundaries: Pennines to the left, North Sea to the right, Hull down below, just like the hull of a ship. They might be a bit vaguer about the northern termination but will probably associate it (approximately correctly) with the notch in the coast formed by the river Tees.

But my friend from the Yorkshire Society does not like the term county at all when it comes to Yorkshire. 'The better and more accurate word is "region", though even better would be the German word *Land* – like Bavaria, to which there are many parallels with Yorkshire!' I might add that the great migraine of Yorkshire local government arises from fact that Yorkshire is big – too big for any one book to encompass it. So this book is about *my* Yorkshire, which – as stated – I view in part from a London perspective.

When on the Tube, I sat in smoking carriages, because Dad – a smoker himself – said 'Smokers are the best people; they'll always look after you.' There were no ashtrays, and the butts would all be aligned in the grooves between the sycamore slats on the carriage floor. One November evening in 1987, a careless smoker sent the ticket hall of King's Cross Underground Station up in flames. By then I was *living* in London, in a shared house in Leytonstone. I was not at home that evening, and when I got in, one of my housemates told me that Dad had called from York half a dozen times. He hadn't said why, but I knew. My regular flits back to Yorkshire from London, which tended to occur at weekends, made me such a regular at the Cross that there must have seemed a reasonable chance I'd been caught up in a Friday night fire – clearly just the kind of fate awaiting a young Yorkshire person adrift from their moorings.

I had moved full-time to London in 1984, the year of the miners' strike, which – since the Yorkshire miners were in the vanguard of that fight against pit closures – was symptomatic of the North–South divide, much spoken of in the Thatcher years. The North suffered worst from the recession of the early 1980s, just as it had done from that of the 1920s and 1930s. The staple industries of the North – coal, shipbuilding, weaving – had been dying for decades before Margaret Thatcher came to power. The miners' strike of

1984 was about the closure of twenty pits; Harold Wilson had closed 300. The Thatcherite free-market panaceas – a house price boom triggered by the 'right to buy' scheme for council house tenants and the financial de-regulation of the Big Bang – benefited the South more than the North. It seems reasonable to suggest that Thatcher was negligent of the North, and through this she gave New Labour the ammunition to target her as anti-Northern. Gordon Brown exploited the North—South divide for political advantage: Thatcher had 'attacked the North' and 'systematically destroyed' its economy. The divide would persist under New Labour, but the rhetorical heat died down.

Writing in *The Times* on 24 October 2020, Robert Crampton, who's from Hull, recalled the North—South divide of the 1980s as 'poisonous', and fretted that it might be opening up again, as a result of resistance from the North to underfunded lockdowns imposed from London by Boris Johnson. Johnson's background could be described as cosmopolitan, since he was born in Manhattan, and spent part of his childhood in Washington DC and Brussels. But when you factor in childhood stints in Oxford, Somerset and London, and the fact that he made his political name as Mayor of London, it all adds up to pure southern-ness. Even so, the North fell for his dubious charms in the 2019 election, and the 'Red Wall' of safe Northern Labour seats became blue. I think of this much as if an old girlfriend had taken up with some notorious cad – none of my business really, but vexing nonetheless. How has the Conservative Party, led by this 'southern show-off' (in the words of Andy Burnham, Mayor of Manchester) become the repository of Northern hopes? We might blame Brexit, or the priggishness of the modern Labour Party, or the deindustrialisation that has dissolved the Northern identity; or we might put it down to the shape-shifting nous of Johnson and the Conservative Party.

Robert Crampton decided that the old North–South fight was probably *not* about to kick off again, because there had been a cultural rapprochement since the 1980s: 'You can hear unmoderated Northern accents in broadcast news and current affairs – Chris Mason (West Yorkshire), Nick Robinson (Manchester), Steph McGovern (Middlesbrough) – in a way you didn't when I was grow- ing up . . . North and South,' he added, 'we're all watching American or Danish or Spanish box sets rather than arguing over the merits of *Room at the Top* or *Brideshead Revisited*.'

The miners' strike still reverberates, however. In *Yorkshire: A Lyrical History of England's Greatest County,* Richard Morris writes, 'The defeat changed Yorkshire as a landscape, as a community and as an idea. It also changed Britain. And like the end of the Cold War with which it roughly coincided, we still have no sure idea what this means.'

I'm pretty certain about one consequence of the strike: I determined to become a writer, specialising in the North– South tensions the strike had highlighted, like somebody who picks at a scab, which, in the context of strikes, is not as bad as *being* a scab, but not the most honourable ambition, and the amelioration described by Crampton means it is not one that any young writer would entertain today.

I had better say something about the formulation of this ambition.

Educationally, I experienced what is known as a roller- coaster ride. I was probably among the top half-dozen students at my state primary school in York, so I was disap- pointed not to pass the Eleven Plus, and even after all these years I feel compelled to mention that the school in question was run by a 'progressive' headmaster who didn't like the

Eleven Plus, and so didn't coach pupils for it, or prepare them in any way, with the result that only the top two in my year did pass it. This failure made me both more and less Yorkshire. Less in that I was diverted away from Nunthorpe Grammar school, est. 1920, which my father had attended, and was a York landmark, being centrally located, and the breeding ground of some eminent Yorkshiremen (it being a boys' school), including the ex-Liberal Democrat leader Vince Cable – he was head boy – and sometime England football manager Steve McClaren.

On the other hand, attending Ashfield Secondary Modern, which was in a new building on the edge of town (sufficiently undistinguished to have been flattened a few years after I left), made me more Yorkshire in the sense that it consigned me to a more working-class and industrial milieu than would have obtained at the grammar school. I have a CSE Grade 1 in woodwork, for example, which, I will have readers know, is an 'O-level equivalent'. I probably scored 100 per cent in woodwork theory, but only scraped through the practical thanks to the intervention of the hardest kid in the school, who was on the same workbench as me, and was so appalled to see me planing against the grain that he silently walked over and, crossly gesturing at me to step aside, reversed the position of my piece of wood in the vice, thereby nobly risking his own disqualification from the exam, which would have been disastrous for him, given that he was an excellent woodworker. Today he is a successful joiner in York, probably earning more money than me.

I did get to the grammar school eventually – to attend the sixth form where, after a slow start, I got the hang of essay writing. After a mock exam, one of the teachers said, 'Just remind me – which boys were down to do Oxbridge?'

and when I saw another secondary modern transferee raise his hand, I was so indignant that he had been co-opted to this elite cohort that I raised my hand, even though I was *not* down to do Oxbridge, no teacher having seen fit to put me down. But somehow no objection was ever raised to my becoming a 'history boy', to almost quote the title of Alan Bennett's autobiographical play about Oxbridge applicants at a Sheffield grammar school – a title dating from a more gendered time. The play was first performed in 2004. I went 'up' (as we Oxonians annoy people by saying) in 1981, but I was aware at the time I applied of the Bennett-ian precedent. The careers of J. B. Priestley and Michael Palin also suggested that the path from more-or-less working-class Yorkshire to Oxford could lead on to a successful media career.

There seemed a particularly strong connection between Oxford and Yorkshire in 1981, since *Brideshead Revisited* was serialised on TV in that year, and the scenes featuring the family of Sebastian Flyte, the gorgeous toff, were filmed at Castle Howard, near York. To underline the connection, it turned out a daily train connected York and Oxford directly, albeit as part of its meandering course from Aberdeen to Cornwall.

Naturally, my three years at Oxford only increased my North–South complex. I was very aware of my Yorkshire accent and so were other people. One tutorial partner of mine said, 'Your accent sounds Yorkshire-but-trying-to-be-posh,' which was devastating, since he really was posh. Particularly perilous was the Yorkshire 'u' sound, which seems to be visually represented by the shape of the letter, being a sudden plunge. I would modify my pronunciation of 'pub' to something more like 'pab'. The plunging 'u' might also be involved in the word 'love', but that hardly ever came up during my university years, whereas 'pub' came up on a daily basis.

I got to know some old-Etonians, who were more tolerant of provincials than southern minor public-school types, being more socially confident. They had more 'off', in Yorkshire terms. I became quite close with one particular OE. He carried a picture of his family home in his wallet, and, early in our acquaintance, he showed me this snap, explaining, 'It's only half the house, really. It's too big to fit on a single photograph.' After our finals, we had a more-or-less formal parting over a glass of whisky in his rooms. 'I suppose this is goodbye,' he said. 'I doubt we will be meeting much in the future. It's a shame, but our lives will take us on different paths.' That was true enough, and I was soon back to the North—South rat run, living tenuously in London and returning frequently to Yorkshire from King's Cross.

But I don't want to denigrate my time in Oxford; that would be ungrateful. I have never again had the same sense of well-being as I experienced on early summer evenings there, with mellow church bells directing some undergraduates towards evensong, and reminding me that it was time for an aperitif in a lovely little wood-panelled pub called the Bear. Some Japanese tourists once asked to photograph me as I lounged in the doorway, sipping white wine and smoking a cigarette while dressed in my academic gown, suit and — I fear — a bow tie. Naturally, I consented to be photographed, adopting various *Brideshead*-ian poses for numerous snaps, and in that moment I briefly transcended my Yorkshireness.

I loved being at Oxford, and Dad loved me being there as well, his letters expressing such happy Yorkshire sentiments as, 'I'm saving an absolute fortune on breakfast cereal.'

His letters to me were always signed off with a Yorkshire reticence – 'regards', not 'love' – and I try to keep that up with my own sons. 'Love' is too emotionally demanding; no need to spell it out. I was disappointed that, on the one day that Dad actually took that meandering train to come and see me in Oxford, a grey drizzle was falling, and the town did not look its best. As I collected Dad from Oxford's particularly ugly railway station, he said, 'Where's all these bloody dreaming spires, then?'

In London, I pursued a faltering career in journalism, but I'd return to York at least once a month, on my 'Priv'. What would happen is that I would run out of money, or just lose heart, so I'd go home to scrounge off Dad and have a couple of evenings in the relatively cheap pleasure grounds of the York pubs. I continued to return home regularly even after I'd forfeited my Priv Ticket, having supposedly become gainfully employed as a journalist. I had many tense moments at that Lloyd's Bank cashpoint near the Cross, since I was always overdrawn. As a rule, the machine coughed up the necessary thirty quid, and I'd go into the ticket office, which used to be located in a plastic-looking canopy attached to the front of the station, obscuring the elegance of Cubitt's façade.

It was usually late on a Friday night, and there was no guarantee there'd be any affordable tickets left. Back then, the tickets were ready-made, not printed on demand as today. Under the white fluorescent lights, with fag smoke writhing in the glare, I'd join the queue for 'immediate travel'. As each successive customer was served, the clerk would reach into a big white drawer – like a drawer in a 1970s fitted kitchen – and magnanimously hand over the means of returning to the Yorkshire comfort zone. But some of the clerks – all Londoners – would retreat through a back

door for a tea break just as I approached, as if tormenting
me, knowing I hadn't the means to survive another week
in the capital, and perhaps attributing this to my refusal to
buckle down to a lowly clerk's job like their own. It might
be five minutes until another Londoner (or the same one
again) would reappear holding a coffee mug and the keys to
the important drawer. It seemed to me that I was recognised
as a regular by some of these clerks, and I feared they were
on the brink of saying, 'I wish you'd bloody make up your
mind where you want to live,' or 'Another week of failure
in London, eh?'

After I'd secured the ticket there would ideally be time
and money left for a celebratory pint in the Duke of York –
the one on the departure platform. It was not a charming
pub. Reviews written online before its closure survive in
a ghostly way: 'As everyone is transient you cannot expect
much of an atmosphere . . . Station pub . . . overpriced and
served a transient clientele . . . Toilets show which Northern
football teams have passed through in recent years and the
names of their "firms".' But I was a transient too; like the
Grand Old Duke of York himself, I was neither up nor
down. The whole of that departure platform – which had
once contained a tea room, both a 'general' and a ladies'
waiting room, a booking office and an enquiry office –
seemed festive because it was the start of the journey home.
By contrast, there were no facilities on the arrival platform
on the opposite side. That was bleak and businesslike. You
weren't meant to hang around once you'd arrived, and if
King's Cross per se ever did become your destination in
the 1970s and 1980s, that would have meant you were on
the skids.

In 1986 I lost my nerve and trained as a barrister, while
picking up scraps of journalism on the side. The training

kept me in London, but my aim was to be a barrister on the Northern Circuit, which sounded a very nice gravy train to be aboard, and we will be seeing what became of that plan as my ambition to write reasserted itself.

The Professionals

I sought to become a Professional Northerner, specifically a Professional Yorkshireman, which is the main franchise within the brand. The term is not in the *Oxford English Dictionary*, but I think most people have some idea of its meaning. On 20 July 2018, Anthony Clavane (a Yorkshireman) defined 'Professional Yorkshireman' in the *Yorkshire Post* as 'a label lazily applied to anyone born in the Broad Acres who has made it down south'. He adds, 'It is a form of insult and implies the chap in question is dour, has a penchant for flat caps and whippets and constantly prattles into a microphone about the wonders of God's Own County.'

It was an 'insult' I wouldn't have minded being applied to me, just as I wouldn't really have minded being called a 'hack' or a writer of 'potboilers'. 'Professional Yorkshireman' implies a certain industriousness and competence, and it is a back-handed compliment to Yorkshire, a testament to its specialness, because nobody speaks of 'Professional Lancastrians', for instance. To my mind, the basic definition of a Professional Yorkshireman is someone who lets you know he's from Yorkshire on a very regular basis. A classic example would be Dickie Bird, the retired cricket umpire who was born, and still lives, in Barnsley. In August 2021, he was interviewed over about half a page of the *Sunday Times*. The word 'Yorkshire' occurred eight times in the piece, and in the accompanying photograph Bird was wearing two lapel badges: one in the shape of a letter 'Y' (standing presumably for Yorkshire), the other depicting a white rose, symbol of Yorkshire.

Michael Parkinson would be another example. When, in 1977, he was riding high as a chat show host, Peter Cook said, 'I think most people know by now that Michael Parkinson hails from Barnsley. I will donate £5 to any charity (unconnected with Barnsley) for every Parkinson programme that omits the word "Barnsley". I know it will be hard, Michael, but it can be done.'

In my formative years, it seemed Professional Yorkshiremen were everywhere. Jack Hargreaves and Fred Trueman were both signalling their down-to-earth ruminative Yorkshire wisdom by smoking pipes on TV – and on children's TV at that. Hargreaves did his smoking on *How* (a show in which things were relentlessly explained), Trueman on Indoor League, which – really baffling scheduling, this – showcased pub games during the children's teatime slot. Trueman not only smoked on this show, but also drank beer from a glass with a handle, which underlined the Yorkshire brand, as did his sign-off, 'Ah'll si thee' (Yorkshire for 'I'll see you'), presumably to the bafflement of many, since the show was broadcast nationally.

The phrase 'Professional Yorkshirewoman' has never tripped off anyone's tongue, perhaps because 'Yorkshire-woman' itself is an awkward compound. I grew up instinctively thinking that all very Yorkshire people were Yorkshire*men*, just as I instinctively thought that all dogs were male (cats being the females of the species). Professional

Yorkshirewomen do exist, though, and you might say that the first of them was Charlotte Brontë, who lived long enough, just, to reach the uplands of literary fame. The leading professional Yorkshirewoman of today is Amanda Owen, self-styled 'Yorkshire Shepherdess' of Swaledale and Channel 5. She certainly talks the talk: 'The snowflake generation, they can't do anything. They don't know anything about how to look after themselves, or a work ethic, all of that has gone out of the window. It's our fault as parents.' She and her husband Clive have nine children, and she has quite frequently given birth by the side of the road, but she made a point of having some of her recent children at home ('I got so fed up with spoiling people's picnics and all the rest of it').

Her predecessor, in a sense, is Hannah Hauxwell (1926–2018), who ran a farm single-handedly in the Pennines with no electricity or running water and a single cow, which produced one calf every year for market. She was the subject of a hit Yorkshire TV documentary of 1972 called *Too Long a Winter*, produced by Barry Cockroft, who – as a co-founder of Yorkshire Television and with a reputation as 'the chronicler of the Dales' – was certainly a Professional Yorkshire*man*.

I somehow missed Hannah Hauxwell at the time, possibly because I snobbishly boycotted Independent Television, except for the *South Bank Show*, presented by that Professional Cumbrian Melvyn Bragg. In 2019, I paid 50p for two Hauxwell books – spin-offs from the TV programmes – from the cluttered second-hand bookshop opposite the railway station in Pickering. *Innocent Abroad* (1991) is about what happened when Barry Cockroft and his film crew took Hannah to Europe, including Switzerland, where she maintained her Yorkshire tone: 'After Saint

Martin, I went on an even worse road . . .' *Hannah's North Country* (1993) opens with some remarks by Hauxwell that beg a familiar question where Professional Yorkshireness is concerned: Are you moaning about your lot, or crowing about it?

> You see, I was in chains to Low Birk Hatt Farm, my family home in Baldersdale and the only home I had ever known until well past pensionable age. I suppose I shall always be wedded to that place in my heart. Cruel circumstances obliged me to leave . . . Another bad winter could have brought me down.

But perhaps there was some poetry to this moaning. 'It was the speech mannerisms of Hannah that initially caught people's attention,' wrote Cockroft, in the Preface to *Innocent Abroad*. 'The words appeared to float from her lips like a progression of musical chords.' We are concerned with two things here: the Yorkshire accent and the Yorkshire tone.

As Robert Crampton suggested, accent is not such an issue as it was in the 1980s, when the North–South divide was fracturing the country. The benchmark of Received Pronunciation still obtained. An Englishman was still, in the words of Wyndham Lewis, 'branded on his tongue'. Yorkshire accents were not yet being used to advertise financial services, the implication of those ads being that a plain-speaking Yorkshire person is too guileless (or too dim) to rip you off. When Yorkshire was a more distinct place, the opposite implication had applied, at least as far as North Yorkshire was concerned. 'Where the West Riding men were known for their stubborn truculence towards strangers', writes Michael Bradford in *The Fight for Yorkshire*, 'the horse-loving men of the of the North were famous for their double dealing and acute bargaining power. The phrase "Yorkshire Bite" was used to denote this.'

My accent became a fraught issue at Oxford, but it had been mutable from an early age. In our street, about half the men went to work in lounge suits, half in boiler suits, and my father, as one of the former, tried to stop me talking like one of the latter. He would come down hard on the contracted negative, 'I'n't it?', or 'Gerroff'. He also tried to cure me of definite article reduction – the working-class Yorkshire habit of replacing 'the' with either the letter 't' ('On Ilkley Moor Bar T'at') or a glottal stop. When I began to write novels set in Yorkshire (and most of my novels *are* set in Yorkshire) the question of whether to enunciate 'the' had been settled in favour, but the question of how to represent a Yorkshire version of 'the' on the page began to arise.

In recent years, I have acted every Christmas in plays – usually one-act drawing-room comedies – put on by my friend, the author Mathew Sturgis. Being Northern, I play the broad comedy parts: yokels, servants. At the drinks party that always follows, some stranger might congratulate me on my performance, and my 'really authentic Yorkshire accent', but as the small talk proceeds, they're listening to me with a cocked ear. 'But it's obviously your *real* accent,' they blurt, which is tantamount to revoking the praise. Those plays, incidentally, are staged in the big living room of a flat in Powis Terrace, Notting Hill. The room was a staging post for Northerners on the make in London, in that it used to be David Hockney's studio and became a focal point of a social scene involving Northerners attending the Royal College of Art. In *Re-Make Re-Model: the Art School Roots of Roxy Music*, Michael Bracewell quotes Bryan Ferry: 'The first night I ever spent in London was in David Hockney's studio in Powis Terrace.'

In 1973, David Hockney starred in a film about his own life called *A Bigger Splash*, and in this, the natural order seems reversed, because here is a man from Bradford being courted by Mayfair types, who moan that Hockney is not productive enough to satisfy the demand for his work. 'Well, that's too bad, in't it?' says Hockney, languorously lighting another fag.

I have occasionally exaggerated my Yorkshire accent in readings and TV programmes, thinking the context or market required it, and it once got back to me that a London neighbour had been discussing one of my TV programmes in a local shop: 'Did you see Andrew Martin camping up his Yorkshire accent on TV?' It is possible to take a pride in the Yorkshire accent, whereas I don't usually detect deliberate exaggeration when I hear, say, a Glaswegian accent. In *Does Accent Matter?* (1989), John Honey, drawing on 'some fairly systematic experiments', proposed a hierarchy of acceptability in accents as follows:

1. Mainstream RP
2. Educated Scottish
3. Educated Irish; Educated Welsh
4. Northern (with Yorkshire generally high); West Country
5. London, Liverpool, Glaswegian and West Midlands.

Honey suggests that the Yorkshire accent is one of the non-standard accents thought compatible with 'educatedness'. But he does acknowledge that it has long been the aim of Yorkshire 'gentry' to educate their children outside the county, to insulate them from its accent, a tendency he dates back to class consciousness arising from the passing of the 1832 Reform Act. The 'right' school within Yorkshire might do the job equally well. Attendance at Scarborough

College was enough to extinguish the Yorkshire accent of Ian Carmichael (who was born in Hull) to the extent that he played the snobbish Lord Peter Wimsey on TV and radio.

I certainly don't like the London accent. In the globalised Cross, the automated female announcer – known as 'Anne' – has a London (or perhaps an Estuarine) accent, and when she says, 'Please join the train now [pronounced to rhyme with 'miaow'] as it is ready to leave,' she brings out the Henry Higgins in me.

When I board the train to York today, I luxuriate in the Yorkshire accents and phrases around me: people saying 'Tara' to those waving them off from the platform, or perhaps 'I aren't bothered where I sit' instead of 'I'm not bothered'; people saying 'smashing' to mean 'good', or 'were' instead of 'was', as in 'I were that tired,' and people overusing the word 'like' – not to mean 'said' (a habit now almost universal) but as a sort of charmingly pointless add-on: 'We'll have a coffee later on, like.' These phrases seem to refute the globalised branding of the East Coast Main Line trains, which are bland electro-diesels called Azumas. They are made in Japan, and prior to their introduction they were heralded by posters on the previous generation of trains: 'AZUMA. IT'S FAST. IT'S CRAZY FAST . . . It's like a train and a laser made a baby while on holiday in Japan . . .'

On the train, I will quicky pick up the two Yorkshire tones. The first is disclosed by some remark of a pithiness that's just not possible among southerners: one Yorkshireman asking another for assistance with a suitcase might say, 'Cop 'od', meaning 'cop hold' or 'grab hold'. The second tone is more langorous and dreamy. Once, on a train about to leave King's Cross, I heard a woman who was possibly a Londoner ask a man who was definitely from Yorkshire, 'Does this train terminate at Leeds?' 'Some of it does,' he drawlingly replied, and he let her taste the strangeness of those words before explaining that the train divided at Leeds, part of it continuing to Skipton.

Let us deal with 'Cop 'od' first.

This has the bluntness associated with the county, the tone of hard men working in heavy industry, or of the peremptory catchphrases – containing the merest glimmer of humour, like a small spark struck from a flint – that you tend to see on coffee mugs or tea towels: 'See all, think all, say nowt'; 'If ever tha does owt for nowt mek sure it's for thissen'; 'Where there's muck there's brass', or the surprisingly self-deprecating 'Yorkshire born an' Yorkshire bred, strong in t'arm and thick in t'head'. This is the terse tone referred to by Mrs Gaskell when she discusses the Yorkshire character in *The Life of Charlotte Brontë* (1857):

> Even an inhabitant of the neighbouring county of Lancaster is struck by the peculiar force of character which the Yorkshiremen display. This makes them interesting as a race; while, at the same time, as individuals, the remarkable degree of self-sufficiency they possess gives them an air of independence rather apt to repel a stranger.

Mrs Gaskell says of West Riding people, 'They are not emotional,' but this is only half the story. Think of all the shouting that goes on in those Yorkshire 'kitchen-sink' dramas, from *Room at The Top* to *Kes*. Not too far into any given literary depiction of Yorkshireness, the emotional reticence gives way to the opposite. In *Wuthering Heights*, by Charlotte's younger and wilder sister, Emily, Catherine Earnshaw wastes away and dies through love of charismatic Heathcliff, whose low social status prevents her marrying him. On the opening page Heathcliff is described as 'Exaggeratedly reserved'. But here he is 150 pages later, having learnt of Catherine's death: '"May she wake in torment!" he cried, with frightful vehemence, stamping his foot, and groaning in a sudden paroxysm of ungovernable passion.' After urging the shade of Cathy to haunt him, he dashes his head against a tree trunk and 'lifting up his eyes, howled, not like a man, but like a savage beast getting goaded to death with knives and spears.'

Then again, in *The Brontë Myth*, Lucasta Miller describes *Wuthering Heights* as 'terse' and 'laconic', which it often is — for instance when Catherine says of Heathcliff: 'he's more myself than I am.' I find in this, and many other Yorkshire novels or dramas, a certain neglect of the middle ground. Everyone's either raving or mumbling monosyllabically.

Insofar as the Yorkshire voice *is* terse and laconic, this might be associated with the workplace. Not much time for witty quips at the coalface, or on the factory floor, and they probably wouldn't be audible anyway. And there's no virtue in individualism and self-confidence in that setting, whereas the cockney sole trader had to cry his wares; he had a patter. 'A child of the north', wrote Alan Bennett in *Untold Stories*, 'I don't care for cockneys or their much-advertised Blitz-defeating cheerfulness: all that knees-up, thumbs in the lapels down at the old Bull and Bush cockney sparrerdom has always left me cold.'

Now let us consider that reply to the question about whether the train terminated at Leeds: 'Some of it does.'

I find in this a whimsicality, a slow entanglement with words, that is a less often-noted part of the Yorkshire tone, perhaps arising from the more sedate pace of life to be had in the county's suburbs and villages. It is captured by the comedian Graham Fellows, who was born in Sheffield, and whose alter ego – in TV and radio programmes – is the equable, Sheffield-based retiree, John Shuttleworth. In 'his' book, *Two Margarines and Other Domestic Dilemmas*, Shuttleworth fills us in on his CV: 'I used to work for Comet, demonstrating audio equipment, and before that, I was a security guard for a sweet factory in the Rotherham area. Obviously, I can't say where for security reasons.' When I interviewed Fellows for the *Daily Telegraph* of 25 October, 1997, he described Shuttleworth's main characteristic as 'steadiness', a quality also discoverable in Fellows's own Yorkshire father: 'He's the sort of man, if you come to see him by a new route, he'll immediately look it up on the map.' Shuttleworth is transfixed by the minutiae of life. He doesn't eat pork pies, but instead '*buffet* pork pies'; he 'elects' not to wear his roll-neck sweater and feels obliged to note that the seats in a restaurant are in 'banquette formation'.

You get that same quality – a sort of poetic pedantry – in Alan Bennett's characters, or Reeves & Mortimer (those sons of Leeds and Middlesbrough, who once explained to a friend of mine, 'Mars Bars aren't funny; Revels are funny.'). You used to get it in *Last of the Summer Wine*, written by Roy Clarke – in the earliest episodes, when it came over, according to Simon Armitage in *All Points North*, as 'a minimalist existential dialogue written by Samuel Beckett'. It is important to mention some instances of Yorkshire humour because it is a commodity thought to be in short supply. The most famous Yorkshire joke is about Yorkshiremen, not by them. In the Four Yorkshiremen sketch, four Tykes-made-good seek to outdo each other in describing the lowliness of their origins ('We had it *tough* . . .') The sketch was written – in 1967 for an ITV comedy series called *At Last the 1948 Show* – by Tim Brooke-Taylor, John Cleese, Graham Chapman and Marty Feldman, none of whom are from

Yorkshire. The sketch was made famous by *Monty Python*, who revisited the North–South divide in a sketch where Graham Chapman is a gruff and boorish London playwright, whose effete son flew the nest to become a miner in Yorkshire: 'Hampstead wasn't good enough for you; you had to go poncing off to Barnsley with all your coal-mining friends.' The son responds by criticising his father's lifestyle: 'I'll tell you what's wrong with you. Your head's addled with novels and poems, you come home every evening reeking of Chateau La Tour . . . And look what you've done to mother! She's worn out with meeting film stars, attending premieres and giving gala luncheons.'

In *Pies and Prejudice: In Search of the North,* Stuart Maconie, from Merseyside, wrote of the attitude of his fellow Lancastrians towards Yorkshire people: 'We each nurture deeply held prejudices against one another. They think we are soft and a bit silly. Easily led and somehow lightweight. We think they are humourless and mean-spirited, arrogant and dull.' In *Lancashire, Where Women Die of Love*, Charles Nevin writes of the importance of the Pennines as a cultural boundary: on the west side, a people of 'lightness and wit'; to the east, 'smothering gloom'. He adds, 'It is an essential truth that comics come from Lancashire and don't come from Yorkshire', and he attributes this to the Scandinavian influence to the east, the Celtic one to the west, although Nevin admits he has to tread carefully here, since his wife is Norwegian. Nevin believes that 'whimsy' is a key characteristic of Lancashire. He finds it in Lancastrian Stan Laurel's continuing to write skits for himself and Oliver Hardy after Hardy had died. In support of his theory, he turns to toponymy (the name Southport, for example, to denote a town that is neither in the south nor a port) and to news stories: 'Where else, for example, would a bull actually find its way into a china shop? Lancaster, 2003. Where else, for another, would a man end a 12-hour siege after police gave way to his one demand, an egg and mayonnaise sandwich? Blackpool, 2003.'

When it comes to comedians, Lancashire does seem to have the first team: Stan Laurel (born in 1890 in Ulverston, which was in Lancashire at the time), Frank Randle, Tommy Handley, George Formby, Gracie Fields, Les Dawson, Eric Morecambe, Ken Dodd, Victoria Wood, Peter Kay. Insofar as it is funnier than Yorkshire, Lancashire is perhaps less Northern, and it has had a strain of working-class Toryism absent from Yorkshire until Brexit and Boris Johnson turned the Red Wall blue. (A historian of the North once suggested to me that this political tendency had its not very honourable origin in a xenophobic resentment of Irish migrants.) 'For better or worse, and I have to say it's the latter', Maconie writes in *Pies and Prejudice*, 'Yorkshire has become emblematic, axiomatic, symptomatic of the North in the hearts and minds of the South. It speaks of bullishness, lack of sophistication, dour self-sufficiency. The words that spring to mind are "bluff" and "no nonsense".' He adds, 'And that is a myth.' But for the moment we are dealing with mythologies.

In 2010, I wrote and narrated a BBC documentary called *1960: The Year of the North*, which pointed out a paradox. In 1957, Harold Macmillan declared, in his patrician way, that 'most of our people have never had it so good'. The North was still 'the engine room of Britain', but this prosperity, and increased permissiveness, shook things up, generating more diverse and inner-directed discontents. A 'new wave' of writing by 'angry young men' of the North – and very often Yorkshire – would be generated. They were called 'kitchen-sink' writers, to denote their concern with unheroic, quotidian subjects, rather than their willingness to do any housework. The term was used by the art critic David Sylvester, in the December 1954 issue of *Encounter*, to describe the work of four social realist painters (John Bratby, Derrick Greaves, Edward Middleditch and Jack Smith) who, he said, 'take us back from the studio to the kitchen'. We will come to the authors to whom this term was applied in a moment, and to the cultural momentum of 1960, but first we should note that there had been a previous wave before this 'new' one.

'The compass needle of the 1930s pointed unequivocally northwards,' writes Peter Davidson in *The Idea of North*.

> North was the inevitable destination for the 1930s, given the two leading preoccupations of the writers of the period: social concern focusing on the troubled and decaying industries of the north of England; and that complex of survivor guilt and hero–worship felt by many members of the Auden generation towards fathers and brothers who had fought, or were killed, in the First World War.

Davidson discusses the romanticisation by W. H. Auden of industrial and Northern landscapes, to the extent that there is a volume called *W. H. Auden, Pennine Poet* (by Alan Myers and Robert Forsythe), although Auden's North extended all the way to the Arctic Circle. 'Again and again in the 1930s,' writes Davidson, 'the north was equated with authenticity or heroism,' and he places George Orwell's *The Road to Wigan Pier* (1936) in that context, but there is also this by Orwell, from his essay of 1941, *England Your England*:

A Yorkshireman in the south will always take care to let you know that he regards you as inferior. If you ask him why, he will explain that it is only in the north that life is 'real' life, that the industrial work done on the north is the only 'real' work, that the north is inhabited by 'real' people, the south merely by rentiers and parasites.

Among the second wave of kitchen-sink writers I found my main career models. When I thought of the term 'author', I pictured these people. Not all of them were from Yorkshire. Alan Sillitoe, for example, is from Nottingham, and his novel of 1958, *Saturday Night and Sunday Morning* – starring Arthur Seaton, a stroppy, womanising welder with too much take-home pay for his own good – is set in that town. Sillitoe might as well have been from Yorkshire, though. The Arctic Monkeys, who are – to slightly over-simplify – from Sheffield, used a Seaton pronouncement, 'Whatever people say I am, that's what I'm not,' as the title of their debut album. When I read Sillitoe's other famous book, *The Loneliness of the Long-Distance Runner*, the peevish, droll narrative seems to have a Yorkshire accent, perhaps because I've seen the film, in which Tom Courtenay (from Hull) stars.

But Yorkshire can claim more kitchen-sink authors than any other county. In 1957, *Room at the Top* by John Braine was published. Braine was from Bradford. The novel was filmed and later adapted for TV. Two years later, there was *Billy Liar* (1959) by Leeds-born Keith Waterhouse, which was subsequently turned into a film, a musical and a TV series. *A Kind of Loving* (1960) by Stan Barstow, from Horbury near Wakefield, became a film, a television series, a theatrical play and a radio play. Also out in 1960 was *This Sporting Life*, by David Storey, from Wakefield itself. It became a film.

This penumbra of adaptations haunts me today, as proving the extent to which the books penetrated the culture at the time. (Only one of my own books has been adapted. The novel, set in Yorkshire, was dramatised for a play at the Stephen Joseph Theatre, Scarborough, about which I was very pleased, but still: one really wants to take Yorkshire to the *world*.) I apprehended these works in my teens or early twenties – that is, in the late 1970s or early 1980s, and they seemed to be providing the definitive view of Yorkshire. Jarvis Cocker, from Sheffield, apparently thought the same. In *Moving the Goalposts: A Yorkshire Tragedy*, Anthony Clavane quotes Cocker as saying that 'the "kitchen-sink dramas" ... were inspirational touchstones for people like me in the indie bands of the 1980s.'

I recently revisited some of these works. I watched the film of *Room at the Top*, and its sequel, *Life at The Top*. In the first, Joe Lampton is torn between his true love and the more tactical liaison with the boss's daughter. The second film sees him cynically married to the boss's daughter but tempted by a metropolitan actress. Both films are extremely torrid, with very little 'reserve', least of all 'exaggerated'. Tonally, they reminded me of more beautifully filmed versions of *EastEnders*, and I think the self-pitying Lampton comes over as more sinister than intended, because of the dead-eyed performance by Laurence Harvey (born in Lithuania) whose Yorkshire accent sounds alien and robotic.

Lampton escapes to London in *Life at the Top*, but soon scuttles back to Yorkshire. Whilst most of the kitchen-sink authors moved south, London is too big a hill to climb for their characters. In *Billy Liar*, the over-imaginative undertaker's clerk, Billy Fisher, played by Tom Courtenay, seems on the point of breaking away from Stradhoughton (Bradford) in company with bohemian Liz, played in the film by Julie Christie as the only woman in Bradford unencumbered by a hat, headscarf or hairnet. But of course, he bottles it. The film, written by Waterhouse and Willis Hall, is the funniest of the kitchen-sinks and the most iconoclastic. Billy Fisher refutes the supposed Northern virtue of communitarianism: 'I don't like knowing everybody – or becoming a part of things.' That struck a guilty chord with me, because neither do I. Billy wishes to exchange Yorkshire life for his personal dreamworld of Ambrosia, rather than the big time in London.

In *The Watchers on the Shore*, Stan Barstow's sequel to *A Kind of Loving*, Vic Brown does actually move from Cressley in Yorkshire to Longford in Essex, which is (supposedly, since it doesn't exist) only forty miles from London. He has 'collywobbles at the thought of leaving', but 'I know why I *have* to go: to get out, once and for all, of this dead, dreary, do-as-you've-always-done atmosphere to somewhere where I can stand on my own two feet in some good free air.'

Dad was offered a big promotion in 1974 that would have taken him from York to British Rail headquarters in London. He too had collywobbles – and fair enough, since he was the recently widowed father of two children. A couple of years later, he told me why he'd turned down the offer: 'I was petrified.' The discrepancy in house prices between north and south wasn't a factor because there wasn't much of one at the time. In *The Watchers on the Shore*, Vic's wife Ingrid (the one with whom he has only 'a kind of loving') speculates, almost as an afterthought: 'I bet it costs more to live there than it does here.'

The Watchers on the Shore contains self-satire by Barstow. His hero, Vic, meets Wilf Cotton, successful author of two Northern kitchen-sink plays with the superbly dreary titles, *Jack Told My Father* and *Day After Day*. Vic suggests that being from Yorkshire is 'like blue blood in the theatre', but Wilf says, 'People won't take north-country working-class stuff for its novelty value any more. It's got to be good in its own right.'

Strange to think, in the globalised modern world, that there was once an excess of Yorkshireness in the media. My friend Tim Lott, whose father worked in a greengrocer's shop in West London, can claim to be that rare thing, a working-class novelist. His books feature working-class Londoners, and he is a student of the whole subject of working-class authorship. He thinks the Yorkshire kitchen-sink men had a very lucky break. 'The point is not that they overshadowed Southern working-class writers — but that there were no working-class Southern writers published, perhaps because they weren't "exotic" enough for southern publishers.'

Of the above-mentioned novelists, one who particularly interests me is David Storey, the son of a miner who gravitated to Kentish Town, north London. If I attempted to fictionalise the importance of the North—South train shuttle in my own creative life, I might create a character like the young Storey, who was torn artistically between literature and painting. The latter seemed to be winning out when he secured a place at the Slade School of Fine Art in London. At the same time, he was playing professional rugby league for Leeds. This double life, he recalled, when interviewed by James Campbell for the *Guardian* of 31 January 2004, 'had a very poor effect on the other players, who were all young coal miners — this artist swanning in for matches. At the Slade, meanwhile, I was seen as a bit of an oaf. I only really felt at home on the train, where the two different parts of my life came together.'

While on the train he'd write novels — half a dozen

unpublished ones until *This Sporting Life* was accepted. Whereas most of the kitchen-sinkers were one-hit wonders, Storey hung around. He won the Booker Prize in 1976 for *Saville*.

In this survey of kitchen-sinks, I have kept back that relative latecomer, *A Kestrel for a Knave*, by Barry Hines, which was published in 1968 and filmed by Ken Loach in 1969 as *Kes*. Jarvis Cocker's addendum to his praise of those writers was, 'But of course, the daddy of them all is *Kes*.'

I've read the book, and I've seen the film many times. Billy Casper, growing up in an oppressive South Yorkshire pit village, finds escape from the dourness of life when he steals a fledgling kestrel and begins learning falconry, using a stolen instruction book. It does not end happily, of course. The film was regarded with reverence in my boyhood, and we were shown it in school. The message was: 'Take note. This is who you are – or who you would be if you came from a grittier part of Yorkshire.' The poet and broadcaster Ian McMillan *did* come from a grittier Yorkshire place, namely Barnsley, where he still lives. (He is the 'Bard of Barnsley'.). It seems that, for the young McMillan, *A Kestrel for a Knave* was as liberating and uplifting as the kestrel was for Billy. On 21 March 2016, he wrote in the *Guardian,* 'What really made me grin and bang the settee arm with my pudgy fist was the way the characters spoke: they talked just like me. Somehow Hines ... managed to get that minimalist Barnsley poetry down on the page without the apostrophes flying round the paragraphs like racing pigeons.' *Kes* also struck me as powerful, but I can't have been viewing it from the right angle, because the main feeling it left me with was that I wanted to see more of the amusingly pugnacious games teacher, Mr Sugden, played by Brian Glover. He removes his tracksuit top to reveal a Man

United number 9 shirt, fitting his tubby form too tightly.
'I'm Charlton today, lad,' he explains, 'all over the field . . .
It's too cold for t'striker. Besides, Denis Law's in the wash.'
In other words, I liked the funny bits, where Hines was
writing with the levity of a Waterhouse.

Kes was the high watermark of Yorkshire Kitchen-
Sinkery as traditionally understood. A new genre emerged,
nominally about Yorkshire but also more globalised and
generic, and less real, in the sense of having happy end-
ings. This genre is characterised by Anthony Clavane, as
'the American/Thatcherite dream of the individual who,
against all the odds, makes good', and these new heroes,
he contends, are found in *The Full Monty* (unemployed
men from Sheffield become strippers) or *Billy Elliot* (miner's
son becomes a ballet dancer). The West End musical (and
now film) *Everybody's Talking About Jamie*, about a Sheffield
schoolboy who wants to be a drag queen, is in the same
genre. We might also mention the film *God's Own Country*
(2017), about a homosexual relationship on a Yorkshire hill
farm. The implication is that for a young man to abandon
machismo is more transgressive in repressed Yorkshire than
elsewhere. There's a hint of this in *Billy Liar*, when Billy's
exasperated father says of his whimsical son, 'He's like a
lass himself.' But in a way these heroes are not new. All of
Yorkshire kitchen-sinkery was about escaping Yorkshire;
about Yorkshireness not being enough.

I suppose I assumed I would pen my own kitchen-sink
novel, and it would be in the traditional mode: serious and
miserable.* In the meantime, I would write journalism.

One of my early commissions was to cover the Edinburgh
Book Festival. It would have been 1989 or so. On the train

---

*   In the event, I wrote crime fiction.

back to London, I travelled with the brassy *Daily Express* columnist Jean Rook, who – it gradually dawned on me – was *interviewing* me for some reason or other. I was half flattered, half alarmed. Clive James said of Jean Rook that she was 'unusually prone to writing and talking in cliches', and when she wrote up our chat she reached for 'Northern Yuppie'. Rook, who was from Hull, probably regarded me with suspicion for having remained on the train after York – in other words for being so presumptuous as to do what she'd done and move south.

One of my early targets was a page in the *Guardian* called Grassroots, on which ran Northern features, as though the paper were attempting to atone for having dropped the prefix 'Manchester' from its name. I sent them an account of a mouse fair in Cleckheaton. It was rejected by Grassroots but taken by the new *Independent*. It was a decent piece; I'd got lucky with some mouse fanciers who'd bred what they called a 'blue' mouse (in practice it was a sort of RAF grey). But other pieces read queasily now. I had a decade-long association with the paper called at the time the *London Evening Standard* ('London' was dropped in 2018), which, given that geographical specification, was very generous in letting me talk up Yorkshire. On 20 November 2001, I wrote a piece pegged to the apparent unpopularity of Jamie Oliver (who's from Essex) in the North. 'But there are lots more reasons why Northerners don't like the South,' ran the standfirst. 'Yorkshireman Andrew Martin explains.' One of the Northern bugbears, I alleged, was the term 'Home Counties': 'Why shouldn't Northumberland, Yorkshire, Lancashire and Cumbria be classified as the Home Counties? They're home to the people who live there, aren't they?' At the time, I had a column in the *New Statesman* called Northside – not bad going for somebody who lived in London.* The general theme was 'It's nice up North' (to quote the title of the film in which Graham Fellows stars as John Shuttleworth). I wrote about the pleasantly slower pace of life in Yorkshire: a butcher's shop in York had a chair for customers to sit down on while they waited; I noted that in Yorkshire, pedestrians on zebra crossings don't feel obliged to scurry across waving a craven thanks to the driver, as they do in London, where everyone crosses under sufferance.

In any given week back then, I might take the train north to get another dose of Yorkshireness for the column, thereby spending at least as much as the actual fee. Some of my articles crashed straight into the North–South divide. A piece for the *Telegraph* about a scheme to re-locate people from a poor London borough to Huddersfield elicited a letter from a Yorkshire reader: 'ridiculously patronising' was her general theme. About ten years ago, I wrote an article for the *Guardian* in praise of York. A friend of mine who actually does live in York, said, 'I read your article online. Did you see the comments from readers?' Before I could get out the words, 'I never read those, and I don't want to know what they said,' she continued, 'They all said, "If he likes York so much why doesn't he live here?"'

I don't often write journalism about Yorkshire these days. There isn't a market for it. I mainly write about Yorkshire in novels, and *historical* novels at that; and this present book is largely (but I hope not entirely) retrospective. I'm much surer about what Yorkshire used to be than what it is today. 'Professional Yorkshireman' is not quite a dead genre, but it is dying. Jimmy Savile went down with the ship; or it might be said that he scuttled the ship. When, as a boy, I watched Savile on TV, he scared me. He was *hard*, being from the

---

* At the time, I would do events in York bookshops billed as 'Local Author'.

hard town of Leeds. Geoff Boycott, from quite near Leeds, was also hard – still is, and in recent years, he seems to have been maintaining the old-fashioned Yorkshire tone single-handedly. I found him compelling on *Test Match Special*, for his knowledge of the game and sheer truculence. During 2019, his last season on the programme, another commentator (some urbane Southerner) welcomed him to the microphone with 'Good morning, Geoffrey,' but Geoffrey was not interested in the goodness of the morning. Instead, he said, 'Well, the new ball's gone through faster because it's *harder*.'

Alan Bennett is also from Leeds. He embodies the dreamy Yorkshire tone, but he too is hard in his own way, more acerbic than most people think, and certainly a survivor – almost the last man standing among the truly famous 'Professionals'. (I have never, by the way, considered Professional Yorkshire-ness incompatible with true talent.) Simon Armitage is up there as well. Most people know Judi Dench is from Yorkshire (from York, indeed), but they might not be so sure about Ben Kingsley (born Krishna Pandit Bhanji in Snainton, North Yorks) or the Kaiser Chiefs (Leeds), or Leigh Francis, aka Keith Lemon (also Leeds), or the late Diana Rigg (Doncaster). The exciting – and marketable – edginess that some Northerners once embodied is now more likely to be detected in persons of a BAME background.

I never really achieved lift-off as a Professional Yorkshireman, for which I blame the declining demand for Yorkshireness. I tell myself I was simply born at the wrong time to emulate, say, J. B. Priestley. In *Yorkshire: A Lyrical History of England's Greatest County*, Richard Morris writes that J. B. Priestley 'repeatedly celebrated the "high places" intercalated between West Riding conurbations.' But he also had a taste for the 'high places' in north London. In 1928, when he was thirty-four, Priestley left Bradford for a big flat in Well Walk, Hampstead. In 1931, the success of *The Good Companions* enabled him to buy a Georgian mansion in Highgate formerly occupied by Samuel Taylor Coleridge. There are commemorative plaques on both buildings. (Priestley did move back to the Yorkshire 'high places' posthumously. After his death in 1986, his ashes were scattered at Hubberholme.)[*]

I too live in Highgate – not through literary success but because I married a woman who had made sound investments in London property before I met her. And I will probably *stay* here, because my wife – born in Canada and raised in London – would never move to Yorkshire. She feels 'at home' in London, whereas her word for me is 'displaced'. I sometimes think that, like David Storey, I only feel at home on the train to Yorkshire.

---

[*] I frequent the Mayfair tobacconists where Priestley bought his pipe tobacco. He was a 'miserable bugger', apparently.

The Critical Mass

Our train is pulling away for Yorkshire.

These days, I am always glad to depart from the Cross. It has lost its hold over me, and all its gritty glamour. The station is no longer redolent of either Yorkshire or London. There is nothing but trains in the modern King's Cross, and since those trains are not very characterful or diverse, the whole station is bleak. Since 2012, all the facilities have been bundled into another canopy pitched against the side of the station, but this one stands to the side rather than the front, hence its name, the Western Concourse. (The other one didn't have a name.) It houses all the usual chains: Boots, Pret, Costa, W. H. Smith and that international queue of people waiting to be photographed in the Harry Potter pose. It is globalised, like the whole of the King's Cross Central development, which houses a French bank, the British headquarters of YouTube and Google's main UK office. At the heart of the regenerated railway lands is Coal Drops Yard. In this two-storey structure, the coal trains from Yorkshire once unloaded, presumably with the trains on the upper storey, the coal crashing down into the lower one. Today, it's small shops ('boutique retail') and bars and restaurants ('foodie hotspots'). Historic numbered signs aligned to the brick arches of the Drops remain in situ, and speak of 'North London Freight Depot', but what all this had to do with the actual North is, I would have thought, fading rapidly from public memory.

There's still a certain amount of Yorkshire-style plain speaking: Gasworks Tunnel and Railway Street survive under those names. There's still a train called the *Flying Scotsman*, but it's an obscure and wispy phenomenon compared to the old one, and it only runs from north to south, rather than both ways as the old one did. A couple of years ago, a friend of mine who lives in Yorkshire said, 'It's a longer journey from Yorkshire to London than it is the other way,' by which he meant that it's more tiring and demanding to go from north to south, since you seem to be travelling from the slow-paced past to the dynamic future.

Heading north, it takes about twenty minutes to escape the netherworld of the London suburbs, past the Emirates Stadium on the right, which is doubly alienating, being named after a foreign airline, and bearing Stalinist murals of giant footballers in a comradely embrace, and then baleful Alexandra Palace to the left, which would resemble a haunted house it if were prettier. When the train has finally done with London, it doesn't find a new centre of gravity for a while, unless you count, say, Stevenage as a place.

After an hour, the train goes through the historic county of Huntingdonshire, which is pretty negligible as a topographical entity: 359 square miles compared to Yorkshire's 4,600. Huntingdonshire has a population of 177,000, whereas Yorkshire has 5.4 million – about the same as Scotland. Huntingdonshire would not presume to call itself 'God's Own County', which Yorkshire does, along with (and possibly even more grandiosely) 'God's Own *Country*'. There is no Huntingdonshire Day, as far as I know, whereas

Yorkshire Day occurs on 1 August. It does in Yorkshire, anyway, and the celebrations are convened by the Yorkshire Society, which was founded in 1980. Another compliment Yorkshire has bestowed on itself is 'the Broad Acres'. John Speed, mapmaker, supplied a commentary to his Yorkshire map of 1627, in which Yorkshire is described as 'this great Province', 'so worthy a country', 'this Nation', 'this great region'. Yorkshire is 'farre greater and more numerous in the Circuit of her miles, than any Shire of England.' In *West Riding Sketches* (1874), James Burnley wrote: 'It is probable, I think, that the Yorkshireman's pride in his native place indirectly proceeds, in a great measure, from the fact that the county to which he belongs is the largest shire in the three kingdoms.'

On 8 May 2014, Simon Jenkins wrote a *Guardian* piece headlined, 'Mighty Yorkshire is another country in waiting.' The 'peg' was one of those small news events that seemed designed to trigger big statements: 'If little Cornwall can now be afforded "European minority status" why not the mighty province of York?' There have been plenty of opportunities to argue for Yorkshire's independence in recent times. In 1998, Scotland and Wales were devolved. Why not Yorkshire? In 1999, when the Greater London Authority was created, there was an opportunity to say that London was being favoured as usual. The failure of the North-East to vote for devolution when given the chance to do so in the referendum of 2004 might have taken the wind out of any Yorkshire Nationalist's sails − or strengthened their conviction that the county must go it alone.

In 2016, Manchester became the flagship of the Northern Powerhouse (sorry for mixed metaphor), having elected the first Metro Mayor with devolved powers under the provisions of the Cities and Local Government

Devolution Act of 2016. Meanwhile, Yorkshire couldn't get its act together. Sheffield City Region eventually got its mayor in 2018. A West Yorkshire Metro Mayor was not elected until 2021.

In 2014 – the year the Jenkins piece appeared – I was commissioned to write about the Yorkshire Party for an article published in the European edition of *Newsweek* on 8 December. I attended a meeting of the party – newly founded by two Yorkshire businessmen, Richard Carter and Stewart Arnold – in Milnsbridge, a suburb of Huddersfield in the Colne Valley. It was a scene of unmoderated Yorkshireness: a black canal, a colossal railway viaduct, the lowering South Pennines. After a supper of fish and chips, eaten from paper while sheltering from some of the rain (but not the wind) under the viaduct, I walked into a dark, terraced street. As a church clock struck seven, a door was propped open, and a triangle of light spilled out from what had been the Milnsbridge Socialist Club, now reinvented as the Red and the Green Club, a co-operative venture. Over the next half hour, a couple of dozen people turned up, most of them collecting a pint of a Yorkshire real ale, Black Sheep. ('Born and bred in Masham, North Yorkshire', boasts the brewery.) A prime mover in the revival of the club was Professor Paul Salveson, a sixty-two-year-old former Labour councillor and an advocate of the Northern working-class traditions of mutuality and self-help, which he has applied to the imperiled railway branch lines of Britain. Salveson, who began his career as a train guard at Blackburn, founded the Community Rail movement, which has saved many British branch lines by enlisting local communities in their upkeep. He contrasts this 'bottom-up' approach with the statist, 'top-down' mentality of the Labour Party, and the centralisation of British government since the War. Salveson contended that the needs of Yorkshire could not be met from London.

During the meeting, I became increasingly aggrieved on behalf of my native county, especially on learning that 'historic' Yorkshire contains three of the ten poorest regions in Northern Europe. The Yorkshire Party was — and is — progressive, striving not to appear parochial. At the time of the meeting, it was called Yorkshire First, the name later abandoned for accidentally echoing that of the far-right 'Britain First'. Salveson, whose surname is Norwegian, had a neat soundbite here: 'Yorkshire was *founded* by migrants!' (Danish Vikings.)

A woman at the meeting worried that the party was too male — also that it romanticised Yorkshire. She cited the party's website, which displayed a photograph of pretty scenery. Carter responded that the iconography of the party was evolving, and that a third of those who had taken 'the Yorkshire pledge' (a declaration of support for the party) were women. But he acknowledged that 'Yorkshire' and 'Yorkshireman' were commonly elided, and that a Yorkshireman was taken to be a distinct type, namely an old-school plain speaker. Carter called this 'the Geoff Boycott problem'. Another woman at the meeting — a student at Huddersfield University — said that all the good internships were in the capital; that the migration of young people to the south was an issue for even the most successful Yorkshire towns. (At this point, my feeling of indignation on behalf of my native county was overtaken by a feeling of guilt for having been part of this brain drain.)

A show of hands indicated strong support for a Salveson candidacy in Colne Valley, a three-way marginal with a Tory incumbent. He didn't do very well, as it turned out, and when I last spoke to him, a couple of years ago, he admitted to having 'gone over to the dark side' (moved to Lancashire), but he remains a thought-provoking writer on matters Northern. I spoke to the Yorkshire Party's co-founder, Stewart Arnold, just after the European referendum. All of Yorkshire voted to leave except the most prosperous towns: Leeds, Harrogate and York. Arnold was a Remainer, but he now saw an opportunity to move on. He'd spoken to one Leave voter after the vote, who said, 'That's Brussels sorted, now we sort London.' Arnold still thinks Yorkshire is a very devolve-able unit, being so big, and with natural borders: 'It's got the critical mass if you want to do stuff.' If independence-for-Yorkshire ever became a realisable cause, I would feel obliged to support it, but it would be hypocritical of me to *argue* for it, having left the county for London.

Our train has arrived at Peterborough, which is in Cambridgeshire, but has become a London commuter town. A lot of Tube train drivers live there, I was once told. I don't mind hearing London accents after Peterborough, but their owners had better play by Northern rules. Once, when I was in First Class with my wife while heading north on the ECML, I was complaining about a certain magazine editor while a man on the other side of the gangway periodically fielded phone calls in urbane Southern tones. He got up to go to the loo and when he returned, I noticed his fly was open, so I said, 'Your fly's open.' He nodded thanks but blushed; he was annoyed. As he sat down, he said, 'Apparently so is yours, metaphorically speaking.'

'I'm sorry?'

'With regard to that editor you were talking about.' (His implication, I assumed, was that I had been somehow negligent, or committed some faux pas, in my dealings with that person.)

When we'd got off the train, my wife said, 'The trouble was that you told him his fly was open in a very Yorkshire way.'

'But I just told him *straight*.'

'Exactly.'

As our train heads north, there seems nothing to grasp onto. England does a poor show of providing salient features on the first 170 miles of the ECML, and you can see how Yorkshire has developed its superiority complex. We arrive at Grantham. I seem to have been on the train a while, but this is definitely not a Northern town – can't be, since Margaret Thatcher was born there. But it's not a Southern place, either. Grantham's in Lincolnshire. It's also in the East Midlands, which is classed as a mere 'region'; the *West* Midlands, on the other hand, is one of those dreaded Metropolitan Counties, as well as being a Unitary Authority and Ceremonial County. You could say that one virtue of the West Midlands is that it neatly corrals the ugliest towns in Britain: Birmingham, Wolverhampton and Coventry – or at least, the towns generally considered the ugliest. I feel sorry for the Midlands, perpetually drowned out by the North–South slanging match; the very word 'Midlands' is only used in utilitarian contexts like 'East Midlands Airport'.

Robert Shore is the author of an entertaining ebook called *Fifty Great Things to Come Out of the Midlands*. 'As for the Midlands, he writes,

> well, as a badge of identity, it's not like coming from the North, is it? Few people would know where to draw the boundary lines that separate the coastline-free Midlands from the North and South of England, those two monolithic and self-mythologising geographical constructs that sit above and below it on the geographical map.

The fifty great things, incidentally, include the Industrial Revolution – because of Isaac Watt, Josiah Wedgwood, Joseph Priestley (discoverer of oxygen) – and Robbie Williams, who's from Stoke.

We come to Newark, where the Nottingham–Lincoln line crosses the ECML on what is the last flat crossing in Britain; the train gives a judder that tells me Yorkshire is approaching. It's always a moment of relief: London has gone.

Our gateway to God's Own County is Doncaster, a less auspicious one, admittedly, than Sheffield on the line from St Pancras. In any word association game, Doncaster would once have triggered 'coal mining', 'locomotive and carriage building' and 'horse racing' (because of the St Leger). To the left, as the train approaches the station today, is what used to be 'the Plant', where locos and carriages were built until 2008 or so. The *Flying Scotsman* locomotive was built at the Plant, and people on the train would have been able to view the fumaceous works from carriages that were probably also made there. Today, there are sparser signs of railway engineering. (An American company still carries out some carriage refurbishment on the site.)

Doncaster now makes a self-effacing statement. Its calling card is its proximity, by road and rail links, to other places: distribution. There is Doncaster iPort, or Doncaster Inland Port, an international rail terminal opened in 2018. There is an Amazon 'logistics facility': a great, blank slab of a building, entirely uningratiating; and there are two other Amazon hubs at Doncaster. Doncaster iPort can easily be confused with Doncaster International Railport, opened in 1995, which was originally known as Direct for Europe Doncaster.

In the *Guardian* of 11 October 2018, John Harris looked at how Doncaster as a town might be asserting itself against the anonymity of its 'strange, uncertain edgelands' by adapting its town centre to provide what digital retailers cannot. In describing some imaginative council initiatives taking place in the long shadow of these 'Leviathan' warehouses – a new arts centre; a Cultural and Learning Centre, new bars and cafés – Harris wrote of the fate of English towns becoming an 'obsession' among politicians, 'many of which [the towns] seemed to express their collective fears by voting for Brexit', and Doncaster was 69 per cent 'Leave'. I would add to Harris's analysis that the desire to reclaim a sense of place is perhaps especially strong in Yorkshire, the county being so proud of its topography.

Just north of Doncaster, any passenger looking left would once have seen long lines of coal trucks on colliery railways. Today, the train rolls past Drax power station, whose cooling towers look like an industrial Stonehenge, or the funnels of some great distant liner – one that is perpetually steaming away from Yorkshire, its connections to the county's coal having faded away. The last Yorkshire coal mine, Kellingley pit, closed in 2016, signalling the end of deep-level mining not only in Yorkshire but also in the UK. Today, Drax burns imported biomass brought to it by quarter mile-long trains from Immingham, Tyneside, Liverpool and Hull. Some of the Yorkshire coal it used to burn came from the Selby Coalfield, which opened in 1993 and closed in 2004. The opening caused the East Coast Main Line to have to divert. If it hadn't diverted, trains would have had to run slow for fear of causing subsidence in the mine. In industrial (and somehow Yorkshire) language, slowdowns over mines are called 'pitfall slacks', but a prettier phrase would have been invented for the apologetic on-board announcements.

The old route was more picturesque. The line crossed

the Ouse at Selby, and you were suddenly intimate with that little town, and right alongside its affronted-looking Abbey. Then the line crossed the Ouse again at the village of Naburn, where the old railway bridge now dreams its days away in a thickening wood. After Naburn, the line passed the village of Bishopthorpe, where my grandfather was born in a cottage on the main street; then it ran past my alma mater, Ashfield Secondary Modern school. In, say, a maths lesson on a rainy Wednesday afternoon, I'd watch the fast trains to London from the classroom windows and dream of launching myself in the Metropolis.

Now, the train approaches York across some bland fields, which give way to a sprawling Tesco. But the ugliness of the Tesco's is soon counteracted by York Station, which is all the grander for being built on a curve, like a Georgian crescent. The span of the iron roof is 800 feet, and it's technically demanding to make a structure like that on a curve.

The arrival of my train at York is announced by automated 'Anne', who has followed me from London, so I am not greeted by a Yorkshire accent, but then I never was. In my boyhood, York had a live station announcer, but she sounded like a member of the royal family. I used to think she must have availed herself of the elocution lessons offered in the window of a smart stationery shop in the suburb of Acomb, near where I lived: Mrs Something's Academy. The most beautiful girl at my secondary school had taken lessons there. Her parents took the *Yorkshire Post*, so they were what I considered 'county' people (prosperous, slightly countrified), and when I suggested to her that her equally beautiful mother had ginger hair, she severely corrected me: 'Auburn'. With its silver cups and framed certificates for achievements in elocution or drama, and newspaper clippings attesting to pupils' success in TV and film, that window display seemed to me a little shrine venerating London and escape from Yorkshire. But we ourselves will not be escaping Yorkshire for a while.

YORK

Living in the Past

If I'm in funds on arrival from London, I take a taxi to my York base – my stepmother's house – and a conversation with the driver might ensue. 'Where've you come in from?' he might ask, as we pull away from the station forecourt. 'London,' I trepidatiously reply, and a silence might descend.* Perhaps I will offer some conciliatory remark. If the weather's fine in York but wasn't in London, I might say, with exaggerated Yorkshire accent, 'It's chucking it down in London, you know,' or perhaps I'll essay 'siling down', which is how Dad described heavy rain. Whether this is a Yorkshire term, I'm not sure, but I've never heard it in London.

If things haven't been going well in London, I'll take a bus. A couple of years ago when I did that, a sign on the lower deck read, 'Have a safe and comfy journey' – a Shuttleworth-ism. As I travel to my stepmother's house, I imagine the people left on the train gossiping about York, confident, as the train pulls away from the city, that all the

---

* On one of my return visits, the same question was put to me in a York pub by a York man with whom I was about to play a game of pool – it was winner-stays-on and he was a stranger to me. When I replied, 'London,' he said, 'Sorry I asked,' and the game was played in silence.

Yorkies will have got off. I imagine them saying things like, 'It's a nice place, but not proper Yorkshire.' Once, when I'd stayed on the train beyond York, I heard a Geordie voice say, 'It's more like bloody Godalming than a Northern town.' (On the same occasion, I overheard an American woman pointing at the Minster, which comes into view after the station, and saying, 'Look, there's the castle!')

York is *not* like Godalming, or anywhere else in Surrey. It usually has a Labour MP, and I'd like to see how the person who made that remark handles himself at midnight in Micklegate. (We'll be going to Micklegate.) But I've always felt that York was, in Yorkshire terms, embarrassingly genteel; that it could only be said to be a Yorkshire sort of place if you ignored the rest of the county. As we have seen, York stood aloof from the Ridings. It's perfectly possible to pick up a book about Yorkshire and find no mention in the index of the city after which the county was named. The gloomier and more social-realist the book the less likely you are to find an entry for York. This is true, for example, of *A Yorkshire Tragedy*, Anthony Clavane's brilliant but depressing survey of how the communitarian aspects of Yorkshire sport dwindled because of de-industrialisation. York's two salubrious industries, railways and chocolate-making, have certainly declined, but the slack has been taken up by service industries. When I was growing up in 1970s York, there was only one proper restaurant in the town, if you ignored pubs and takeaways. It was a trattoria, Ristorante Bari, which occupied one of the charmingly buckled buildings in the medieval street called the Shambles, and it was advertised by still photographs projected on the safety curtain of the long-gone ABC cinema. 'Come to Ristorante Bari,' a voice half-Yorkshire and half-Italian urged, 'the ideal place for your birthday party or wedding celebration.' Everyone did go there, and the restaurant survived until about the time I started writing this book. Ten or so years ago, I asked the manager what he thought was the secret of this longevity. He said, 'Well, it's a bit unique, this place, intit?'

'How do you mean?' I asked.

'Well, Italian, intit?'

He seemed unaware that by then there were plenty of Italian restaurants among the three hundred or so in York, now that the city's main industry by far is leisure and tourism.

Being sentimental about York, I was delighted at the persistence of the restaurant, and depressed by its closure. This same sentimentality makes me look away from any broadcast or print story about trouble that might be occurring in contemporary York. I like to think that really bad York events are all in the past.

The city was ravaged by William the Conqueror, for instance. On the night of 16 March 1190, 150 York Jews besieged in Clifford's Tower, the keep of York Castle, were massacred or committed suicide rather than renounce their faith. (When I told my wife, who's Jewish and Canadian, about this episode, she said, 'That might explain the funny feeling I always have when I go to York.') In 1536, Richard Aske, a leader of the Pilgrimage of Grace (a Northern rebellion against the dissolution of the monasteries) was hung in chains from that same Tower. The Battle of Marston Moor, which took place eight miles south-west of York on 2 July 1644, signified the collapse of York as a Royalist redoubt in the Civil War: there were 4,000 Royalist casualties. In his social survey of York conducted in 1901, *Poverty: A Study of Town Life*, Seebohm Rowntree coined the term 'poverty line', and concluded that 3,000 families in the city lived below it, especially in the districts of Hungate and

Walmgate, where the housing was consequently improved, but these remained 'tough' areas for decades afterwards. Police constables patrolled in twos, and Dad recalled how – as a boy in the 1930s – he and *his* father were walking the stretch of the Bar Walls bounding Walmgate when they encountered some men sitting on the walls and blocking the way while playing a game of jacks or knucklebones. My grandfather said 'Excuse me' to the men, who made no response at all. So he and Dad climbed down from the Walls.

York's history, of which there is such a lot, always seemed at variance with that of the rest of the county. Take the role played by topography. The most celebrated aspect of God's Own County is the hills, of which York has hardly any worth the name, although St Helen's railway bridge, which lay between our suburban house and the centre of town, felt like one, especially when the ramshackle pushrod I was riding was stuck in third gear. York is flat, lying in the centre of that southern-sounding concept: a vale. I used to feel guilty that the rivers rushing down from the Pennines – Swale, Ure, Nidd, Wharf, where they might have powered mills – drained into York's river, the slow, complacent Ouse, bringing alluvium (or something like that) to its flood plain, and making the Vale of York so fertile. So the other rivers did all the work and the Ouse took the credit.

This relative flatness made York the original transport hub. It's what attracted the Romans, and at junior school we drew self-congratulatory maps showing Eboracum nestled cosily at the confluence of the Ouse and the Foss, with arrows indicating the inflow of seaborne supplies along the Humber and the Ouse, along with the corn-growing Wolds to the East and the forerunner of the A1 to the west. At first, Eboracum was a military camp for the fight against the

Brigantes, dwellers of the Pennine hills: an early instance of York against Yorkshire, you might say. In *c*.AD 213, Eboracum became the capital of Lower Britannia. Under the Vikings, it became Jórvik, a trading axis of international dimensions. When Viking Jórvik became York in early medieval times, it was a city second only to London, and that was still arguably the case until the nineteenth century.

We felt we had been blessed by history. It was as though we occupied a living room stuffed with heirlooms and trophies. In York, things conspired to slow down time and preserve the past. Waterlogging, caused by its low-lying situation and clay substratum, preserved relics for the archaeologists to find. There was little Victorian or post-Victorian development to disrupt the historic core. In the Second World War, York was not much bombed. In the 1940s, its quaintest and most famous street, the Shambles, was renovated – an early example of a local authority conservation scheme. In 1946, the York Civic Trust was founded, from justified wariness of the post-war 'spirit of renewal' that would go on to wreck so many towns.

In 1968, the Civic Trust was involved in commissioning the Esher Report, by Lord Esher, which would lead to the spring cleaning of the relatively few industrial eyesores of central York. In 1970, in celebration of the Silver Jubilee of the Civic Trust, the car park was cleared from the biggest of York's central squares, Exhibition Square, and a fountain erected instead. This was the theme of my formative years: conservation, York discovering its own beauty. In *Why York is Special*, a pamphlet published in 2006 by the Civic Trust, Ron Cooke writes that 'conservation took root in York just in time to preserve the essential qualities of the ancient city – and that it arrived in most other English cities just too late.' In the same pamphlet, George Pace, architectural historian, writes that 'propinquity', created by the constriction of the Bar Walls, is the key to York's specialness: the 'spider's web of streets, lanes, snickets', the 'numberless little irregular places, squares, piazzas, spatial leaks, keyholes and the like'.

I regarded the medieval (originally Roman) Bar Walls as a kind of fairy ring; all the magic of York was inside them. I would never have become a writer – certainly not a writer of historical fiction – were it not for my many hours of daydreaming in central York. It distressed me that Dad didn't like going into the centre of town: 'Too many bloody tourists.' But tourists proved you lived in a nice place, and an interesting one. The ten-minute bus journey to the centre was rapid time travel: Victorian, Georgian, medieval, Roman, yet with the dominant shades of masonry fairly consistently pink and white – festive colours – and everything low and cosily huddled except the Minster, that great white ghost in the very centre.

I became aware, while living in London and writing about the Tube, that a man more influential than me had also regarded central York as a haven or urban ideal. Frank Pick, second-in-command of the London Underground in the inter-war years, integrated what had been a disparate collection of railways into a coherent Tube network by the creation of a common visual style. He had grown up in York, and the effect of the city upon him is discussed in *The Avant-Garde in Interwar England: Medieval Modernism and the London Underground,* by Michael T. Saler. The book is about 'how the nineteenth-century English arts and crafts merged with the twentieth-century avant-garde, romantic medievalism with visual modernism'. Saler places Pick at the centre of that movement, contending that the physical layout of York, with its towering cathedral and ancient Roman wall encircling the city, left an indelible impression on him. York could be grasped as a civic community: the whole was more than the sum of its parts, which Pick did not find to be true for London.

By making the Tube coherent, manageable, orderly – York-like qualities – Pick sought to make London likewise. Pick was also an enthusiastic supporter of the London County Council's proposal of 1935 to set up a green belt that would contain the sprawl of London. 'The green belt would be the modern version of the "sacred circle" of the York city wall,' writes Saler. It would 'help transform London from its current cosmopolitan chaos to the "provincial" cosmos of Pick's desire.' According to this argument, millions of Tube travellers in London have experienced York even if they've never been there.

The magnesium limestone of the Minster and the Bar Walls was black during my early childhood, as it would have been during Pick's. I thought that was their natural colour, and York had a tarnished silver look under grey skies and rain. In the early Seventies, as the Tower of the Minster was being propped up, it was also cleaned, and what had been a black rotten tooth became a gleaming white molar. Sometimes today, in the right weather, the limestone of Minster and Walls has a lunar glow.

In 1971, the important medieval street, Stonegate, was pedestrianised. The street became, in effect, a stage set or a museum exhibit, like the mock-streets created in the York Castle Museum. York pioneered pedestrianisation. This, and the rejection of a scheme for an inner ring road, boosted my sanguinity about the city: cars were bad, and trains were

good, and I was on the right side of the argument, since Dad
worked on the railways. In 1971, the York Archaeological
Trust began some trial excavations, just in case the road
scheme should be approved, leading to the entombment
of many treasures under tons of tarmac. These excavations
became a full-blown dig between 1976 and 1981 when a
hippyish cohort of students from York and around the world
worked in a football pitch-sized hole at Coppergate. There
was a viewing area for passing shoppers and the sifting of the
mud in this hole* – the burrowing into the past – appeared
to be the dominant activity of central York.

As a boy, I inhabited the York past in diverse extra-
curricular ways. In 1976, aged fourteen, I performed in the
York Mystery Plays, held in the Museum Gardens – the
precincts of the ruined St Mary's Abbey – which are stuffed
with listed buildings and ancient monuments. The audition
and rehearsals were held in an old sorting office off nearby
Lendal, or, as the several Americans involved in the production incorrectly called it, 'Lendal *Street*'. At the audition,
I stood on the makeshift stage, and the director, standing
at the other end of the room, said something I didn't hear.
I said, 'Pardon?' and the director turned to her assistant
and nodded. They could hear me clearly, so I had landed
a speaking part – that of Herod's Messenger. I can be seen
in costume for the role, standing next to King Herod, in
a photograph in Paul Chrystal's excellent book, *York in the
1970s*. The photograph is in black and white, which is just
as well, since the costume involved a pink corduroy smock
and green tights. During a dress rehearsal, I was interviewed
by a journalist from BBC *Woman's Hour*. She said, 'What
do you think about the fact that the plays are funded by the

---

*   Now the Jorvik Centre.

ratepayer?' I said, 'I didn't know they *were* funded by the ratepayer.' I don't think the interview was used.

King Herod was an English teacher at one of the many York private schools, and he turned out to be a very nice man, who had a big influence on me. He advised me to listen to Radio 3, which I have done ever since. But he played free and easy with the script. He liked to improvise while hamming up the panto villain stuff by walking into the audience and belabouring people with a black pudding-like soft truncheon. On the opening night, as I waited by the side of the Abbey ruins to go on and give him the first of my messages (potentially significant news from Bethlehem), I realised that he was too busy joshing with the audience for me to deliver my cue. It would be up to me when to enter. The strain of trying to decide what to do, combined with the tremendous heat of that evening (1976, remember), caused me to throw up, which I did down the side of the remains of a Roman column, the first of many times I have vomited among York antiquities. Most of the subsequent incidents were alcohol-related, York having (it used to be said) a pub for every day of the year within the Bar Walls. Now it's more like a hundred. In the one called the Roman Bath on St Sampson's Square, I used to look through the glass-screened hole in the floor that gave a view of a lately discovered Roman thermae or bathing complex while waiting for my mate Ali – who was sixteen like me, but looked eighteen and had (almost) a moustache – to get the drinks in.

I went to parties at which the above-mentioned student archaeologists were present. It's thirsty work, all that sifting through the mud for doubloons. They liked prog rock, and there was a fittingly medieval look to their kaftans and knee-high boots. The vibe was that of the Jethro Tull song,

'Living in the Past'. As a teenager, I was into rock music, and every Saturday I would come into town to buy a couple of second-hand LPs; then I'd repair to the Minster to sit on a pew reading the *NME*. I used to love going to the Minster; I enjoyed directing tourists there, and I made a point of not agreeing with the York taxi drivers who complained when the road to the side of it was blocked off, to protect it from vibration. I enjoyed climbing the narrow stone steps to the Tower, always magnanimously stepping aside to allow enormous wheezing Americans to descend. After the fire of 1984, which badly damaged the South Transept – to the extent that you could see the sky – I asked a nun if the Tower was still open to visitors. 'Don't be so stupid,' she said, and I have looked differently at nuns ever since. In 2003, an admission charge was imposed on anyone who couldn't prove York residency, thereby exposing my diminishing Yorkshireness.

Aged nineteen, when I was waiting to go to university, I formed a band with my mate Dave. We played our second gig in the upstairs wood-panelled function room of the Black Swan pub on Peaseholme Green, which dates from 1417 and has a mainly seventeenth-century interior. Illegal cock fights used to be held in that room. The landlord asked us not to play too loud, or the pub might collapse.* In about the same year, I went to a nightclub that used to be in Lady Peckett's Yard, a dark medieval courtyard, to watch Joy Division, supported by Sheffield electronic avant-gardists Cabaret Voltaire. My life was full of such collisions of pop culture and medieval surroundings.

Much of my drinking was done on Micklegate, an ancient thoroughfare heralded by Micklegate Bar. That's not a pub,

---

* 'About as tight as a circus net', one muso in the audience was heard to say of our performance.

but a gateway in the city walls. There were, however, at least a dozen pubs on Micklegate (some of which are now quite avant-garde restaurants), and there was a challenge called the 'Micklegate Run', by which you would have a pint in every pub. An elementary injunction to York tourists was, 'Don't go to Micklegate on a Saturday night.' There was a night-club on the street, located in an elegant Georgian building and with the very 1970s name of Ziggy's. If you went to Ziggy's on a weekend when a race meeting had been held on York's beautiful eighteenth-century racecourse (the grandstand dates, in part, from 1754), the bouncers would not have their customary swagger, and would enquire nervously, 'You're not from Wakey, are you, lads?' mean-ing, 'You're not a coal miner from Wakefield, are you, and looking to continue the heavy drinking that you started on the racecourse?' I was so evidently not a coal miner from Wakefield that I was surprised they asked. But I was also flattered because the miners were hard. I once tried to get into Ziggy's with a friend of mine from Oxford University. I was privately doubtful of his prospects, since he wore a white Arran jumper. Sure enough, he was turned away. It was done in a friendly enough way: 'It's the jumper, mate. It's just not Ziggy's.' (Whereas my velvet jacket, drainpipe cords and Chelsea boots would have been nodded through, had I been crass enough to abandon my friend.)

A couple of years later, when I was living in London, I returned to York with this friend. I met him at Nunnery Lane car park, and from there we would have to run the Micklegate gauntlet to access the middle of town. Again, I was anxious on behalf of my friend, who this time wore a tweed suit and a hat − a sort of homburg. We had pro-gressed halfway along Micklegate without comment, even though my friend was discoursing about novels in a surely provocative manner. Then we passed a bloke of about our own age, lounging outside a pub, cigarette in hand. As we approached, he was staring at the hat with contempt. We passed directly in front of him, and nothing was said, but he was only gauging the most appropriate insult. When we were about ten yards past him, he pronounced his verdict: 'You're a pair of fucking gobshites.' We'd got off pretty lightly, I thought.

On any given early evening, I have noticed on my recent return visits, the streets of central York are criss-crossed by men in black caped-coats and top hats: when they encounter each other, they do not raise their hats in friendly greeting because they are all rivals of each other: they are the hosts of the York 'ghost walks'. They carry Victorian doctors' bags, like so many Dr Jekylls, and when I joined one of these walks, the host used this bag to store the ticket money he'd collected from everyone who'd turned up on a certain cobbled courtyard to join the tour. When everyone had paid up, he dashed off around some gabled corner and remained out of sight for half a minute or so. When he sauntered back into view, he said, 'For some of you, that's going to be the biggest fright you'll have all evening.'

He was right. York was much more ghostly in the 1970s, before Lord Esher and his Report had eliminated the dark corners, which were not so much factories as breweries, coal merchants' premises, warehouses, printing works – places that tended to be closed and shuttered in the evening. Just off the above-mentioned Stonegate, there used to be a collection of dowdy, blank courtyards and alleys. If York was a stage set, this was backstage when the theatre was dark. This district has all been developed now, with stylish bijou shops and restaurants. For a while, it was billed as York's Restaurant

Quarter, and there were many signs directing you to it. A few years ago, I dined in a restaurant there that was somehow international in its presentation. Sushi, perhaps? I can't recall, and it's gone now, but there were three clocks on the wall showing different times to demonstrate the cosmopolitanism of the place. They were labelled 'Paris', 'Tokyo', 'New York', but no clock showed the time in Old York.

This is the kind of jaundiced reflection that a middle-aged man is likely to indulge in, I admit. When returning to York, I look out for the landmarks that betoken the city but that seem vulnerable and are on my mental critical list. One was the Army and Navy Stores, on the corner of Fossgate and Pavement. Here you could buy utility clothing for work or dandification purposes: army surplus clobber, railway-men's jackets, chef's hats, boiler suits, steel-capped boots. It smelt of boot polish and wood polish, because a lot of the stock was kept in wooden cabinets. It was countrified: you could buy sleeping bags, gas stoves, and a 'survival' kit that incorporated in a little pouch all you would need if lost on the moors: a plastic poncho, a needle and thread, a fishing hook and line and a small penknife. I asked more than once to view this, but never dared buy it, always detecting in the assistant's eyes a scepticism about my ability to use any component of it except the poncho. In the Army and Navy, I bought the gas mask bag that served as my school satchel, and the ex-RAF greatcoat onto the sleeve of which I sewed a cloth hammer and sickle badge, being somewhat of a Wolfie Smith.* The shop closed in 2013. It is now a bar. Also on the critical list was Bulmer's, a sprawling second-hand shop near Monk Bar on Lord Mayor's Walk, which occupied

---

* For the benefit of younger readers, Wolfie Smith – a character from a 1970s sitcom called *Citizen Smith* – was a self-styled urban guerrilla from Tooting, south London. When I became aware of the Clash, they reminded me of Wolfie Smith.

premises formerly owned by a harness maker. Bulmer's, like the Army and Navy, was countrified and violently inclined. You could buy a rusty catapult, a crossbow, an old airgun, a gasmask, a pair of dusty binoculars. Bulmer's was about adventure and self-realisation, so it's fitting that you could also buy a second-hand electric guitar there. (Fitted kitchens are now sold on the premises.)

Ken Spelman, second-hand bookseller's of Mickelgate, was – and is – on the list, but it survives: a wonderfully sleepy shop, with many books of Yorkshire topography and cartography and a real fire in winter. Also still extant, because it's Grade 2 listed, is a tall, graceful chimney that had been built in 1899 in Walmgate. This being relatively un-industrial York, it is not a factory chimney; it was attached to a rubbish-burning furnace resonantly named the York 'Destructor' and now demolished. The chimney is one of two in York to make it into *Our Grimy Heritage*, by Walter Pickles, a celebration of chimneys. Oddly enough, there are only two entries for Leeds as well (although Halifax has thirteen). The other York one – an elegant 'octagonal stack' on the banks of the Ouse – was also not a factory chimney. It belonged to the York and County Press, publishers of the York evening paper, which remains a model regional paper, but was also more Yorkshire in the past, in that it was called the *Yorkshire Evening Press*, as opposed to its modern incarnation: *The Press*.

I wrote a piece for the *Financial Times* magazine, published in June 2006, called 'Home Truths'. It was a chronicle of York's lost industry, and therefore of lost Yorkshireness. I compared the British Sugar factory at York unfavourably with a new call centre which, to my mind – by the distressing intangibility of its product – epitomised the post-industrial service industries:

I cycle on still heading south, aiming for the chimney of the York Sugar Factory. A notice outside the reception says, 'Number of accident-free days: 49', and I wonder why that's worth boasting about. Forty-nine doesn't seem that many. But there's a kind of dark glamour to the notice. Factory work is dangerous, which is partly why it's associated with masculinity. The building – a great tangle of pipes and silos – looks to me a fit place for a young man to test himself in a way that the CPP call centre, for example, does not. And yet the future of the factory is uncertain. Too much sugar is produced in the European Union and the business is under pressure.

British Sugar closed that factory in the following year; there are homes on the site now. For the article, I spoke to Micheal Gallagher, a clinical psychologist who'd once lived in York, and had a background in labour studies. 'The effect on young men of working in services as opposed to manufacturing has not been much studied,' he said, 'but it should be, given the high rates of suicide and depression among them.' I did not run past him my theory about service and leisure industries, which is to the effect that the Yorkshire character and tone of voice – as adumbrated by Mrs Gaskell – is particularly unsuited to asking, 'Would you like a top-up for the coffee, sir?' Jobs in the leisure industries are also generally badly paid, and today there are people working in York who cannot afford to live in York. They might live in, say, the outskirts of Leeds, whereas the high-rolling professionals of Leeds like to live in York because it's prettier.

I also interviewed the assistant director of economic development at York Council for the piece, and when I spoke of the 'ever-growing service sector', he bristled somewhat. 'A bigger change here', he said coolly, 'is the growth of high-quality jobs in the knowledge-based service industries that now employ 9,000 people in the city, as many as are employed in tourism.' He mentioned specifically the Science Park at the University. At the time, I ran this past a friend of mine who still lived in York and worked for the council. 'It *sounds* like bullshit,' he said, 'but it happens to be true.' In today's York, we might put the businesses of the Biotech Campus at Sand Hutton (just outside York) in the same future-facing category.

The successful young professionals of York often aspire to live in South Bank, an area of dignified red-brick Victorian terraces close to the centre of town. I was born in a two-up, two-down in South Bank, but when I was two, we moved to the housing estate on the edge of York I have already mentioned, my parents wanting an extra bedroom and a bit of garden, as opposed to a back yard. As a boy, I would return to South Bank on my bike and congratulate myself on having escaped the place: it was usually raining as I biked along the cobbled alleys – 'ginnels', in Yorkshire-speak – between the rectilinear lines of backyards; the dreary *Coronation Street* music spooled in my head; the houses seemed occluded with their net curtained windows; the men generally wore grey belted macs and flat caps, and hobnailed boots that echoed down these ginnels – a lonely sound. The women sported curlers and hairnets.

Whenever I visit South Bank today, I am amazed to see the canvas tote bags and electric bikes of the cheerful inhabitants, and sunlight in the streets. A house on the South Bank street on which I was born is now worth about £360,000; a house in the street I grew up in is worth a bit less than £200,000. My parents wanted to escape the inner city – even if it was only the inner city of York – just as London people had been abandoning Islington for, say, Finchley. But in my parents' case there was perhaps an additional element: they wanted to swap a very Northern-seeming place for a less Northern-seeming place. Today, that Northern-ness has been reinvented, with bay trees in the back yards, and even – occasionally – public-spiritedly stationed *outside* the back gate, to bring a touch of colour to the ginnels.

Trains

York was an important railway town in the most glamorous and exciting way: not because it was a *big* town, but because it was a junction. In the railways' Edwardian heyday, when York was the HQ of the North Eastern Railway, its engine sheds would also have accommodated overnight the visiting engines of the Great Western Railway, the London & North Western, the Lancashire & Yorkshire, the Great Central, the Great Eastern and the Midland Railway. (I could go on.) Even today, York is the second busiest station in Yorkshire after Leeds, and ahead of Sheffield, even though Sheffield has more than twice the population of York: half a million against 200,000. To my mind this gives York some much-needed Northern credibility, because I do think of railways as a Northern product. (The Stockton & Darlington opened in 1830, whereas the first line to reach London – the London & Birmingham – didn't do so until 1840.)

York remains a railway town. The train operating companies, Northern, LNER and Grand Central have offices in York, and some freight companies have rail yards; Network Rail has an office in York; there's also the Railway Museum. When I was born, in 1962, the railway credentials of the city could be more simply stated: it hosted the headquarters of the North Eastern Region of British Railways, which occupied an attractive, neo-Georgian building dating from 1906. (The only regional HQ of BR to be located outside London, since all the other regions radiated from the capital.)

I was vaguely aware that two or three Georges were responsible for York's railway eminence. Of the two principal Georges, one was a goodie and one a baddie. There was a statue to the goodie, George Leeman. He stood, gleaming white like an angel, on a plinth near a pretty garden in Station Rise. The baddie was called George Hudson. There was no statue to him. One had an idea of his physical form (short and fat) from satirical cartoons in history books, in which he was described, in what seemed like an ironic way, as the Railway King. A street located a couple of minutes' walk from the station was named after him, but George Hudson Street had a dismal atmosphere, and never seemed to see the sun. There were some glowering Victorian frontages, but also a multi-story car park and a bland 1970s office block. It was more like a street in Leeds than York. There was a pub on the junction between George Hudson Street and Micklegate called the Railway King, and in the 1970s it was the only one in York with bouncers on the door. It was a hard pub. On one of its exterior walls, a dark plaque had been mounted. It's still there, and so is the pub, which is now called Popworld. The plaque (which is not completely grammatical) reads:

GEORGE HUDSON STREET

Originally called Hudson Street in memory of George Hudson MP. The Railway King, three times Lord Mayor of York who laid the foundations of the city's railway prosperity. It was changed to Railway Street when he fell from Grace in 1849. It was renamed George Hudson Street on the 14th December 1971, being the one hundredth anniversary of his death.

Hudson's York & North Midland Railway – engineered by his friend, George Stephenson – connected York to London via Normanton, which is south of Leeds; it also connected to the Leeds–Selby line. Hudson was not responsible for the main railway route going north from York (to Darlington), but he did build lines connecting York to Scarborough and Whitby. So it can be said that if he didn't fulfil his alleged ambition to 'mek all t'railways cum ter York', he directed a lot of them that way. In 1844, Hudson was in charge of over 1,000 miles of railway. But he was dethroned after he was discovered to be a confidence trickster: he had paid dividends out of capital, not profits. George Leeman succeeded Hudson as chairman of one of the Hudson lines – the York, Newcastle & Berwick Railway – and helped uncover his shady dealings. Leeman was MP for York between 1865 and 1868 and was highly regarded in the city.

Hudson's network became the North Eastern Railway, which company built the neo-Georgian building mentioned above, where Dad worked for thirty years in BR days. It was known as Head Office, and I was never allowed in. So I would stand on the doorstep like a Victorian urchin, waiting for the echo of Dad's footsteps as he came along the wide stone corridor into the marble entrance hall. If Dad said something and, not quite hearing him, you responded in the traditional Yorkshire manner – 'Eh?'– he would stand on his dignity in a comic way: 'Eh? To me? Head Office?'

There was another railway office building opposite Head

Office: Hudson House, built in the 1970s when George Hudson was being rehabilitated. It housed younger men than Head Office, with longer hair, and often beards. They did not necessarily wear suits, as Dad did, but sports jackets, and their tie knots were tubular, not equilateral triangles like Dad's Windsor knots. (My own tie knots were also tubular, but if I was ever going off to an important interview, Dad would polish my shoes and make a Windsor knot for me, tying it on his thigh.) I did go into Hudson House. When I was seventeen, I worked there in the early evenings, cleaning the floors of the deserted offices with a buffing machine. I noticed that soft porn magazines were circulated in BR internal-mail envelopes, with each man listed on the envelope ticking off that he'd seen it.

In-between Head Office and Hudson House was a lower, older building that had been part of the complex of the original York Station, about 500 yards east of the present one, and just inside the City Walls, whereas the present one is just outside. This venerable building had been part of the hotel connected to that first station, but when I was a boy, it was used as a bike shed for railway workers. Being Dad's son, I was allowed to use it – a considerable privilege. It was the best bike shed in York: bang in the middle of town, under full cover and guarded day and night. In the school holidays, at the end of a day lounging about with my friends in the Museum Gardens, I might collect my bike from there and coincide with Dad, collecting his after his day's work, and we'd ride home together.

I have written many books about railways, fiction and non-fiction. A reviewer of one of them said that I was born 'into the railway purple', and my privileges did not stop at the bike-shed access. The main perk was the free first-class travel, mentioned in the previous chapter. There was my membership of the railway golf club mentioned in the Preface, which was founded by the York Railway Institute. The Institute was in a tall, ugly, Edwardian building on Queen Street, just outside the station. It incorporated two wide billiard halls, suffused in green gloom, some classrooms, a lecture hall, a bar, a theatre and a reading room. I learnt to play snooker and billiards at the Institute, and Dad joked that proficiency at these games was 'a sign of a misspent youth', but if playing a full-grown man – perhaps a train driver – I would be on my best behaviour, immediately retreating from the table with genuflections if I should accidentally touch the cue ball with my hand.[*]

At the time, the Institute was at the heart of a red-brick railway colony. Alongside it was a great hall that, until 1905, was York Locomotive Erecting Shop Number 2. In my day, it had become a gymnasium, and I had trampolining lessons there, but there was always something primitive about it, what with the five-foot-wide clock on the end wall, and riveted, juddering pipes in the changing rooms. I was assistant stage manager at a couple of amateur drama productions in the theatre on the top floor of the Institute, where the actors – railway employees – could never quite escape their day job, since the station announcements would waft over to the Institute, and drift in through any open windows.

I was a regular visitor to York's first railway museum, opened in 1927, which was also on Queen Street. There were a few locos, stuffed and mounted on plinths. Unlike in the new, airy National Rail Museum in the city, there seemed no possibility of their ever having a run outside. For the real connoisseur (or anybody sufficiently bored) there was the 'small exhibits collection' featuring things

---

[*] 'While billiards are good, study is better,' said Alexander Kaye Butterworth, chairman of the North Eastern Railway, at the AGM of the Institute in 1907.

like station clocks, and the desks of long-dead railwaymen. In Queen Street, I found the only public community to which I have ever really belonged, or it found me, and I think of this as a Northern – if not specifically Yorkshire – experience. In 1910, the *Railway Magazine* noted that the North Eastern Railway had risen particularly well to the challenge of providing 'facilities which provide both education and recreation, and by means of which their employés [sic] ... may find that companionship which is necessary to develop the social side of human nature'. The article described other NER institutes – at Blyth, Darlington, Hull, Newcastle, Shildon.

If I went into York Station, which I did regularly – as often merely to observe trains as to catch one – I would recognise people from the Institute, and vice versa. I liked being on the station at night, when the high volume of parcels traffic (all gone now) made the place seem Christmassy. It was a world as cosy and comforting as a first-class compartment. Stations had porters in those days, and I was twice mistaken for one on York Station – possibly on account of a second-hand charcoal-coloured suit I used to wear, which had the dowdy formality of a railway uniform, or perhaps, railways being in my blood, I had the physiognomy of a railwayman.* Just as the Institute was the focal point of the Queen Street railway buildings, so the station was the focus of the railway lands, a sprawl of what were known as 'yards' (sidings), 'shops' (workshops) and 'sheds' (engine sheds) – and there was also the mysterious, shadowy, largely nocturnal, goods station. The distant clank of shunting at the Dringhouses Marshalling Yard resounded through the York nights in a comforting way. In the late 1960s and early

---

* I wore that suit at Oxford, until some toff passing by in a quadrangle said, 'Your ensemble is pure charity shop.'

1970s, about 850 wagons – many containing Rowntree's chocolate – were sorted into about thirty trains. The marshalling yard closed in 1987, and for two reasons. First, freight trains were suffering a loss of diversity: the 'trainload' concept determined they be made of identical wagons carrying identical goods, rather than a variety of wagons carrying a variety of goods. Second, Rowntree's decided to send their chocolate by road (and I was once nearly killed on my bike by a Rowntree's articulated lorry blazoned with 'Have a Break, Have a Kit-Kat', which would have been a bathetic end). Sometimes today in London, I think I hear the clanking of shunting at 3 a.m., before realising that it's only some aural hallucination.

The railway lands gradually lost their trains and tracks, and the railways lost their primacy in York, a function of the decline of industry, especially coal mining, and the shifting of freight from rail to roads. There is something furtive about such railway activity as occurs there today. Lines of sealed wagons, their contents unguessable; a man in high-vis and hard hat walking over an expanse of scrub that used to be tracks. The Carriage Works, which bordered the railway lands, died a fitful death *as* a carriage works in the early twenty-first century. Today, it's used for the maintaining the Railhead Treatment Train, which cleans tracks. The *Wagon* Works was entirely flattened recently. The railway lands, also known as the York Eye or the Teardrop, are largely empty, so that York is like the Polo Mints made in the city: there's a hole in the middle. The site is earmarked for 'residential neighborhoods, cultural spaces, and a high-quality commercial quarter', and this is a work in progress. Even the station is not such a railway-ish place as before. With the electrification of the East Coast Main Line in the late 1980s, there was a clear-out of tracks, so it always looks half empty to me. What used to be the signal box is a Costa Coffee; at the time of writing, the booking hall (as I called it; officially it was the 'travel centre') is being converted to accommodate a Pret a Manger and an outlet for York Gin, a new, diminished booking hall having been created in what was formerly the ladies' lavatory.

The former bike shed is now part of the York Council offices. Hudson House was demolished in 2018, replaced by Hudson Quarter (expensive flats). A new railway office, George Stephenson House, stands nearby and accommodates a Northern office of Network Rail. Dad's office – *Head Office* – is now a five-star hotel, the Grand. When it opened, he was offered a guided tour, and it turned out that his old office had become the Whisky Lounge, where he was assured, over a hundred single malts are available. In the basement there's a spa, sauna, swimming pool and beauty treatment rooms. To access these, you walk through a thick steel door. It's propped open, but intimidating nonetheless, and surely perplexing to those who don't know that the North Eastern Railway kept the cash in the basement. The next-door office, formerly belonging to Yorkshire General Life Assurance, is also being converted into a hotel (a Malmaison), and if that particularly grim building can be so converted, nothing in York is safe from the globalised leisure industry. (Incidentally, 'Yorkshire General Life Assurance' used to be written on the risers of all the steps of the York Station footbridge; they'd make you worried about the financial consequence of tripping and injuring yourself as you ran for a train.)

The Queen Street Railway Museum closed in 1973; the National Rail Museum on Leeman Road opened in 1975, in what had been the York North Engine Shed, and this was a victory for York in the North–South battle. The

nearest thing Britain had to a national railway museum at
the time was in Clapham, South London. Lord Montague
of Beaulieu tabled a special debate in the House of Lords,
arguing that any future transport museum should also be in
London. A petition to that effect was signed by 122 MPs,
but this was outweighed by a public petition of 90,000 sig-
natures, and the campaigning on York's behalf by Baroness
Lee, formerly Jenny Lee MP, Minister for the Arts under
Harold Wilson.

In 2015, I spoke at an event commemorating the forti-
eth anniversary of the Museum. Dad came along, in what
was the last year of his life. He seemed uncharacteristically
garrulous and vocal, possibly because of the medication he
was on. At the reception afterwards, he had a glass of wine,
and it went to his head. I introduced him to the curator of
the museum, and when the brief conversation had ended,
and the curator had turned aside, but not quite departed,
Dad said to me, 'In the old museum, there was no need for
a curator. The whole operation was run perfectly well by a
Grade 4 clerk.'

The York Railway Institute, as mentioned, is now
abstractly titled Y.I. The rooms have been subdivided.
Certainly, the snooker hall has lost its moody, Edward
Hopper aspect. As for Dad's other perks . . . the 'Priv Ticket'
provisions of the privatised railways are complicated, but
not as generous or nationally applicable as in the days of
BR. Nor is there the same job security. Dad worked with
a sign on his desk reading 'I'm surrounded by idiots,' and
it was only half in jest. He would tell me lurid tales of the
incompetence and misdemeanours of some his colleagues,
and I would say, 'But haven't they been sacked?'

'Nobody is *ever* sacked,' he would reply. He retired at
fifty-five, on two-thirds of his salary by way of redundancy

payment and with a generous pension about to kick in.

The Queen Street Bridge, built to traverse tracks that connected the 1887 York Station with the sidings of the old one (1841), which were last used in 1967, is about to be demolished. The bridge screened those shadowy, hallowed spaces of my childhood (the Institute and Gymnasium) from the world at large. Light will be let in, and my memories will fade, as when the door is opened on a darkroom, although if anyone's interested, my railway novels, supposedly set in Edwardian York, owe much to the city of the 1970s. British Rail and York between them gave me a stable and secure childhood, even though my mother had died when I was nine – a thought that prompts a recollection.

Sense of Security

One evening when I was at Oxford University, I walked into the shared bathroom of the house I lived in during my second year, and when I switched on the light, a wild-looking man leapt out of the bathtub, in which he'd been sleeping, having somehow broken into the house. He followed me back to my room, to which I'd fled, demanding with menaces that I let him in and make him a cup of tea, which I did. I offered him a digestive biscuit from a nearly full packet. He took one biscuit from the packet, handed it to me, and kept the rest for himself. He then began quizzing me while prowling around the room. 'Where are you from originally?' he demanded.

I told him.

'York?' he said, 'A walled city. Gives people a false sense of security.'

The man – who, as I later discovered, had escaped from a secure psychiatric unit – was fine after that. Maybe the very word 'York' had calmed him down.

If I were to select the epicentre of York's essentially festive spirit, I'd say it was the racecourse on a race day. Equipped with his retirement 'Priv' Dad was a keen gambler on all the Yorkshire racecourses. He liked to boast that he'd had a bet every weekday of his life since he was fifteen, and that first bet (which was a *winning* bet), made with a bookie's runner loitering on a York street corner, was illegal, not so much because Dad was under-age as because betting on horses away from a course was illegal. But of all the courses, York was his favourite, and his ashes are scattered upon it.

York Racecourse is sited on the Knavesmire, a vast area of open land south of the city centre, which is part of one of York's four ancient 'strays', ancient areas of common land. (Harrogate also has a stray.) As a Freeman of the city, Dad's dad – my grandad – had the right to graze sheep on the Knavesmire, although he never availed himself of the privilege, not actually possessing any sheep. I often went to York races with Dad, and it was like going to a carnival. I would have a toffee apple, and glass of lemonade with a cocktail cherry on a plastic sword. You were part of a sea of people, all baking in the sun, at least in my memory. (When I was researching an eighteenth-century novel set in York, I read that when all the horse-drawn coaches that converged on the Knavesmire for a race meeting were parked up, the coachmen would lie sunbathing on their roofs.) Floating over the throng was the urbane voice of the course announcer. I was mildly indignant that he didn't have a York accent, but I liked the way he announced a photo finish in his mid-Atlantic tones: 'Phodergraph . . . phodergraph.' The bookmakers fascinated me. They seemed Dickensian, florid men shouting the odds from little stepladders. When you handed over your stake, they lobbed it into a Gladstone bag on which their name was painted in blistering emulsion paint. They all had assistants – quieter, clerkly men – who would chalk up the odds on the little blackboards fixed to a pole that rose up behind the steps. There was a right way of putting a bet on with these blokes, and it involved not

saying anything plodding and obvious such as 'I'd like fifty
pence to win on Jimsun.' When Dad did it, it was all just
quick numbers, something like 'Fours on three at two.' Of
course, the bookies didn't mind what you said as long as
you paid your stake, and then the clerkly man would peel
off a card from a pack like a card sharp and give it to you
while looking to the next punter, or mug. When I was next
to Dad in the grandstand, and a race was approaching its
climax, Dad would suddenly seem to disappear from my
sidelong glance. He was crouching down, in the posture of
a jockey whipping the horse home.

When my mother died in York County Hospital in 1971,
my sister and I were staying in the house of Dad's brother,
George, just outside Beverley. So Dad travelled out from
York to break the news. I had not for a minute thought
my mother would die, but as soon as I saw Dad, I knew
something was up. He wore his full going-to-the-races rig:
hand-made suede boots, pressed slacks, his best sports coat,
with the *Racing Post* in his pocket. I sensed that he was for
some reason trying to boost his own morale.

In 2005, the Royal Ascot meeting was held at York
because the Ascot course was being rebuilt. For the first time
ever, I saw the name of my hometown on a *London Evening
Standard* bill: 'Runners and Riders at York'. I attended the
meeting, for an article that appeared in the *Guardian* on 16
June. On the day of the meeting, sleet was falling on the
hundreds of top-hatted southerners. As I was making notes
in the Royal Enclosure, a prosperous-looking Yorkshireman
approached me: 'They're not as rich as they look,' he said.
'It's all corporate.' As the weather worsened, I felt sorry for
a woman who said, in a cut-glass accent, 'This dress is in a
flouncy, Gypsy style that's all wrong for this weather.'

Ten years later, I knew Dad was ill when there was a race

meeting at York and he didn't go. He'd also stopped going to the betting shop. 'I don't feel lucky,' he told my sister. But I think he had been lucky to live in York, and so was I.

Chocolate

An article in the *Yorkshire Post* of August 2018 began, 'From chocolate to sweets to mints, Yorkshire has invented and manufactured some of not only the nation's, but the world's best loved sweets and chocolate, with many calling it the confectionery capital of the world.' The piece did not say why this might be, but contributory factors must include the presence in the county of some leading Quakers, who were in a sense consigned by religious discrimination to chocolate-making, as we will be discovering; the abundance of locally grown sugar beet; and the presence of a ready market in the urban areas.

And Yorkshire has a sweet tooth. The need for carbohydrates to ward off the relative cold might come into it, and then there is the tradition, or – as people prefer to say now – the 'culture'. If my father had bramble crumble and custard, he put a dessertspoonful of sugar on it. When I was first married to my Southern wife, I'd do the same, to her horror. ('The custard is *already* sweet!') If you want to see the evidence, go to Kirkgate Market in Leeds, where sweets are retailed in what look like wholesale quantities. (And we *will* be going there.) For a more upmarket instance of the same phenomenon, go to Bettys tea rooms.

Bettys displays a partisanship reminiscent of that of Yorkshire County Cricket Club, which, until 1992, would only pick players born within the historic county of Yorkshire (which, by the way, proves that the historic county existed). There is no Bettys outside Yorkshire, and a Bettys signifies a smart town, much as a Waitrose does down south. They are to be found in York (which had two until very recently), Harrogate (also two), Ilkley and Northallerton.

The first Bettys tea room was opened in Harrogate in 1919, by a Swiss-born confectioner, Fredrick Belmont. He and his tea rooms are invested with a mystique. Apparently, he ended up in Yorkshire by accident. Newly arrived in Britain, he boarded a Bradford train at King's Cross with no firm idea of where he was going. Nobody knows why Bettys are called Bettys (except perhaps the Belmont family, who still run the firm). My favourite theory is that the meeting to decide the name was interrupted by a young girl called Betty, but it might have been on account of Betty Lupton, who ran the Harrogate Spa in the early nineteenth century. And there ought to be an apostrophe in Bettys, especially given the gentility of the company, but there isn't.

The York Bettys, on St Helen's Square, is the biggest. It opened in 1937 and is elegantly wood-panelled, like the RMS *Queen Mary*, which inspired its interior décor. I usually have a chocolate éclair when I go there, but the *famous* Bettys cake is the Fat Rascal, which is a combination of a rock cake and scone, made to look like a sort of bug, with almonds for teeth and cherries for eyes. I associate Bettys with what Dad called the 'county set'. They might have been educated at St Peters School, York, 'the Eton of the North'. The men of the county set were pink-faced, which clashed with their green tweeds. You'd see them, probably on the other side of a barrier, in the select part of York Racecourse, beribboned with accreditations like prize bulls. They were fat, Pickwickian men, in the days when fatness signified prosperity, rather than its opposite, as today. They must have eaten too many Fat Rascals.

But back to sweets.

In *Confectionery in Yorkshire Through Time*, Paul Chrystal writes that, 'Yorkshire has been home to more confectionery companies over the years than any other region of Britain.' It is not easy to make such a trenchant statement about the current situation.

Yorkshire and confectionery mainly intersected around Pontefract in West Yorkshire, and the sweet was liquorice. The liquorice plant was brought from the Mediterranean to Pontefract by Dominican monks in the 1560s. It grew well, and the liquorice juice was considered healthful. Pontefract cakes, resembling primitive coins, were first made in the eighteenth century. Liquorice is one of two peculiar crops associated with Yorkshire. The other is rhubarb, grown in the Rhubarb Triangle of Wakefield, Leeds and Morley, and sometimes 'forced' in dark sheds (the darkness keeps the rhubarb sweet), where it is harvested by candlelight. It strikes me that a rhubarb flower would better represent Yorkshire than the white rose. Rhubarb has a Yorkshire tone, being an unglamorous fruit that divides opinion and is produced in semi-industrial circumstances. Rhubarb has been embraced by that leading Yorkshire patriot, Geoff Boycott. Apparently, he eats a great deal of it, and he will say of a poor attempt at a cricket stroke, 'Me old mum could have hit that with a stick of rhubarb.'

Yorkshire was an appropriate setting for the no-nonsense Pontefract cake. 'No one would praise the Pontefract cake as an aesthetic wonder,' writes Nicholas Whittaker in *Sweet Talk: The Secret History of Confectionery.*

> It looks like, let's face it, a slug that's got on the wrong side of an industrial boot. But its no-frills appearance – no pretty colours, no sparkle, no scent, no sugariness – was all to the good. It encouraged a non-sissy reputation that advertisers were happy to exploit. 'Men like them. They are the smoker's sweet. They have class appeal and mass appeal.'

In 1900, a dozen firms were making liquorice in Pontefract. One of them was Wilkinson's, whose factory is now operated by retro-sweet specialists, Tangerine Confectionery. Another of the original Pontefract liquorice makers was Dunhill's, now owned by Haribo, who still make liquorice in Pontefract.

Further afield, and beyond the realm of liquorice, there is still Farrah's in Harrogate, known for toffee. The firm of Dobson's still makes Yorkshire Mixture and other old-fashioned-sounding boiled sweets at its factory in Elland, Calderdale. In Doncaster, there was the Nuttall's factory, from which Mintoes emanated. The factory is now an Aldi; Mintoes are no longer made. There was Needler's in Hull, whose factory is now a housing estate; the company is owned by a Northamptonshire firm. In Sheffield, there was (since the 1840s) Maynard's, famous for wine gums, which merged with Bassett's in 1990. In 1998 Maynard Bassett's was acquired by Cadbury, which is owned by Mondelez International (formerly Kraft). Wine gums are still made in Sheffield, but the chocolatier Thorntons, founded in Sheffield in 1911, now manufactures in Derbyshire, under the ownership of the Italian firm, Ferrero. There was – and still is – the Mackintosh's sweet factory in Halifax, but Mackintosh's was acquired by Rowntree's in 1969, and Rowntree's was acquired by Nestlé in 1988.

The names associated with York were Rowntree's, Terry's and Craven's, the latter making sweets that challenged your teeth: sugared almonds, humbugs and toffee. The original Craven's factory was bang in the middle of town, at Coppergate; the firm moved to Poppleton, on the edge of the city, in the 1970s, and the demolition of the first factory facilitated the Viking excavation mentioned earlier. Today, the Poppleton factory is used by Tangerine Confectionery.

Above all, York had (and still, in a way, has) Rowntree's, whose factory would on certain days of the week generate a chocolatey fug over the city that was half delicious and half nauseating, a sort of benign pollution, like a conceit from a children's story: 'And in this town, there was no horrible dirty smoke in the air, but only the smell of lots of lovely chocolate being made!'

Rowntree's first factory, established in 1869, occupied in the site of a former iron works on the riverbank in the middle of town. A product called Elect Cocoa was developed. It was not greasy, unlike all previous cocoas. In 1890, production was moved to a 150-acre site at New Earswick, a village three miles north of York, where Joseph Rowntree developed a 'garden' or 'model' village for his employees and other workers. It was designed by Raymond Unwin and Barry Parker, who had designed the garden cities of Welwyn and Letchworth. There were neat, pretty houses with neat pretty gardens, each with two fruit trees, and there was a non-denominational Folk Hall, a swimming pool and sport pitches, but there was no pub. The Rowntrees, as Peter Terry, scion of York's other famous chocolate-making family once told me, 'were all dead

against drink'. They were Quakers, like those other choc-
olatiers, the Frys and the Cadburys, whose bosky garden
village at Bournville had influenced Joseph Rowntree at
New Earswick. Being Quakers, all the above were barred
from the church, so they expressed their morality through
manufacturing, and they hoped that cocoa would displace
alcohol. Hitler had hoped much the same. When Joseph's
son, Seebohm, conducted his social survey, he counted the
number of York pubs, reaching the appalled conclusion that
there was one for every 230 people in a city of 46,000; he
also neurotically counted the pub entrances.

In his survey, Seebohm described York as 'a typical provincial city', but the Rowntrees were major contributors to
the specialness of York, and I took full advantage of their
philanthropy. I spent many afternoons of my school holidays in somnolent riverside Rowntree's Park, which the
Rowntrees bequeathed to the city in memory of the York
dead of the First World War, and also (it was rumoured) to
block the expansion of the first Terry's factory, adjacent on
the riverbank. There was something melancholic about the
park. In the 1930s, Dad was a regular there, swimming in
the lido and lounging about on the open-air terraces afterwards. The lido was popular with Great War veterans, and
he would try to ask them about the War, but they would
refuse point blank to discuss it. He knew one young man, a
contemporary of his, who tried to dive into the water from
the viewing gallery. He didn't make it, and smashed his head
open on the tiles at the side of the bath, with fatal results. I
too became a regular at the lido. I would lie on my towel up
in the gallery and gaze up at the tops of the poplar trees that
acted as a wind break. The lido was demolished in 1985, but
the poplars remained, albeit now purposeless. They looked
about half the size I remember from my childhood.

I acted in plays at the Joseph Rowntree Theatre, an Art
Deco building of the 1930s. The green room really was
green, and the mirrors really did have light bulbs surrounding them. I usually acted in smaller venues, like the York
Arts Centre, which occupied the premises of a medieval
church on Micklegate (and which was a nightclub, last time
I looked), but the Jo-Ro was a real theatre, as signified by the
fact that I was normally acting to a 'house' consisting largely
of empty velvet seats. The theatre was directly opposite the
factory. Comedy films and westerns used to be shown there
at lunchtime for the workers. Aged fourteen, I emerged at
about eleven o'clock from playing Abdullah, an Arab street
urchin in *Camino Real* by Tennessee Williams. (A piece of
casting that would be frowned on today.) As usual, I had
accidentally-on-purpose left much of my eyeliner on for the
journey home and, as I waited for the bus, with the orange
lights of the factory windows blazing before me, creating –
in conjunction with the chocolate smell – a Christmassy
effect, I congratulated myself on being me, likely future
star of stage and screen, and not a factory worker, even if
the factory in question was prefixed with the word 'garden'.

My Auntie Dot and my Uncle Peter, and Dad's good
friend Bob Dixon, worked at Rowntree's. Many of the girls
at my secondary school went to work for a while 'choccie-
bashing' (packing chocolates) at Rowntree's or Terry's. Yes,
it was a dead-end job, but it did not have that connotation.
It seemed more a case of joining a pleasant social club until
they got married.

My grandfather had worked at the Rowntree's factory
between 1926 and 1958 as a fitter on chocolate-wrapping
machines. Before that he'd spent three years as a railwayman, working for the London & North Eastern Railway,
and before that he'd worked at Leetham's Flour Mill on

the banks of the Foss, which is today a block of flats, but was for a while – after it ceased to be a flour mill – part of the Rowntree's empire. My grandfather belonged to the Yorkshire working class, albeit the skilled working class. Towards the end of his life, his memory – or that part of it he expressed – became a stuck record, and he must have told me a hundred times how, in order to walk to Leetham's from the outlying village of Bishopthorpe where he lived, he would wake up at four and drink a cup of cocoa left for him overnight in the oven by his mother. 'Can you imagine it?' he repeatedly asked me. 'You can't imagine it, can you?' Eventually, he might deign to ask me a question about myself: 'Still clerking down south, are you?' he would sneeringly ask.

'No, Grandad,' I would reply. 'I'm studying at Oxford University.'

'Aye,' he'd say, 'well . . .', as if that were debatable.

I used to feel like flinging his own challenge snobbishly back at him: 'You can't imagine it, can you?' Leetham's obviously left a scar, whereas his work at salubrious Rowntree's evidently did not; it never came up, anyhow.

My grandfather drank cocoa every day of his life, and in his later years he lived very near York's other big chocolate factory, Terry's. But he was not a very chocolatey person. He was not what you'd call sweet, and his dour personality was hard to square with the jaunty slogans of his employer. What did this reserved monosyllabic man with a pale-blue faraway gaze (his favourite word was 'Yonder') make of the 'Lovabubble', which Aero was alleged to be? What could 'Get together with Rolo' have meant to a man who, according to Dad, had 'no friends at all', unless you counted his wife and six children? He never went to the pub. His sole entertainment was taking solo bike rides, or going alone to the York Music Hall, the first of the two evening performances – 'early doors' – when he would sometimes be the only person in the audience; and he never laughed.

As an employee and ex-employee of Rowntree's he possessed a card that entitled him to very heavily discounted chocolate. This was slightly duff, albeit edible, chocolate given to him from some outlet at the factory in bags labelled, in order of increasing severity, 'Mis-shapes', 'Rejects', 'Waste'. These he kept in what ought to have been the fruit bowl on his sideboard, but he never ate fruit or anything not involving fat, which did him no harm, since he died at ninety-six, and was still cycling his lonely way about York at ninety-four.

There was something very Yorkshire about the giving of 'waste'. It was not offered or received with any great enthusiasm – it hardly could be, given that it was 'waste' – and the transaction was usually conducted along the following lines:

My grandad (indicating the fruit bowl): You might want some of that.

Me: Oh, yeah, ta.

The chocolate had some pigmentary defect whereby it was described as 'blue', but, like the above-mentioned Cleckheaton mouse, it was more grey than blue. It was pitted and scarred, and insufficiently diverse. The paper bag might have the subtitle 'Dairy Box', and the first one you bit into would be one of the less appetising flavours from that collection, say the glass-like mint cracknel. You'd bite into the next one: mint cracknel again, and so on for the next five, until you might chance on something slightly more appealing: the one with a hazlenut in it, for example – but the sheer luxury of the raspberry one – my favourite – always seemed elusive.

My grandfather, as mentioned, lived near York's other chocolate factory, Terry's. The Terrys were not Quakers, but they were philanthropic Tory Paternalists. There was no garden village for their workers, but their factory, built in 1924, was a garden factory, with fishpond, bowling green, tennis court, football pitch. It was neo-Georgian, in warm red brick, with a clocktower that gave it a restful cathedral-like air. The numerals on the white, illuminated clockface spelt the words 'TERRY' and 'YORK'.

Terry's lent a certain opulence to York. Half a mile down the road from the factory, on the edge of the countryside, was a mansion called Middlethorpe Hall that had been occupied by Francis Terry, grandson of the founder, and chairman of the company in the early twentieth century. When I was a toddler, Dad would clip a small, supplementary seat onto the crossbar of his bike, and we would ride out to Middlethorpe Hall to look at the stone eagle on the roof. The firm kept a smart cake and confectionery shop in St Helen's Square in the middle of York, with the Celebration Restaurant, wood-panelled and candlelit, at the rear, which rivalled Bettys tearoom for the custom of the county set. The restaurant closed in 1985 (it survives as a cocktail bar), to be succeeded by the smaller, but equally genteel, Terry's Tea Room in the Dean Court Hotel opposite the Minster. On the walls of the Tea Room, alongside Terry's memorabilia, this inscription was displayed:

Four centuries ago, Cortes sent home to Spain the first chocolate and cacao beans as part of the spoils from his conquest of Mexico. In the New World this chocolate, Theobroma – the food of the Gods – was believed to be a

supreme gift of divine origin, and certain kinds, reserved
for the emperor Montezuma himself, were served only in
golden vessels in honour of the giver.

Hence Terry's All Gold, introduced in 1931, counter-
part to Rowntree's Black Magic, but with a slightly more
elevated tone and a higher RRP. Eileen, a friend of my
stepmother's, played hockey for Terry's while she worked
there in the 1950s, and the team were kitted out in the All
Gold colours: 'gold socks, gold shirts, brown skirts'. That's
the swankiness of Terry's for you; they were the BBC to
Rowntree's ITV. The most famous Terry's product, the
Chocolate Orange, had a similar indulgent exoticism to
All Gold, and the logo used to involve a desert island with
two palm trees and the words 'Terry' and 'York', an odd
conjunction of the tropical and the Yorkshire.

Eileen's mother had worked at Terry's in the 1920s as
a hand coverer (putting the fillings inside the chocolates
and inscribing them with decorative marks). When she left
Terry's and applied to Rowntree's, she was seen as a 'catch'
and immediately fast-tracked to the top-of-the range brands.
According to Eileen, her mother was highly regarded not
only because of her Terry's experience, but also because she
had the inestimable natural advantage for a hand coverer:
'She had cold hands; they didn't melt the chocolate. That
also meant she could make good pastry. I've got hot hands.'

I interviewed Peter Terry for a piece about York and
chocolate that appeared in *Granta* magazine in 2005 (*Granta
89: The Factory*). He had been the last family member to
occupy a senior position in the firm, and he'd retired in
1987. I met him at his house, an Edwardian mansion in
large grounds north of York. It had been designed by Fred
Rowntree, a member of the rival chocolate clan, and there

had at one time been cottages in the garden for convalescing Rowntree workers. The house had a slightly battered elegance. I sat on a sagging velvet sofa as I waited for Mr Terry – a graduate of Marlborough School and Pembroke College, Cambridge – to come through from a lunch party he'd been hosting. When, early in the interview, he told me that the Rowntrees 'were dead against drink' he was finishing off a glass of wine. But Peter Terry had liked the Rowntrees and felt no rivalry towards them. As far as he was concerned, the firms did different things.

They used the cocoa beans from West Africa, which had a purply colour before roasting. We preferred beans from the West Indies or Malaysia, which were light brown, and had a finer taste. All Gold was five shillings a pound, whereas Black Magic was two shillings eleven. But then you shouldn't expect a Rolls-Royce to cost the same a Morris Minor.

Peter Terry spoke of the Terry's factory in the past tense. The firm had been acquired by Kraft, who would close it down later in 2005, to shift production to cheaper sites in East Europe. 'The factory was so clean,' said Mr Terry. 'To have a big dirty furnace somewhere . . . it wouldn't do at all. And I felt it appropriate that York should have light industry, because York is such a beautiful place.'

That seemed to express my feelings. I never did regard Rowntree's or Terry's as true factories in the Yorkshire sense. The product they made was too frivolous. In the war, the top of the Terry's clocktower was used as a lookout post, and there's something *Dad's Army*-ish about this. I'm reminded of Captain Mainwaring's frequent command, 'Rendezvous at the Novelty Rock Emporium.' It also

seemed comical as I cycled past Rowntree's factory, that
such a whimsical thing as Kit-Kat should have high-rise
buildings dedicated to its production, and – stranger still –
the one for the two-finger Kit-Kat was higher than the one
where the four-finger version was made.

After Rowntree's was acquired by Nestlé in 1988 the
Rowntree's factory seemed to me to turn its back on York.
Between then and the time of my *Granta* article, the numbers employed had dropped from 5,000 to 2,000. When
I contacted Nestlé's in connection with that article, they
never replied (and when I told Peter Terry of this, he shook
his head at such ungentlemanly behaviour). Nestlé's had
seemed matey enough when, as manufacturers of Milky
Bar, their name was pronounced 'Nessles', but when they
took over at York they flew the Swiss flag from the roof
of the factory and insisted on the acute accent. 'Nestlé
have always come across as a faceless multinational,' writes
Nicholas Whittaker in *Sweet Talk: The Secret History of
Confectionery*: 'distant, icy and secretive, as fondly regarded
as the CIA or Swiss bankers.'

Only a few Nestlé products carry the Rowntree name:
Jelly Tots, Fruit Gums and Fruit Pastilles – not Kit-Kats, the
product I associate most strongly with York. I used to like
removing the paper sleeve and slicing through the foil along
the gaps between the fingers of chocolate. It made pleasingly
straight lines. Some anal-retentive types would roll the foil,
bogey-like, into a simulacrum of a ball bearing. But now all
four-finger Kit-Kats are in flow-wrapped plastic packaging.
(The two-finger jobs are still in foil.) Any modification
of this product seems to erase part of my life story. The
appearance of 'Chunky' Kit-Kats was unsettling enough,
but now there are also whisky, caramel, green tea and apple
pie-flavoured Kit-Kats among other heresies. These are

stocked in my local corner shop, and they originate in Japan, where Kit-Kat has become a cult among Japanese students, who regard them as *omamori*, or good luck charms, because 'Kit-Kat' sounds like *kitto katsu*, which means, 'You will overcome.' In a way, they were similarly used in the York of my boyhood. My mother would prepare me for my junior school trips by making me a packed lunch, neatly arranged in a Tupperware box, and a two-finger Kit-Kat would always be the last – and best – addition: something by way of a going-away present from her to me.

Part of the York factory – the so-called Almond and Cream Buildings – has been sold off, and smart flats called the Cocoa Works have been created within, while the ex-Terry's factory is a mixed-use residential and commercial development called the Chocolate Works. Residents have their own private access to the adjacent York racecourse, and at least one resident (I was told by someone connected to the development) used to work in the factory, which, given that factory work is usually of a humble order, whereas the flats are distinctly posh, must have been a very satisfying transition to make. The word 'Terry's' survives on the clockface of the clocktower, and on the light boxes above the gateposts at the main entrance, which glow goldenly, evoking the famous chocolate box.

There are several bijou chocolate outlets in York, some of which also manufacture on a small scale, but the original Rowntree's shop in central York is now a Pizza Hut. There is a permanent exhibition, York's Chocolate Story. ('It's fun, quirky, educational and finishes off with a taste sensation!') One display is devoted to George Harris, chairman of Rowntree's from 1941 and a marketing genius. He invented Smarties (which were made using button-making technology), Aero, Black Magic and Dairy Box, and he rechristened what had been the ploddingly named Chocolate Crisp ('a snack that a man could take to work in his pack-up') as Kit-Kat. It was largely thanks to Harris that Rowntree's focused its business on York where, after the War, it employed over 10,000 people. Surely, he is a candidate for a statue in the city, although he was not *from* York (he was born in Glasgow), and he was not philanthropic, unlike the Rowntree family into which he had married.

York's Chocolate Story is different from other retrospective York attractions, because this story continues: 3.5 million Kit-Kats are made in York every day, and the discounted chocolate continues to circulate. Until recently, my stepmother belonged to a York social club that was regularly visited by a man who had a car boot full of 'waste', and he'd take orders if, say, anyone wanted some waste mint Aeros. 'The odd thing was that he'd never worked at Rowntree's or Nestlé's,' my stepmother told me. 'He was a carpet fitter, I think.'

LEEDS

Many Stories Told

Whereas the York of my boyhood seemed well-conserved and museum-like, Leeds inhabited the all-too-real modern world. Leeds is about 20 miles south of York, but it seemed more Northern. Heavy things happened there. Leeds had a crematorium before York, and Dad's brother, Uncle Frank, who died a few years before I was born, was cremated there. When Dad died, I inherited a small black metal box containing a small archive of Uncle Frank's life. From this I know that a brass plate bearing his name appeared in the Upper Woodland Glade of Leeds Crematorium until the end of its contracted term in 1983. I find it particularly unfair that he should end up in Leeds, since this lonely and dreamy character had dedicated his adult life to escaping Yorkshire.

He had worked as a clerk for Yorkshire Farmers Limited at 51 Skeldergate, York. In 1950, he left them to join the Pure Seed Company in Linton, Cambridgeshire, but he gave that up to move to London, where he lived in a hostel, in the surprisingly prestigious address of 71 Princes Gate, SW7. He couldn't find work in London, partly because the Pure Seed Company wouldn't give him a reference, Frank having left them after only a few months. In 1952, Uncle Frank was in Canada, where for some worrying reason he subscribed to a counselling service offered by the Toronto Young Men's Christian Association, who reported that 'The ability to reason and handle concepts using words is very noticeably above average.' On the other hand, 'The majority of people with scores like yours do not like meeting and dealing with people with a view to promoting or selling something. Nor do they like dealing with machinery and tools.' The following year, Uncle Frank was in America, in Washington. The black box contains a sightseeing brochure entitled 'Seeing the Nation's Capital', which invited visitors to tick off the sights as they saw them, and Uncle Frank ticked all of them (Lincoln Memorial, Arlington National Cemetery, Capitol, Naval Observatory etc.) except the Zoological Park. Uncle Frank was back in London in 1958, when he died of a sudden illness. He was twenty-nine years old.

Whereas York's prison had been demolished in 1935, Leeds had Armley, that squat castle on a hill that stands as a warning to the whole town, its message underlined by the graveyard opposite. And Leeds turned its back on the innocent whimsy of the Fat Rascal, in that its Bettys had closed in 1974. Leeds was not only more Northern than York, it was also more like the rest of the world. For example, the air rights above the railway station had been sold, so there was a tower block on it, among other high-rises, of which there were none in York; and Leeds had riots – the Chapeltown Riots, arising from racial tensions in that relatively deprived area, which came around almost as reliably as the Olympics, in 1975, 1981 and 1987; hence, I think, the hit song 'I Predict a Riot' by Leeds band the Kaiser Chiefs. Leeds also had the Yorkshire Ripper, in the sense that most of Sutcliffe's attacks were carried out there.

Sutcliffe was born in Bingley and living in Sheffield when arrested, but it seemed to me that Leeds had made Sutcliffe as surely as it had made Jimmy Savile.

In Leeds, unlike York, the traffic noise was general, a constant susurration you couldn't escape from, partly thanks to the baffling and dispiriting ring road, built in the 1960s. Dad maintained it was 'impossible' to drive into Leeds because of this – a matter of 'can't get there from here'. York didn't get its ring road until two decades later, when it obliterated many of my childhood cycling routes. Unlike York, Leeds was not pretty. It had that signifier of industry, a black canal, the Leeds & Liverpool, not easy to distinguish from its river, the equally black and sullen Aire, loitering nearby in the general vicinity of the back of the railway station. In *All Points North*, Simon Armitage writes that 'The skyline of the city looks like a drawing board where ideas of all types have been tried and tested, then built properly somewhere else.' As I approached Leeds's sprawling, shapeless railway station on a smoke-belching diesel multiple unit from York, I'd be passing buildings that had half fallen down, entire factories abandoned, with every window systematically smashed. The terraced houses and streets that appear like cross-hatching on any Victorian map of Leeds were made of red brick – reminiscent of some dermatological flare-up – as were the factories and mills that disrupted the cross-hatching, but presumably did not provide any psychological release from it. According to my builder friend, Paul, the brickwork of Leeds is particularly ugly: 'English Garden Wall Bond – very basic, and there's no rhythm to it.'*

---

* The colour of a town's brick or stone is a crucial determinant of one's impression of a place. Stan Barstow based Cressley in *A Kind of Loving* on Dewsbury, not Wakefield, because he preferred the stone of the former to the red brick of the latter.

I would ride the train to Leeds to kill the boredom of a Sunday, or perhaps to masochistically compound it. Most of the shops would be shut; rain would be falling from a grey sky. One shop near the station was open, though: a dusty and understocked newsagent's whose proprietor sold me single cigarettes, which was illegal, and when I paid him he'd say, 'Thankinyew' in that whiney Leeds accent.

In a way, it was not necessary to go to Leeds to experience it. The hardest kids in York cleaved to Leeds – to the football team, I mean – and if some flinty-looking skinhead came up to you on a York backstreet and asked who you supported, the correct answer was Leeds. I thought everyone knew that. But when I and my friend Phil were so approached in a York backstreet in about 1975, Phil said, 'We support York.'

'Hold on a minute,' I said, 'I don't support York,' which saved me from the fate that befell Phil: he was stabbed in the thigh with a sharp object, probably not a knife. On the face of it, this was triple treachery: Phil co-opting me to his York-supporting stance (he really did support York); me disavowing any such allegiance; and the hard lads supporting Leeds instead of their own town's team. But I don't think *I* was treacherous, in that I really did *not* support York, or indeed anyone.

The 1970s Leeds were the classic Leeds United and, according to a book about the team, *The Unforgiven*, by Rob Bagchi and Paul Rogerson, Leeds, with its aspiration to be a 'motorway city' (the A58M was the first 'urban motorway' in Britain)[*] and its habit of knocking down handsome Victorian buildings, was the classic 1970s city. The team, known for being aggressive and negative, were

---

[*] The legend 'Leeds, Motorway City of the Seventies' was used as a postmark stamp for the city.

also very Seventies, in the sense of being tasteless. They combined hard play with sentimentality: waving to their fans from the centre circle before every home game and wearing tabs on their socks bearing their autographs. The players had superbly dour, although not necessarily Yorkshire, names: Gray, Sprake, Madeley, Reaney, Cooper and, best of all, Norman Hunter. Fewer than half the team were Yorkshiremen, but Leeds United had a very Northern identity. The manager, Don Revie, believed that 'seven London policemen' had prevented him from telling the captain, Billy Bremner, to close down the game in the 1970 Cup Final against Chelsea.

Jack Charlton ('Big Jack') was possibly the hardest of the lot. It was said he kept a 'little black book' of those players he 'owed one'. There's a film online of Jack, viewed from the back, felling an opponent with what appears a mere shrug. It's a head butt, expertly done. If another Leeds player criticised Jack's play in the dressing room, he'd fling a cup of tea at him. I interviewed Charlton for a piece in the *Daily Mail* on 5 November 1994. The cue for the interview was the publication of a book about his managing Ireland at the recent World Cup, and I approached him in the London bookshop where he was doing a book signing. The pen seemed too small in his hand, and his legs were squeezed awkwardly under the table. 'Hello,' I said, 'I'm Andrew Martin; I've come to interview you for the *Daily Mail*.' He shook my hand, but then turned to his publicist and said, 'Has John approved this?', a reference to his agent. When he was told that John had indeed approved it, he muttered, 'That's the trouble, John approves everything.' I liked Jack after a while, though. If he was occasionally rude, he was completely un-grand, and at one point he offered me a cig-arette from his packet of ten. In the course of the interview, we crossed a London square and Jack stopped to buy an *Evening Standard*. The newspaper vendor nearly fainted, but he rallied sufficiently to say, as Jack loped off with paper in hand, 'I hope you'll be taking over Spurs, Jack!' But Jack just waved away the idea, 'Not me, pal!' It was a nice assertion of Northern power over London, although I kept having to remind myself that Jack was not a Yorkshireman. He had a house in the Dales at the time, and his wife, Pat, was Yorkshire (he met her at a dance in Leeds in 1957, where he was giving out the spot prizes, although that didn't impress Pat: 'I'm funny like that'). Much though I'd like to claim Jack for Yorkshire, he was born in Ashington, Northumberland.

A feature film about the Leeds team, *The Damned United*, based on David Peace's compelling novel of that name, is instructive about Yorkshireness, in that Brian Clough is shown as being too arch and elliptical for the Leeds lot, even though he was a Yorkshireman himself, born in Middlesbrough. It's the clash between those two Yorkshire tones, the dreamy and the dour.

I went once to Elland Road to see this team, taken by a neighbour whose sons were Leeds fans to the extent of having bought the record the team recorded to mark their appearance in the 1972 FA Cup Final. I couldn't see the pitch because of the big blokes standing all around me. There was no question of asking them to shuffle aside slightly, so that a young boy might see, and there'd be no question of them agreeing if I had asked.

In 1975, Leeds fans rioted at the European Cup Final in Paris, and as a result the club was banned from Europe for two years. I thought of Leeds fans as the epitome of evil, and a Leeds fan in the singular seems to be given that role in Tony Harrison's long poem, *V,* in which Harrison describes the desecration of his parents' grave by a Leeds-supporting skinhead's graffiti. The narrator challenges the skinhead, whose responses are expletive-laden. When Harrison read the poem on Channel 4 in 1987, there was outrage from the Mary Whitehouse faction at this 'cascade of left-wing obscenities', but the poem, written in the form of Gray's 'Elegy Written in a Country Churchyard', surely expresses the conservative sentiment of anti-vandalism.

Leeds meant trouble or, to put it in a Yorkshire way, bother. Once, while walking down Briggate, I stopped to buy a communist newspaper off a thin, jittery, furtive-looking man. Apparently astonished at having made a sale, he drew me out of the rain into a shop doorway, where he asked for my address, which I supplied, being too unworldly to formulate a refusal. A few days later, I received from him a scruffy letter of about half a dozen pages written with a blunt pencil. Amid some spouting of communist theory was the suggestion that I set up a communist cell in York. He appreciated that I might not know about how to go about this, so he supplied the name of a friend of his – a Leeds man who would be addressing a meeting of the Young Socialist League in central York. I was somehow hypnotised or intimidated into going along. The meeting was held in a room above a pub on that street of many pubs, Micklegate. About half a dozen student types were addressed by the man, who had long hair and a straggly Zapata moustache. With his corduroy jacket and desert boots, he could have been a university – or more likely polytechnic – lecturer but, being from Leeds, he was hard, and when I disagreed with his suggestion that Stalin's forcible collectivisation of agriculture in the Soviet Union, and the commensurate murder of many thousand peasants, was justified, and he realised I was ideologically unsound, he simply stopped speaking to me. When I persisted with the subject, he said, 'Do you want to take this outside?' I didn't, so I left. When, a few years later, my several applications for jobs with the BBC went unanswered, Dad said, 'Remember when you were involved with those communists in Leeds? That could have put you on a blacklist.'

Leeds did indeed mean trouble. In 1980, I went to see the Only Ones at Leeds University; the gig finished late, and I and my mate Pete had to spend the night on Leeds Station – a veritable dormitory, it seemed, for the homeless of the city. In that same year, I was on Leeds Station again, late on a winter afternoon, when a man walked past holding a copy of the *Yorkshire Post*, which bore a headline about John Lennon being shot dead. I walked up to the man and said, 'Where did you get that paper?' thinking – in my shocked disorientation – that it was one of those mocked-up ones you could buy, in which the headline proclaims you Prime Minister, or Formula One champion, or anything you like. The man gave me a hard stare. 'I got it at the paper shop,' he said. I had been in various Northern towns that day, and I'd kept hearing Beatles tunes on the radio with no idea why.

One part of Leeds where one might expect to be insulated from such nasty shocks is the leafy suburb of Headingley, where the home ground of Yorkshire County Cricket Club is located. I went there for the first and only time in, I think, 1979. Here, as at Elland Road, I couldn't see, not because there was anybody in the way – the ground was almost empty, as is traditional with County Championship matches – but because the players were too far away. As I sat on a rough wooden plank (today Headingley has tip-up plastic seats), I seemed to be looking mainly at sky. I also got badly sunburned.

When I was at my secondary modern school in York, one of the games teachers played six games for the Yorkshire first team as a medium-fast bowler. I faced him in the nets once. He didn't take a run-up; even so, I couldn't see the ball. The only evidence it had been bowled was my splayed stumps, and he was, as I say, only medium-fast.

I held contradictory ideas about cricket. It was a peaceful game if watched from a distance, but stressful to play. On my summer bike rides around York, I would watch a couple of overs of a village game from the boundary whilst remaining on my bike; I was always quite happy to cycle on, but perhaps I would pause to watch another over at another ground half an hour later. There were always plenty of games available; it is said that, on any given summer weekend, a quarter of all cricket being played in England is played in Yorkshire. But like so many other intensely Yorkshire activities, it seemed to by-pass York. We seldom played cricket at school. No famous Yorkshire player was from York, I believe, and I played only one proper, formal game of cricket at my secondary school. Also, Yorkshire did not have one of its 'outgrounds', or homes-from-home, in York.

Yorkshire played at many outgrounds, as if it were trying to bind the county together, or staging recruiting rallies for the Yorkshire cause. All counties had outgrounds, but the games at the Yorkshire ones were particularly well attended, Yorkshire being such a cricketing county. There was Bramall Lane, Sheffield, at one time known as much for cricket as football. When that ground was rebuilt into a conventional four-sided stadium exclusively for watching Sheffield United, Yorkshire moved to Abbeydale Park in the south-west of the city. There was Acklam Park in Middlesbrough. On *Test Match Special*, one of Fred

Trueman's 'we-had-it-tough' themes was that, in his playing days, he might finish a game against Kent at their Dover ground on a Wednesday evening, only to be required to go again on the Thursday morning at Middlesbrough. There was the Circle Ground at Hull ('Always smelt strongly of fish', recalled the Yorkshire and England legend Ray Illingworth), on which now stands the KC Stadium where the Hull football and rugby league teams play. Yorkshire played at Harrogate, and at Bradford Park Avenue, which at the time of writing Yorkshire might appropriate for the site of their academy. The outgrounds ceased to be used as the specifications for sporting venues became more rigorous. The cricket book publisher Graham Coster tells me that 'They were associated with splintery pavilion floors, trickly showers and no massage tables or exercise bikes.' Nowadays the ground at North Marine Road, Scarborough, is the only outground regularly visited by Yorkshire, and the games they play there attract the highest crowds for County Championship cricket anywhere in the country. The Yorkshire Cricket Festival is held in Scarborough every year, and I have attended, as it were, remotely, hearing the ripples of applause and perhaps even the thwack of leather on willow while pottering around in the North Bay. On a hot day the sound of cricket mingles harmoniously with the that of the sea.

In 2019 Yorkshire finally deigned to play in York for the first time in over a century, Headingley being used for the World Cup of that year, and it was as if Yorkshire itself, rather than just a cricket team of that name, were visiting York.

The Roses matches against Lancashire might have been played at any of the outgrounds, as well as at Headingley. In *A Social History of English Cricket*, Derek Birley describes the 'wonderfully tense' Roses matches of the Edwardian era – tense, yes, but probably also boring because it was essential to win, or at least not to lose. The Yorkshire philosophy was 'Give 'em nowt', while the safety-first motto of the Lancastrians was 'No fours before lunch'. When I was a boy, in the 1970s, the Roses match would be broadcast specially on Yorkshire TV, and I recall staying in to watch it with the curtains closed against the sun but, the game being somehow sacred, Dad would refrain from telling me to 'Go out and get some fresh air.'

But here was another cricketing paradox. When I began to follow cricketing news, Yorkshire County Cricket Club were better known for fighting among themselves than fighting on the pitch against Lancashire, hence the titles of Stuart Rayner's book: *The War of the White Roses: Yorkshire Cricket's Civil War 1968–1986*. The wars were mainly about the mercurial Geoff Boycott, whether or not he was directly involved at any given battle. The question of whether he should be the captain of the team gave way to the question of whether he should play for the county at all. I know two people who've had direct dealings with Boycott; they both found him friendly and helpful. To others, he is the epitome of Yorkshire cussedness, and they see this evinced in his slow scoring at the crease, a function – they contend – of selfishness.

As I watched the Yorkshire regional tea-time news during my teens, the politics of Yorkshire Cricket Club often displaced national politics. I would hear more about the 'Yorkshire Committee' than the Yorkshire team, and that team was increasingly unsuccessful, debilitated by the in-fighting.

Yorkshire have won the county championship more often than any other side, and they won it seven times

between 1958 and 1968, when the surnames of the principal players all seemed to reflect Yorkshire characteristics:
Close, Trueman, Boycott. (And the captain was Ray
Illingworth, whose surname is also the name of a Yorkshire
village.) They played what was almost a different game to
the other counties: harder, more competitive – more like
the Australians.

But Yorkshire wouldn't win another title until 2001
and, the in-fighting aside, the decline is attributed to a
self-denying ordnance. In 1968, it became possible for the
counties to recruit overseas players; Yorkshire alone fores-
wore the privilege. They also refused to recruit anyone
born outside the county, and Yorkshire was, again, alone
in its masochistically strict policy here, the various and
complex residential qualifications of county cricket having
been quite legally dropped by the other counties by the
Second World War. In the twentieth century, up to 1991,
Yorkshire fielded only nine men born outside the county,
and eight of those were amateurs – that is to say, *gentlemen*
amateurs, and in their case a blind eye was deferentially
turned. The last of these was Geoffrey Keighley, an Old
Etonian and Oxford graduate, who played for Yorkshire
in 1951. Despite his Yorkshire-sounding name, he had
been born in France, which was at least not another
English county. The only professional of the nine was Ces
Parkinson, a bowler, who took two wickets for Yorkshire
in a match in 1906, but then it came to light that he had
been born at Eaglescliffe, County Durham, twenty yards
outside the county boundary, so his debut for Yorkshire
was also his swansong. Both strictures were dropped in
1991, when Yorkshire signed the brilliant young Indian
batsman, Sachin Tendulkar. In *Summer's Crown: the Story*

of Cricket's County Championship, Stephen Chalke writes, 'The Yorkshire folk, rising above their reputation for hostility to outsiders, took to him from the start: his charm, his enthusiasm, his modesty. "Don't you have a go at our Sachin," one lady was heard protesting at Sheffield, "he's better than any big-headed Australian."'

But what accounts for the hair shirt in the first place? Pride. Stuart Rayner writes in *The War of the White Roses*, 'It was Yorkshire officialdom to a tee – unashamed pride and stubborn refusal to move with the times mixed with an arrogant belief that those spawned within their boundaries made up some sort of cricketing master race.'

Pride is now a lop-sided word. You can be proud of being gay, trans, black, but territorial pride is taken to be aggressive, especially if the territory concerned – for example, England or America – is more overdog than underdog. Of course, Yorkshire is God's Own County, the Broad Acres – a natural top-dog. But there has also been a chippiness, a justified sense of grievance (mainly in relation to London) that perhaps makes old-fashioned Yorkshire pride not so damnable after all.

But racism is a different matter, and we turn to Azeem Rafiq, and his powerful testimony, before the Commons Culture, Media and Sport Committee in November 2021, about the racist abuse he experienced while playing for Yorkshire between 2008 and 2018. Eleven days beforehand, on 5 November, the chairman of Yorkshire, Roger Hutton, had resigned over the club's handling of Rafiq's allegations, and on 6 November, Chris Waters wrote in the *Yorkshire Post*, 'Forget the famous Yorkshire CCC civil war of the 1970s and 1980s, when Geoffrey Boycott was at the centre of an earthquake. This present crisis makes that one look like a trivial argument about the provision of soap in the Headingley toilets.' He speculated that there might not be such luxuries as toilets at Headingley in the future, and if there were they would be unlikely to have a sponsor, such was the 'incalculable commercial and reputational harm' caused by Rafiq's testimony.

Rafiq said before the select committee that the issues he faced at Yorkshire were 'without doubt' widespread in cricket, and the discrepancy between the number of Asians playing grassroots cricket, and the number playing the first-class game is a nationwide scandal. But I did wonder whether any commentators would trace a connection between the treatment of Rafiq and Yorkshire's sense of being the chosen one among counties (and I'm speaking of the territory now, not the cricket club). In a typically eloquent and powerful piece for *The Times* on 20 November 2021, Janice Turner, who grew up in Doncaster, wrote, 'Inevitably from Yorkshire exceptionalism and a prizing of harsh, unfettered speech, comes racism.' In the piece she discusses her father's 'racism', describing it as a product of his 'all-white life' that would give way to his natural generosity when he did encounter people of different ethnicity. Reading the article, I thought of my own Yorkshire father, equally all-white in his circle of acquaintances and also given occasionally to 'harsh, unfettered speech'. But I never heard him say anything racist. He was one of the Old Labour-progressive type of plain speakers, like, say, Brian Clough; they prided themselves on walking a tightrope: trenchant but not reactionary. And I thought of a Yorkshire friend of mine, who is perhaps my *most* Yorkshire friend, by which I mean he is so blunt, and so regularly critical, that he is also an adversary. But he is not a racist and nor, come to think of it, is he sexist. For what it's worth (probably not very much, given my own background), I don't think Yorkshire is any more or less racist than any other county, and I suspect that racism will out whatever the mode of speech of a given locality. Where were we? Leeds.

In a way, Leeds *is* Yorkshire. It was known as 'the city of a thousand trades' and it has its finger in all the Yorkshire pies. Its rise was based on textiles – the Yorkshire version: wool, and 'heavy wool' at that. It became a textile town despite not being particularly hilly. According to John McGoldrick, Curator of Industrial History at Leeds Museums and Galleries, the Aire powered the water wheels 'by sheer volume of water rather than speed'. Leeds does not seem as countrified as the other textile towns: it's not rimmed with high greenery, but it does have its countrified suburbs. It also had its coal mines.

The textile industry gave rise to engineering, including railway engineering. You might have seen a 'Made in Leeds' nameplate while sauntering along to the dining car of a luxury blue and gold Wagon Lits sleeper service on the Continent (the *Train Bleu*, for instance), since those carriages were built by the firm of Leeds Forge, based at Armley. But Leeds was more likely to be invoked in a gritter setting: the rainy siding of an industrial railway, where the workhorse locomotive (possibly narrow-gauge) might well have been made in Hunslet, that red-brick factoryland of south Leeds.

Leeds' industry was in decline by the 1970s, but a rebirth was just around the corner, and for me, getting to like Leeds was, in part, simply a matter of going there when the shops were open. At the top of the scale is

Victoria Quarter, those ornate and confusingly inter-
connected – and confusingly named – shopping arcades
whose high-end outlets have earned the description
'the Knightsbridge of the North'. But this *is* the North,
with Northern weather, which is why the arcades have
barrel-vaulted glass roofs. Most of these gilded, marbled,
multi-coloured arcades are Victorian, but one of them
only *became* an arcade in 1989 when Victoria Street was
roofed over, with no expense spared. And if you want to
see the county set, go to the County Arcade: they are the
ones walking into the shops and not just sheltering guiltily from the rain. It strikes me, incidentally, that no city
in any other county would use the word 'County' in that
proprietorial way. If they did, even the locals might not
know which county was being referred to.

The wide social range of Leeds is reflected in the close
juxtaposition of the glitzy arcades and Kirkgate Market,
which is also Victorian, but doesn't boast of the fact. This,
the largest indoor market in Europe, is a cornucopia of
vulgar Yorkshire delights. It's a beautiful space: soaring
ornate ironwork topped by angled glass, with the festive
aspect of a winter gardens at the seaside.

Kirkgate Market would confirm every prim southerner's
worst idea of a Yorkshire diet. In the little cafés, demar-
cated by pastel-coloured wooden booths, you can get
cheese and chips in a sandwich. Every type of Yorkshire
stodge is available: teacakes, parkin, custard pies, and I
can duplicate the sort of tea (evening meal) I might have
eaten after school in 1974: mince on toast followed by
Battenberg cake, washed down with a mug of tea with two
sugars. In some Kirkgate booths, the tea is served in plastic
beakers and if you don't want sugar you have to say so,

otherwise you get it. In terms of confectionery, all the delicacies of my childhood are still available (whereas they are no longer readily available in York): for example, cinder toffee (which is like primitive lumps of Crunchie), chocolate tools, sherbet strawberries and lemons – although in Kirkgate Market, sherbet might also be called kali, and liquorice 'Spanish'. I heard a young man in Kirkgate Market say to his mate, 'I'm waiting for Dave to get me some pineapple chunks.' (I also heard a woman in one of the cafés say, 'Our young 'un had her first tattoo done on Friday. She didn't flinch. I'm getting my fifteenth done on Friday – I can't wait.')

In 1998, I wrote an article about the Market, in which I mentioned that the chief type of crisps available there are Seabrook Crisps, which are my favourites, having the most pungent flavours. I also like it that they're crinkle-cut, which is possibly a Yorkshire thing. Certainly, we had a spud crinkler in our house when I was growing up. Seabrook Crisps are made in Bradford and have been since 1939 when a man called Charles Brook (who owned a fish and chip shop but wanted to go into potato frying in a bigger way) noticed, when he went to collect some photographs developed by his local chemist, that the man had written 'Seabrook' instead of C. Brook. After my article appeared, I got a letter from Mr Jack Harrison, Sales Director. It began:

Dear Mr Martin,

Your article in the *Independent on Sunday* on Sunday, 2 August 1998 has brought interest and comment from the Seabrook faithful far and wide. Please accept the accompanying crisps with our compliments and I enclose some information on our company which I feel you will find interesting.

More importantly, I would like to offer you a visit to our factories here in Bradford. Once you have tasted our crisps hot from the pan you will be spoilt forever! You mention that you have connections with Yorkshire and perhaps we could incorporate a visit to us when you next return to God's County. We could stock you up to help you endure your exile in the south.

In 2018, Seabrook Crisps were acquired by Calbee Inc., 'the leading snack brand of Japan, as part of their international growth plans'. They're still made in Bradford.

I like crisps because I like fat, which might be a genetic predisposition. The Yorkshire diet was always tipped towards fat and carbohydrates (Yorkshire pudding, for example), because they were cheap and gave an energy boost to people doing physical work. So the fat didn't necessarily make people fat. The saddle bag on Dad's bike had a base of hardboard that was impregnated with fat from all the times he carried home fish and chips or what were called 'scraps' (deep-fried fat, free from either a butcher's or a fish and chip shop), and his own father kept a plastic cup of solidified brown fat in the kitchen of his terraced house in central York, which he melted and used in the preparation of almost every meal he ate. After his meal, he poured the fat back into the cup.

Kirkgate Market suits Saturday afternoons in winter, a time of little treats, with the Leeds United result coming through by osmosis, and the countdown to convivial evening in the form of a butcher shouting out the steadily declining price of half a dozen steaks. The Market has recently been refurbished under the slogan, 'Many stories told, many still to tell.' It is now market*ed* as a tourist destination. Wi-Fi has been installed. New stall holders offer 'street food', as if Seabrook Crisps and stand pies were not already street food.

The Party Town

In *Pies and Prejudice* (2008), Stuart Maconie speaks of Leeds as 'Britain's most improved city, the gentrified jewel of the new north, the Barcelona of the West Riding'. This is reflected in his accommodation; he is staying at 42 The Calls, Leeds' first boutique hotel, housed in a converted warehouse: 'I realised, with mild annoyance, that I'd left the recessed plasma widescreen in the living room switched on and that I could still hear Ray Stubbs on *Grandstand*. Never mind, I'd go through in a minute just as soon as I'd finished my Bombay Sapphire and leafed through the menu one more time. White Crab Meat in a Saffron Aioli looked nice . . .'

The spur for the Leeds revival was what John McGoldrick calls 'the banking renaissance', and the spur for *that* was the Big Bang of 1986, by which financial services were de-regulated. Leeds is the largest legal and financial centre outside London, but it has experienced fast economic growth – and job creation – in many areas and, unlike many of the bigger Northern towns, it has a high ratio of private to public sector jobs. There is a certain balefulness to its success, in that it has been said to suck the life out of surrounding towns like Batley, Dewsbury, Wakefield.* 'Have you seen the migration from here to Leeds every morning?' said a man I got talking to on a platform at Huddersfield railway station a couple of years ago. 'It's like the sardine packer's outing.' (The train was crowded, in other words.) Leeds is the third largest manufacturing centre in the UK (engineering, printing, food and drink, chemicals). It is also successful in IT and computer game development. Grand Theft Auto was partly developed in Leeds. I'd have thought that was pure Los Angeles, but if someone had told me a UK city had a hand in its development, I like to think I'd have guessed Leeds.

In 1987, Leeds extended the hand of welcome to me – an invitation to join its prosperous ride. Having moved to London, I was finding it hard to get off the ground as a Professional Yorkshireman, so I took a law conversion course and qualified as a barrister, which was logical enough, since I'd enjoyed watching murder trials at York Crown Court once I was old enough to sit in the public gallery. (You must be eighteen.) I decided to be a Professional Yorkshireman in the more serious sense of being a barrister on the Northern Circuit, and to this end I undertook a week-long mini-pupillage in Park Square, Leeds, which is in the heart of the commercial district.

The barristers of the chambers would take their lunch in the elegant, tiled café, somewhat Turkish bath-like, of the Art Gallery which, like most of Leeds, had been recently refurbished. I sensed that, if I joined them full-time, I would soon gravitate further along the Headrow to Brodrick's

---

* But Wakefield is staging a strong fightback, with much urban renewal, and a bid to be City of Culture, 2025. A PR for Wakefield told me, 'This Yorkshire cathedral city and district was recently voted one of the UK's chicest destinations by premium interiors brand, Dowsing & Reynolds.'

palatial Town Hall, because surely a Leeds lawyer was likely to be involved in dignified civic 'functions' in that venue. I was assigned a junior barrister to shadow, and on my second morning I was walking through sunny Park Square with him when he paused and pointed out, 'Your left shoelace is undone.' A warning flashed into my mind: *If I come here permanently, it will be the end of Bohemia.* But my minder had mentioned the untied lace in a spirit of pure helpfulness and after I had tied it up, and sprinted along to catch him up, he said, 'You'll have a good life if you come here, you know. You'll make decent money, and of course it goes further in the North. After a couple of years, you'll go around the corner to Clutton's Estate Agents and get yourself a nice converted barn, out Wetherby way. You'll probably take Silk in your forties, and – since I think you're interested in politics – why not find yourself a nice, safe Yorkshire seat to represent?'

To wind up here the story of my legal career ... At the end of my week in the chambers, it was intimated to me informally that I would be offered a pupillage 'with a view' – that is, with the likely prospect of becoming a member of chambers. As I walked away from Park Square towards the railway station and the London train, I diverted into one of those grand, gilded bars of central Leeds, venues for deal-making and back-slapping, where I proceeded to get drunk, partly to celebrate, and partly to drown my confusion, because I didn't know whether I wanted to clasp the hand that Leeds had offered. After a week of agonising, I turned it down, which I immediately regretted, so I tried again for the Northern Circuit, this time applying to a chambers in Sheffield. After another mini-pupillage, I was again offered a pupillage 'with a view'.* This time, the offer

---

* It was much easier to be taken on as a barrister back then than it is today.

was made vocally, by the head of chambers, a burly, bald man in the mould of the charismatic Yorkshire and England cricketer Brian Close (who was known not to flinch when hit, even on the head, by fast-flying cricket balls). The dialogue went like this.

Head of Chambers: You've enjoyed your time here, I hope?

Me: Very much thanks, yes. Learned a lot, too.

H of C: Good. Now I'll be writing to you in due course, but just to say we're minded to offer you the pupillage with a view.

Me: Oh, terrific. Thanks very much.

H of C: But there's something I want to get straight now. If you come here, it's a thirty-year touch. I'm not having you accepting the offer, then buggering off back to London at the first opportunity.

Me (After a period of silence): Course not. Absolutely.

Sitting before that man, I felt as flighty and guiltily irresponsible as Billy Liar. And the way he put it ... it was like being sentenced to thirty years, and by a man who subsequently became an eminent judge. If he *hadn't* put it like that, I would probably have accepted his offer.

The Sheffield debacle was a postscript, and when I think of what might have been, I think of Leeds. On my return visits to the city, I walk around conscious of the departure time of the train that'll take me back to London, whereas I could have been walking around with a Range Rover key fob in my pocket. The vehicle would be in some elite bay near Park Square; there would be a couple of briefs on the passenger seat, tied with pink ribbon. In the back . . . a pair of wellies, and a blanket for my border collie to lie down on.

In 2020, I was in Leeds on a Saturday evening, and wandering around the commercial district, the one part of town that's quiet at that time. (It's busy on a *weekday* evening, when the city's pin-striped high rollers crowd into the marbled bars and restaurants that some of the old banks have become.) I'd just arrived in town and was encumbered with a shoulder bag. I'd tried to check-in at the Queens Hotel, but the queue was too long. I was nostalgically searching for the majestic boozer where I'd got drunk that night after my mini-pupillage. The streets – or should I say the Rows, Parades, Places and Squares – of the commercial district seemed dignified in golden illumination, as in Grimshaw's painting of Park Row (although that painting shames Leeds, since most of the buildings depicted in it have been demolished). Eventually, I saw a man walking towards me. 'Sorry to bother you,' I said, 'but I'm looking for a certain bar . . .' He cut me off with, 'A lap-dancing bar, right?' The exchange could not have happened in York, because lap-dancing bars wouldn't be allowed there.

I wandered into Park Square, where the Leeds red brick really *works*, partly because it's offset by the manicured grass of the central lawn. The Square is dominated by the oriental pink and white extravaganza of St Paul's House, built for a tailoring company in 1877 and used as offices today. I looked towards the chambers where I'd nearly worked; but it's not only barristers who have chambers hereabouts, and places like Pearl Chambers, Zenith Chambers, King's Chambers

and (a bit naff, surely) Cosmic Chambers accommodate other varieties of Professional Yorkshiremen and women.

I walked back to City Square, where young women with hardly any clothes on were flitting about in the rain. Typical attire might be a pair of silky shorts and a top that was, in effect, merely a bra. Some wore sunglasses in their hair, and sashes reading 'Self-Appointed Beauty Queen'. A number of them had congregated under the porch of the Queens. They were negotiating with taxi drivers, who drove up in relays, and the girls would stick their head and shoulders, and therefore also their cleavages, through the open taxi windows. This notion of sexuality in flowing motion . . . it was like the prequel to 'The Whitsun Weddings'. You get a lot of hen parties in York as well, but it occurred to me that Leeds at seven o'clock on a Saturday night is like York at eleven o'clock.

Some of the self-appointed beauty queens were conferring in the Queens Hotel lobby when I finally did check in (and most of them looked the genuine article to me). They were being quite loud, and I raised an eyebrow at the desk clerk, who just shrugged and said, 'Yes, it's quite buzzy. I've just double upgraded you, by the way.'

I like the Queens. There used to be something funereal about its battered monochrome Deco (in November 2011, Jimmy Savile lay in state in the bar, alongside his last half-smoked cigar and a mountain of white roses). The lobby was recently prettified and made colourful; I preferred it before, but the long, wide upstairs corridors still tend to be completely silent in a way I find compelling. After check-in, I walked through to the bar, for a 175 ml glass of Chardonnay. 'That'll be six pounds seventy-five,' said the barman. 'Sorry, it's London prices here.' So I didn't bother having a second, but walked up to my room, where there was a fridge – no mini-bar, just an empty fridge. The hotel obviously knew that most guests would do what I did half an hour later: walk into the Sainsbury's in the railway station and pick up a bottle of white wine for a fiver. Simon Armitage includes in *All Points North* a transcript of a film he made about Saturday night in Leeds that was broadcast on BBC2 in 1996. He writes compellingly of

> Saturday night coming in from the east like a tide
> having waited all week at the edge of the world
> for a green light.

Leeds is a party town, but I was too old for the party. 'All the London kids want to go to Leeds University,' my wife, an educational consultant, once told me, 'and they love it when they get there.'*

---

* She is also a fan of Leeds University aesthetically, especially of the Gothic-revival Great Hall, by Alfred Waterhouse, which is another example of Leeds red brick put to creditable use.

was made vocally, by the head of chambers, a burly, bald man in the mould of the charismatic Yorkshire and England cricketer Brian Close (who was known not to flinch when hit, even on the head, by fast-flying cricket balls). The dialogue went like this.

Head of Chambers: You've enjoyed your time here, I hope?

Me: Very much thanks, yes. Learned a lot, too.

H of C: Good. Now I'll be writing to you in due course, but just to say we're minded to offer you the pupillage with a view.

Me: Oh, terrific. Thanks very much.

H of C: But there's something I want to get straight now. If you come here, it's a thirty-year touch. I'm not having you accepting the offer, then buggering off back to London at the first opportunity.

Me (After a period of silence): Course not. Absolutely.

Sitting before that man, I felt as flighty and guiltily irresponsible as Billy Liar. And the way he put it ... it was like being sentenced to thirty years, and by a man who subsequently became an eminent judge. If he *hadn't* put it like that, I would probably have accepted his offer.

The Sheffield debacle was a postscript, and when I think of what might have been, I think of Leeds. On my return visits to the city, I walk around conscious of the departure time of the train that'll take me back to London, whereas I could have been walking around with a Range Rover key fob in my pocket. The vehicle would be in some elite bay near Park Square; there would be a couple of briefs on the passenger seat, tied with pink ribbon. In the back . . . a pair of wellies, and a blanket for my border collie to lie down on.

In 2020, I was in Leeds on a Saturday evening, and wandering around the commercial district, the one part of town that's quiet at that time. (It's busy on a *weekday* evening, when the city's pin-striped high rollers crowd into the marbled bars and restaurants that some of the old banks have become.) I'd just arrived in town and was encumbered with a shoulder bag. I'd tried to check-in at the Queens Hotel, but the queue was too long. I was nostalgically searching for the majestic boozer where I'd got drunk that night after my mini-pupillage. The streets – or should I say the Rows, Parades, Places and Squares – of the commercial district seemed dignified in golden illumination, as in Grimshaw's painting of Park Row (although that painting shames Leeds, since most of the buildings depicted in it have been demolished). Eventually, I saw a man walking towards me. 'Sorry to bother you,' I said, 'but I'm looking for a certain bar . . .' He cut me off with, 'A lap-dancing bar, right?' The exchange could not have happened in York, because lap-dancing bars wouldn't be allowed there.

I wandered into Park Square, where the Leeds red brick really *works*, partly because it's offset by the manicured grass of the central lawn. The Square is dominated by the oriental pink and white extravaganza of St Paul's House, built for a tailoring company in 1877 and used as offices today. I looked towards the chambers where I'd nearly worked; but it's not only barristers who have chambers hereabouts, and places like Pearl Chambers, Zenith Chambers, King's Chambers

Hunslet

When I was in Leeds in 2019, I did something I'd never done before, at least not as a pedestrian: I entered South Leeds — that is, the city south of the Aire — and I did it by crossing Leeds Bridge. In 1888, Louis Le Prince, a Frenchman resident in Leeds, pointed a camera from a window belonging to an ironmonger's (the window is still there) that overlooked this bridge, and made what is considered the second earliest cinema film. Le Prince had also made what is considered the first film, earlier in the same year, showing some happy friends walking — for two seconds — around the garden of a large house in Roundhay, Leeds. The Leeds Bridge film shows — also for two seconds — what must have been a continuous, almost mechanical, process ongoing for a hundred years: a heavily laden wagon is going north over the bridge; another is going south. A flare of white light in the film lends the scene a luminous, magical aspect, but it must have been utterly routine. Perhaps the wagons were coming from, or going to, the vast goods sidings of the Midland Railway that fumed away near the south side of the Bridge on a site that is today the Crown Point Shopping Village.

South Leeds, and in particular Hunslet, was the focus of

Leeds' engineering. In 2019, I conducted some historical research in Leeds armed with a map of the city dating from 1908 (and it was embarrassing to have to admit the date when somebody came up to me asking directions). I could make out traces of the 1908 world: a surviving factory wall; an area of scrub denoting a demolished factory. But even a modern map of the area wouldn't have been much use because South Leeds is a work in progress, with sleek tower blocks and other developments sprouting from the industrial graveyard. The mansion that used to be the headquarters of Tetley's Brewery stood, apparently bewildered, amid the building sites, even though it has found a modern use as an arts centre.

I was engaged in some historical research for a book about heritage railways, trying to trace the route of a railway that had connected a coal mine at Middleton, just south of Leeds, to coal staithes on the river Aire. The Middleton Railway – which began operations in in the 1760s, its wagons hauled along the rails by horses – brought industrial Leeds to life; it was God touching Adam's finger. In 1812, it was the first railway to make commercial use of a locomotive – an engine called *Salamanca*, designed by Matthew Murray, an engineer who worked in the Leeds textile industry. This being Leeds, some balefulness was involved, since the line was also the site of the first steam railway fatality, when a boy called John Bruce fell beneath the engine, alongside which he had been enthusiastically running. The line was also the first to employ a man officially described as an engine driver, until he was killed by a boiler explosion in 1834.

It proved impossible to trace the line, although I did figure out that what had been its terminal station, close to the Aire, is today a large Pets at Home store. The decisive clue was that there had been a gasworks over the road from

Left: a surviving bit of old King's Cross, when it was more Yorkshire-orientated than today. Right: Andrew, his parents and grandfather in their York backyard.

Left: Andrew at Scarborough. Right: Andrew as Herod's messenger in York Mystery Plays, 1976, a part he landed because of his loud voice.

Right: York Mystery Plays crowd scene. A challenge: spot Andrew.

Above: York salubrity on a
lovely day. Right: the R.I. gym,
formerly a loco-erecting shop.

Above: exotic Terry's.
Above right: less exotic
Rowntree's. Right: the
Whisky lounge of the
Grand Hotel, York, formerly
Andrew's father's office.

Above: Andrew and his father at the National Railway Museum, York, 2006.

Above and left: Andrew at the NRM. (He often goes there.) Yorkshire forward was a Regional Development Agency. It contributed to the NRM's purchase of *Flying Scotsman*.

Left: a dentist's nightmare in Kirkgate Market, Leeds.

Above left: in Park Square, Leeds, a golden future might have awaited Andrew.
Above right: Deco lift doors in the Queen's Hotel, Leeds.

Right: Leeds actually boasting (with typical brazenness) of being a 'Motorway City'. But then it was 1971.

Left: Andrew and son at the end of the Three Peaks Walk in the Dales. (Yes, the boy should have been wearing a hat, too.) Below: Sylvia Plath's grave, with pens stuck in.

Above: Pickering Station on the North Yorkshire Moors Railway. Andrew goes there when stressed. Right: the beach tractor is totemic of Filey.

Left: the Royal Hotel, Scarborough – still quite smart. Directly below: two Whitby scenes

Below: poignant collector boy for blind charity at the St Nicholas Cliff funicular, Scarborough.

Above: the Humber, Hull, in a typically demonstrative mood. Below: view towards Scarborough castle from the third floor of Boyes's Hardware Store, where bath plugs are sold.

Above: start on the descent to idyllic Beck Hole in the North Yorkshire Moors, where another hole was being dug. Below: the Birch Hall Inn, Beck Hole – a perfect pub.

the station, and today there is still a gasworks there, albeit prettified and more office than 'works'. Incidentally, part of the southern end of the Middleton Railway is operated as a preserved or heritage line, and it is the grittiest of the hundred or so British lines of that type, which are normally country branches. Its main station stands amid the hollowed-out red-brick streets of Hunslet. The track runs past a housing estate, an industrial estate, some five-a-side football pitches. It terminates to the south in Middleton Park, where the remains of early coal excavation can still be seen. The trees of the park are part of an ancient woodland, but on my visit they looked grey and sickly, with bin bag tatters in the branches. When the train guard (who worked in IT) checked my ticket, I told him I was a writer, and he said, 'You know, a lot of the media people don't understand the significance of this railway.'

Hunslet is significant to me for two other reasons, or rather because of two other *people*. The first is Keith Waterhouse, who was born in Hunslet in 1929, and who died in London in 2009 – amazing longevity, given how much he drank. He grew up on Low Road, Hunslet, and he took the high road all his adult life. Not long after his death, I wrote something in the *Guardian* to the effect that he would be chiefly remembered for *Billy Liar*. His agent, I think it was, wrote a letter to the paper, saying that I had underestimated Waterhouse's achievement, and that he would be remembered for more than just that one work. I was guiltily reminded of that letter when, for the purposes of this book, I read *City Lights*, Waterhouse's wonderfully vivid memoir of growing up in Hunslet, published in 1994. Waterhouse was born – into a family poor even by the standards of 1930s Hunslet – at No. 17 Low Road, 'now largely urban desert'. The young Waterhouse had 'an affinity with factories'. Hunslet, he recalls, had small 'nook-and-cranny businesses, crammed into small yards or down narrow alleys', but there were also the 'great set-piece mills and factories, sturdy and substantial and standing out like steel engravings against the sulphurous yellow sky: Thwaite Mills; the chemical works; the sweet-smelling coffee works; the fireclay and brick works; Hudswell Clarke's Railway Foundry, shipping locomotives to the Argentine and every dominion of the Empire . . .'

Hunslet also interests me as being the place where the sociologist Richard Hoggart grew up. His seminal work of 1957, *The Uses of Literacy*, examines the steamrollering of working-class street culture by a commercialised mass-market culture. There is a strain of anti-Americanism. Among the pulp literature he castigates are American hard-boiled 'sex novels', and 'American or American-type serial-books of comics, where for page after page big-thighed and big-bosomed girls from Mars step out of their space-machines, and gangsters' molls scream away in high-powered sedans.' The modern word for what Hoggart had put his finger on is 'globalisation'.

He is speaking of 1930s Leeds when he writes,

This is an extremely local life, in which everything is remarkably near. The houses, I said, open on the street; the street itself, compared with those of suburbia or the new housing estates, is narrow; the houses opposite are only just over the cobbles and the shops not much farther.

He mentions that every street has its corner shop and 'if the light is kept on at nights the children make it a meeting place.'

There is a passage about 'the scholarship boy', the child

who has experienced a 'physical uprooting from their class through the medium of the scholarship system'. Hoggart was a scholarship boy, eventually. He initially failed the examination at eleven for the local grammar school (which Keith Waterhouse also failed to get into), but a teacher urged a re-marking on his behalf.

I failed my Eleven Plus, and in my case the verdict has never been overturned. I was expected to pass, but even now I don't believe I could answer any question beginning, 'If John has six apples and Jane has nine . . .' But I made it to the grammar school in the sixth form and when I went to university I did obtain a scholarship, called an Exhibition, which was gratifying but slightly embarrassing to a person of Yorkshire sensibility, being reminiscent of the familiar put-down, 'You're making an exhibition of yourself.' Anyhow, I kept recognising myself in Hoggart's evocation of the scholarship boy. 'He has left his class, at least in spirit, by being in certain ways unusual; and he is still unusual in another class, too tense and over-wound.' The scholarship boy takes 'pride in his own gaucheness at practical things . . . If he tries to be "pally" with working-class people, to show that he is one of them, they "smell it a mile off".' Actually, I don't try to do that, with the result that I am more often thought aloof than ingratiating. Very instructive here was the occasion when a friend of mine from Oxford – a product of Rugby School – walked up to someone in a York pub and said, 'Have you got a light, mate?' 'No,' came the steely reply, 'and I'm not your mate.' The scholarship boy knows he can't go back to his homely origins, but 'he pines for some Nameless Eden where he never was.' Hence, perhaps, this book.

THE COUNTRYSIDE

Rural Romance

In our suburban York house, the display cabinet behind the TV was like the tabernacle in a church: the sacred things were kept there. There was the booze — mainly sherry, the bottles of which lasted from year to year, since it was drunk only at Christmas, and in glasses so small and narrow that it was hard to get the residue out of the bottom. I think Dad assumed it was some sort of preserve, like jam. There were the cartons of duty-free cigarettes, the best china, and the dozen or so books we kept in the house (as opposed to the wave of library books that flowed through every week), and these were sacred by virtue of being concerned with God's Own County. There were a few photographic books of what is called in Yorkshire 'scenery', with captions like, 'The evening milking complete, farmer Thompson takes a moment to contemplate the sunset.' Or 'The view from Sutton Bank Top: you can watch a train start at York and finish at Darlington from here.' There was *Portrait of Yorkshire*, by Harry Scott, which I have retained in my London house. On the cover is the White Horse at Kilburn with a crumbling barn in the foreground. There is a touch of legalese in the dust-jacket biography of the author: 'Mr Scott has an intimate knowledge of Yorkshire

and its people from a long life spent in their midst.' Scott
was born in Plymouth, in 1901, but he more than made up
for that by virtue of having founded, in 1939, the *Yorkshire
Dalesman* magazine, subsequently the *Dalesman*, which he
edited and produced from his cottage in Clapham in the
Dales. In the first number, April 1939, Scott struck a typically stroppy Yorkshire note by declaring that a magazine
devoted to the Yorkshire Dales 'needs no apology'. The
Dalesman, whose circulation is currently around 30,000,
still claims to be 'the country's most popular regional magazine', and it is said that 'For every copy bought, fifteen
people read it,' a statement usually accompanied by some
crack about the stinginess of Yorkshire folk. About ten
years ago, I pitched an article to the *Dalesman*. The editor
said he'd be happy to take it, but there'd be no fee. When
I expressed surprise, he said, 'You make a common mistake
in assuming we pay for articles.'

In my boyhood, the magazine was lying around everywhere. Any second-hand bookshop would have a lucky dip
of old *Dalesman*s, perhaps kept in a shoe box. This, rather
than *Punch*, was the standard fare in doctors' and dentists'
waiting rooms. In the bleak waiting room of our own
local dentists, the context seemed wrong for the magazine:
there was a gas fire where there should have been a coal
one; fluorescent lights where there should have been oil
lamps. The magazine – a bulletin from the real authentic
Yorkshire – would often shame its setting. The correct
place for it was the pocket of a thornproof jacket, where it
would fit snugly, these pockets being relatively large, the
Dalesman relatively small. The soothing flavour of the magazine is given in the contents of *The Dalesman: a Celebration
of 50 Years*, by David Joy. There is a section called 'Folk
of the Broad Acres', including 'Delius in the Dales' and

'Introducing the Brontës'. 'A Year in Yorkshire' includes 'August: Sheep Dipping.'

Things move slowly in the world of the *Dalesman*. The Old Amos cartoon, featuring a typically sagacious old Yorkshireman, has only been drawn by two people, and one was the son of the other. In 1947, the magazine broadened its remit to encompass the whole of the Yorkshire countryside. It is still produced in the Dales, albeit only just – in Skipton, close to the edge. In the early days, Harry Scott would moonlight, doing shifts on the *Craven Herald*, which is said to have been the last paper in Britain to have retained adverts on its front page. It was broadsheet back then; today it's a tabloid, although it prefers the more genteel word 'compact'.

The *Dalesman* has only had seven editors in its history; the best known and longest serving was Bill Mitchell. Alan Bennett narrated a TV film about his retirement from the editor's chair in 1988. Mitchell, mellow and bespectacled, recalls his first meeting with the magazine's founder, Harry Smith: 'He smelt of peat, tweed and tobacco smoke, and he said, "Hail to thee, bright spirit!"' Mitchell described the typical Dalesman as 'realistic and taciturn', adding that 'Taciturnity has been summed up as the ability to say nowt for a long time.' The joke about the number of people who read each edition is perpetuated, and Bennett admits in the film, 'I don't actually buy it. My copy is passed on to me by Irene Plumridge, who works in the *Dalesman* office.'

Our display cabinet in York also held a couple of literary spin-offs from the *Dalesman* – paperbacks denoted by their elegant black borders and the reassuring words, 'A Dalesman Publication'. One of these was *York* by Michael Pocock, who was not from Yorkshire, but Liverpool. We will let him off though, because he was head of history at

Tadcaster Grammar School, and 'a former secretary of the York branch of the Historical Association'.

As my earliest ambition — to be a farmer — gave way to the aspiration to write, I became a great reader of those potted author biographies. The biography of James Herriot was particularly mesmerising. Whilst he wasn't exactly a farmer, he had his wellies planted firmly in Yorkshire mud, being a vet based at Thirsk, in the Dales; on top of which his books had sold in their millions. There were always a couple of Herriots in the cabinet, and very bent and battered they were, because I read them over and over. I associate the books with the taste of Lucozade* and the sight of my thin white bedroom curtains closed against the light of day. They were the only books I could read when I was emerging from one of the migraines that plagued me as a child.

It was the evocation of countryside that provided the balm. Early in the first book, *If Only They Could Talk*, the evocations of the Dales form a crescendo. Here is Herriot, approaching his first encounter with the veterinary practice in Darrowby (a fictional stand-in for Thirsk): 'I had never been in Yorkshire before, but the name had always raised a picture of a county as stodgy and unromantic as its pudding.' A little later, he is speaking of 'a dark tide of heather' lapping the 'mountains'. Then, of Darrowby, 'its setting was beautiful on the pebbly river'. Twenty pages later, when Herriot goes out on a call with his new boss, Siegfried Farnon, we have the climax:

> We took a steep, winding road, climbing higher and still
> higher with the hillside falling away sheer to a dark ravine

---

* Which back then was the opposite of what it is now: a drink for convalescents rather than athletes. The bottles came wrapped in a sort of cellophane shroud, like hospital flowers, or as a reminder of how you might end up if you didn't drink it.

where a rocky stream rushed headlong to the gentler country below ... In the summer dusk, a wild panorama of tumbling fells and peaks rolled away and lost itself in the crimson and gold ribbons of the western sky. To the east, a black mountain overhung us, menacing in its naked bulk. Huge, square-cut boulders littered the lower slopes ...

Unlike the gently moralistic stories themselves, the provenance of the Herriot books is fraught. Herriot's real name was James Alfred Wight; he was born in Sunderland and grew up in Scotland. People misread 'Wight' as 'Wright' and wonder if he's related to Peter Wright, Yorkshire vet, who stars in a TV series called *The Yorkshire Vet* along with another Yorkshire vet, Julian Norton. (Consider the impossibility of a TV series called, say, *The Warwickshire Vet*.) The Herriot books are confusingly bundled. The first two, *If Only They Could Talk* and *It Shouldn't Happen to a Vet*, were later republished in a joint volume called *All Creatures Great and Small*. When I bought a recent edition of this, I got it from a fiction shelf, but the strapline on the cover reads, 'The classic memoirs of a Yorkshire country vet'.

And we must now distinguish between the first TV series, called *All Creatures Great and Small* (1978–90), which drew on other Herriot books besides the first two, and the second, an unexpected triumph for Channel 5 in 2020. 'New Herriot series a huge boost for Dales', ran a headline in the *Craven Herald*. 'The announcement comes just days after the World of James Herriot Museum [in Thirsk] celebrated its twentieth anniversary.' In that same year, a documentary about the *first* series appeared on BBC4. Peter Davison, who played the junior vet, Tristan Farnon, ascribed the success of the series to 'a feeling still in the towns that the country was the ideal place.'

It was likely that while I was off school and reading about the Yorkshire countryside, my colleagues *at* school were also being lead down country byways. The Country Code[*] came up in various lessons, not just geography where it properly belonged. In 1971 a cartoon public information film called *Country Code* was shown on British TV featuring a couple of the Donald McGill postcard type: her big and sexual, him weedy. In the film, they sit in front of a drystone wall, which they have partly dismantled. On the other side of it, their dog (as Petunia observes) 'is having a lovely time playing with those sheep'. The pair are glad that some cows have vacated the field. As Joe says, 'They have taken themselves off for a walk down t' road through that gate I opened – the one marked private.'

It used to irritate me that, from their accents, they were a Yorkshire couple. Surely Tykes, of all people, would know about the Country Code? But then again, the upholder of the Code, the irate farmer who says at the end (more in sorrow than anger by now), 'When folks come out to the country, why, oh, why can't they follow the Country Code?' is also a Yorkshireman. At school, we'd have a refresher on the Code before regular jaunts in minibuses to the Dales or the Moors. A frequent destination was Malham in Airedale, with its glacial lake (the Tarn) and its 260 foot-high wall of limestone (the Cove). At my secondary school, the best walks were organised by the metalwork teacher. Three of us went with him to Malham on Christmas Eve in 1975. There was snow on the ground and the cove was dusted with white. The tarn had been made a very dark blue by the cold, and the water seemed thick, although ice

---

[*]   It evolved from various rural organisations in the 1930s, in response to the popularity among town dwellers of 'hiking'; since 2004, it has been the 'Countryside Code'.

hadn't quite formed. That was one of my happiest days, but as we set off back from our circular walk, I realised that all the shops would be closed when I returned to York, and I still hadn't bought Dad a Christmas present, so I picked up a nice-looking stone, and when I returned home, I wrote 'Malham' on it with a marker pen, and presented it to him, saying, 'It's a paperweight.' He was good enough to keep it on the dressing table in his bedroom for many years.

One of my friends at junior school – with whom I'd visited Malham – was killed when he fell off Malham Cove a year after he'd left school. I think he was with the Scouts or the Venture Scouts. He was an amiable and clever boy, but there was something tragic about him. When we were both ten, I was deputised twice to escort him home from school. On the first occasion he'd been feeling faint; on the second he was very upset, because he'd had to admit that, while looking after the school hamster for a weekend, he'd lost it. (He'd let it out of its cage, and it had gone behind the gas fire.) A few years after his death, one of the teachers at the school I attended for sixth form was blown off a height in the Dales – possibly Malham Cove – and killed. He was a deeply sensible man, and certainly would not have been taking any risk. Schools in, say, Surrey don't have this kind of wastage.

Mindful of the Country Code, I was a great shutter of gates on any walking party. I'd hang about while everyone went through, then I'd make sure the gate was shut fast, either by shooting the bolt or – more satisfying – dropping the steel halter over the gate post. Job done, I'd trot after the party, borne along on a little breeze of piety. Of course, I was never so foolish as to take a drink from a hillside stream without checking to see whether a dead sheep was contaminating the water at a higher level, and I certainly never scrambled over a drystone wall, but always used a stile; and I had been made strongly aware not to hang around near any quantity of cows, since they could knock you down and trample you to death.

I visited the Great Yorkshire Show – held on the Great Yorkshire Showground at Harrogate – several times with school parties. The Great Yorkshire Show is run by the Yorkshire Agricultural Society, and has been since 1838, when it was held in York. The remit of the YAS is partly educational: it is 'passionate about educating future generations about all aspects of farming, food and the countryside'. School groups get discounted entry to the show, and about 6,000 children attend every year. Today, the accent is on the environment and healthy eating, whereas in my day the accent was on telling you how farming worked, and I recall wandering around hot marquees looking at threshing machines and reading of the generous HP terms available for their purchase. There would be exhibitions of hay baling, cheese making, sheep shearing and drystone walling, a skill developed in any county where rock has bubbled up to the surface. But if drystone walling has a home county, it is Yorkshire.

The classic text on the subject is by a Yorkshireman, Arthur Raistrick. *The Story of the Pennine Walls* (1946) mainly concerns the walls of the Dales, and it is a Dalesman Publication, naturally. The book is full of the endearing folksiness associated with the magazine: 'It is still tradition in the Dales that old wallers working on the fell side would, on arriving at the wall in the morning, throw their heaviest hammer some way up the hillside, and declare that as the length to be walled that day.' Sheep sheltering next to a wall in bad weather will keep dry, Raistrick explains, since the rain is wind-borne, therefore coming from the side rather than above, 'and the draughts which come through all dry walls keep the fleece dried out'. Most of the walls were made during the agricultural enclosures between 1780 and 1820, and Raistrick writes that 'The inclosures were a tragedy for the small man; he lost his right of pasturage on the common, lost his bit of land, and was compelled to become a wage labourer in times of falling wages and rising cost of living. It secured the enslavement of the working classes.' This rather jars with the whimsical tone. I had assumed that part of the reason we ought to respect drystone walls was that they had played an honourable role in rural history.

If you ignore their provenance, drystone walls do seem to have the Yorkshire virtues: an almost literal flintiness, an austere beauty (highlighting the green of the fells like so many picture frames), and thrift, since they involve no mortar. In the *Yorkshire Post* of 11 July 2020, the newly installed Archbishop of York, Stephen Cottrell, wrote that when he'd been staying in the Dales recently, he learned of another moralistic aspect of the walls: 'You never put a piece of stone down once you have picked it up.' He explained that, instead of looking at a gap in the wall and trying to find a stone that fits, the waller 'walks across the whole canvas of the wall' to house the stone in his hand. Reading this, I felt a sermon coming on, and sure enough: 'Might this be a picture of the Yorkshire we want to become? One where everyone has a place. One where no one is discarded or put down. One where we work on a big canvas of inclusion, welcome, hospitality and diversity.'

In his book *Re-Make/Re-Model: The Art School Roots of Roxy Music*, Michael Bracewell discusses Anthony Price, who, like David Hockney, had been at Bradford School of Art, and designed clothes for Roxy Music: 'When Anthony Price gave a lecture to fashion students at the Odeon,

Marble Arch, somebody asked how he had got so good at pattern cutting, to which he replied, "By learning how to make drystone walls in Yorkshire."' Price is quoted as saying, 'I was born in 1945, in the Yorkshire Dales between Dent and Hawes and Ribblesdale ... It was just the most idyllic childhood, of animals and wildflowers and mountains – heavenly.' (Bracewell adds that 'Roxy Music, and in particular the deluxe elegance of the Hollywood style designed for the sensibility of the music by Anthony Price, would notably achieve some of their greatest triumphs with working-class audiences in Northern industrial towns and cities.')

Whenever I read the *Dalesman*, or any Dalesman Publication, I felt I was reading about the past, even if the subject of the article was contemporary. It, along with much of the reading matter in our display cabinet, was nostalgic in tone, and could be considered part of a strain of sentimentality that goes back centuries – indeed, to the idea of Eden. But most people would agree that the process intensified in reaction to the industrialisation and urbanisation of the late-nineteenth century. 'The countryside was being settled permanently by some towns-men,' writes Philip Waller in *Town, City and Nation: England 1850–1914*:

it also saw more seasonal visitors. The lure of rugged scenery was well developed from the Romantic period; but the Victorians organised these emotions, through the National Trust (1895) and a miscellany of ramblers' associations. Baden-Powell's Boy Scouts (1907) practised wood-craft and field manoeuvre, while a genteel gypsydom was cultivated by the Camping Club (1901) and the Caravan Club (1907). Literary and artistic celebrities unwittingly acted as mascots for specific locales:

Wordsworth for the Lakes, the Brontës for the Yorkshire moors, Landseer for the Scottish Highlands, Tennyson for the Lincolnshire Wolds, Hardy for Wessex.

The phenomenon was surely exhibited most strongly in Yorkshire. On the literary front, for example, Wessex doesn't exist, and who's heard of the Lincolnshire Wolds? People do not speak of Wordsworth Country, however strongly he is associated with the Lakes, whereas 'Brontë Country', now in common parlance to describe the Pennine hills west of Bradford, was put on the map by a book of 1888 called *The Brontë Country: Its Topography, Antiquities and History* by J. A. Erskine Stuart. On 23 April 1898, *The Times* reported on the inaugural dinner of the Society of Yorkshiremen in London, which had been held the previous night at the Holborn Restaurant. 'The company numbered about 200,' all men, as the name implied. 'In every sphere of action,' said the chairman, 'Yorkshire could claim its share of eminent people.' A long list followed, including Andrew Marvell, Captain Cook, William Wilberforce, Michael Faraday, 'and even Darwin, whose descent could be traced back to a former Mayor of Hull'. (But who is associated much more strongly with Kent.) Three women made the list, although the Society of Yorkshiremen seemed reluctant to acknowledge that they *were* women, referring merely to 'the Brontë family'.

In the second half of the nineteenth century, Yorkshire had become self-conscious about itself, especially about its countryside. A wave of articles, pamphlets and books encouraged people to escape the smoky towns. An early example is *Excursions in Yorkshire by the North Eastern Railway* (1855), by John Phillips, a geologist of York. 'In the later nineteenth century', Richard Morris writes in *Yorkshire: A*

Lyrical History of England's Greatest County, 'regional papers like the *Leeds Mercury* opened "doors of delight" to "tired city workers" by publishing weekly rambles "for all who heed the call of the Greenwood".'

Morris cites the many populist works by Harry Speight (*Nidderdale and the Garden of the Nidd, a Yorkshire Rhineland*) and Edmund Bogg (*A Thousand Miles in Wharfedale*) as being typical of the genre. It is time to consider the *type* of countryside being promoted here.

The Heights

The escapist literature described above was focused on the West Riding, which formerly had the smokiest towns to escape *from*, and still has the most beautiful countryside to escape *to*. Speight, a keen cyclist and rambler, grew up in Bradford, where the 'call of the Greenwood' might have been strongly felt. In *Victorian Cities*, Asa Briggs reports that 'in no decade between 1811 and 1850 did the growth of its population fall below 50 per cent.' In 1844, Bradford was rated 'one of the dirtiest and worst regulated towns in the country' by commissioners reporting on the Health of Towns and Populous Districts. The town's Board of Surveyors reported that the drains of the town were fed into the canal, whose 'noxious' waters were in turn conveyed into the pipes and boilers of mills for the generation of steam; so the water was never cool in summer, and sometimes it caught fire. What with cholera, typhoid and lung disease, life expectancy in the town was little over eighteen; not only were the buildings of the town black with soot, but so also were the sheep on the outlying hills. Bradford had improved by 1897, when it was given city status, but as relatively late as 1931 Walter Wilkinson was asking, in

Puppets in Yorkshire (a droll memoir of being a travelling puppeteer), 'Is there a sun in Bradford?' The poignancy is that the parents of those who felt the call of the Greenwood had probably lived in the Greenwood full-time.

By the late fourteenth century, the West Riding was established as a place for the woollen trade, and the hills had enabled this. Sheep were grazed on their lower slopes; fast streams running down from the Pennines to the Vale of York provided the power for small hillside fulling mills and soft water for scouring. The subsistence farmers of the hills were glad to turn their hand to a bit of weaving. But the weavers were fated to be imprisoned, in effect, in mills. The more dynamic of their brethren – the clothiers – began to employ weavers from outside their own farms, but this was still manufacturing on a small scale, and it was called 'the domestic system'. In their *Yorkshire Tour*, Ella Pontefract and Maria Hartley quote from the diary of a Joseph Rogerson, clothier of Bramley, west of Leeds. His entry for 11 August 1808 reads: 'Very throng in our mill. Mowing oats on Swinnow Close. Got part wool dry out-of-doors. A slubber left us. A great many oats ripe. Got a fine perch out of our dame with a line.' (A slubber prepared the wool for spinning.) Pontefract and Hartley observe, 'The order of the remarks shows how mixed up in Rogerson's mind were the mill and the life of the country.'

Spinning mills began to be built in the valleys, but weaving was still done in the hills. Wool began to be imported to the district, and weekly wool markets began to be held. The one at Leeds was held on a bridge over the Aire – that historically pivotal site we have visited – but others took place in 'cloth halls', the largest and best known of which was the Piece Hall in Halifax, which opened in 1779 and which, with its cupola and courtyard, resembles a Northern version of an Oxford college. Today, it accommodates independent shops.

A couple of years ago, I had a small engagement with the textile trade in Halifax, in that I was writing a book called *Seats of London* about the woollen material – moquette – used to cover the seats on London's Tube trains and buses. The chief manufacturer of these was Holdsworth's, who owned the Shaw Lodge Mill in downtown Halifax. In colour photographs of the mill, it is strange to see hundreds of yards of the seat coverings so familiar from London out of their element in Yorkshire. It's a nice instance of the old North–South balance; of Yorkshire proving its worth to London. David Holdsworth, formerly the production manager at the firm, told me that an inspector from London used to come up to Halifax every few months, 'a Mr Peatfield, a lovely man. He'd check the rolls, and he would take a lead seal on a pink ribbon and clip it to the moquette with a pair of pliers.' Some London Underground carriages used to feature notices proudly announcing: 'The seat coverings in this carriage were manufactured in Halifax, Yorkshire.' The textile industry of West Yorkshire has been in eclipse for decades, and today Shaw Lodge Mill is in part a business complex accommodating many start-ups ('The Calder Valley is a very creative place,' David Holdsworth told me), and what used to be the weaving shed is given over to five indoor football pitches.

(Every building in central Halifax used to be something else, often a mill, and these old mills have been forgiven their tyrannical pasts; and where their chimneys survive, they seem as benign as church steeples. You have the impression that the current residents – Haligonians, they're called – are slightly embarrassed at the grandeur of the buildings they inhabit, which are usually of sandstone – golden today, whereas it would have been black until at least the Clean Air Act of 1959. But they're also proud of their town, and the joke is that Charles Barry built the Italianate Halifax Town Hall, 'having practised on the Houses of Parliament'. John Betjeman described Halifax as a town of 'hidden beauty'. At the time of writing there is a masterplan whose aim, according to the *Yorkshire Post*, is to 'catapult Halifax into the nation's consciousness' with a programme of refurbishments and beautification.)

A Yorkshire firm called Camira Fabrics, which acquired Holdsworth's in 2007, still supplies the majority of the moquettes used on London Tubes and buses. Most of the manufacturing is done in Lithuania, but there's a pleasant circularity in that Camira's headquarters are located in what used to be a water-powered mill, in the hills outside Huddersfield – and so we reconnect with our historical narrative.

As steam power was introduced, the West Riding mills came down to the valley bottoms, to be near the canals and turnpike roads for exporting the wool and bringing in the coal from the West Riding mines, of which there were 450 by the end of the nineteenth century. The mills became factories and were involved in every process of wool manufacturing. 'It was necessary to be up at five o'clock to get to the mill in time,' write Pontefract and Hartley,

and fathers carried the youngest children on their shoulders. In busy times, women and children worked until eleven o'clock at night, sometimes seven days a week, and often they slept in the mill so as to be ready to start again in the morning ... It was these hardships which roused the indignation of a few prominent men and brought Richard Oastler's protest to Parliament, and eventually the Acts limiting working hours and the employment of children.*

If the hills had lost their practical purpose, their romantic allure remained. They brood, and so might any young writer looking up at them, or down from them, since they allow the West Riding towns to be seen and assessed in a single glance. 'If you were going to choose a way of making your way in this world and a place to start from', Simon Armitage has said, 'you might not choose poetry, and you might not choose Huddersfield.'† But then again, if you *did* choose poetry (which would admittedly be perverse) you might well choose Huddersfield, or Halifax, Bradford or Sheffield . . . and by the way, I refer anybody wondering why we are discussing towns in a passage about the countryside to Nikolaus Pevsner's architectural guide to *Yorkshire: West Riding* (1959). He writes of Huddersfield, 'The situation of the town is spectacular, the view of the smoking mills from the hills, or of the hills from the bottom of the valley, impressive if bleak.' Of Halifax: 'The situation of the town is spectacular . . . Hills rise on all sides mostly steep enough to make car driving an adventure.' Of Sheffield: 'None of the big cities of England has such majestic surroundings as Sheffield, and few have such a promising site, hilly, with deeply cut valleys carrying various streams, and green wedges reaching from several directions close to the centre.' In each case, he clearly thinks the towns don't match the hills aesthetically, which seems to me an unfair verdict in the case of Halifax. Only in Bradford do architectural virtues

---

* Oastler, 'the factory king', was a Tory paternalist who pioneered the campaign for the ten-hour working day.
† These words are very widely quoted; indeed, they are available on a fridge magnet, but the exact provenance seems never to be given, and I'm afraid I have not been able to discover it.

edge out any mention of hills. But we have Bradford-born
J. B. Priestley to make up the shortfall. He was always fascinated by the inside-out effect of the town. In his novel of
1946, *Bright Day*, Bradford appears as Bruddersford, which

> was grim but not mean, and the moors were always
> there, and the horizon never without its promise. No
> Bruddersford man could be exiled from the uplands and
> blue air; he always had one foot on the heather; he only
> had to pay his tuppence on the tram and then climb for
> half an hour, to hear the larks and curlews, to feel the old
> rocks warming the sun, to see the harebells trembling in
> the shade.

Here is Angela Carter, who lived in Yorkshire for a while,
writing about Bradford in *New Society*, a piece later collected
in *Nothing Sacred: Selected Writings*. The piece first appeared
in 1970, when the home fires were still burning:

> On some days of Nordic winter sunshine, the polluted
> atmosphere blurs and transfigures the light, so that the
> hitherto sufficiently dark, satanic mills take on a post-
> apocalyptic, Blakean dazzle, as if the New Jerusalem
> had come at last, and the sky above is the colour of ripe
> apricots. A russet mist shrouds the surrounding moorland,
> which is visible from every street, however mean.

The visibility, and availability, of the hills is often cited as
Bradford's saving grace. In any fiction set in Bradford, there
is usually a moment of relief in the hills from fraught town
life. In *Billy Liar*, Billy has an encounter with the elderly
Councillor Duxbury on Stradhaughton Moor ('a kind of
pastoral slum on the edge of town'). Billy snaps out of his

self-indulgent daydreaming long enough to realise that the councillor is being kind to him, so he'd better leave off taking the mickey out of his accent. In the film *Rita, Sue and Bob Too* (1987), written by Andrea Dunbar, most of the sex is had on the moors. Bob, a randy salesman, lives on a depressing modern housing estate. When he first gets the two babysitters, Rita and Sue, in his purple Mondeo, he says, 'Have you been round the moors? We can go up there if you want.' There is no indication that they ever *have* been 'round the moors', but comes the reply, 'We'll go up there then. We're not fussy.' It is only during the scenes set outside the town, when we look down on the lights of Bradford and the few chimneys that were left by 1987 (their defiant upstandingness in league with the priapism of Bob), that we know where the film is located, because the two housing estates could be anywhere.

The moor is Baildon Top, which also crops up in *Streets of Darkness* (2016), a skilful crime novel by A. A. Dhand, who grew up in Bradford. The central character is DI Harry (Hardeep) Virdee, a Sikh who has married a Muslim, with the result that he and his wife are ostracised by their families. The book paints an exaggerated (I hope) picture of racial tension in Bradford, and is generally very down on the city, which is called 'the cesspit of Yorkshire':* 'Thousands of immigrants, welcomed into Bradford to work in the sixties, had found themselves without prospects when the [textile] trade collapsed, unable to educate themselves or find alternative jobs. Bradford crumbled into a bleakness from which it couldn't recover.'

One of the several villains in the novel, Colin Reed, likes

---

* In an interview with BBC News, Dhand said, 'I do regret that line.' He claimed it was his editor's idea. 'I didn't know what a cesspit was until she put that in there.'

to walk on Baildon Moor: 'On a clear summer's day, it gave a view right across the city. Reed knew it well. He walked the moors regularly: respite from the pressures of his job. It could be stressful being one of the most dangerous men in Bradford.'

The Victorian necropolis Undercliffe Cemetery, which stands on one of the outlying hills, features in the novel. With their tall spires, some of the tombs seem as substantial as small churches. The cemetery is a conservation area and Grade II listed, but is still open for business, so there are some Bradfordians who know they will be returning to the Greenwood one day. In the *film* of *Billy Liar* it is the place where Billy has his salutary talk with Councillor Duxbury.

When I was writing an article about Bradford a few years ago, I went to the cemetery with a young Asian woman – not, I stress, for Rita–Sue-and-Bob purposes, but because she gave walking tours of Bradford, and was a kind of ambassador for the city. It was a day of slightly smoky sunshine, and Bradford looked beautiful – certainly more beautiful than its prosperous neighbour, Leeds. Let us hear again from Walter Wilkinson, author of *Puppets in Yorkshire*: 'A city patriotism there certainly is. Why, even a bus conductor, a boy, neglected his other fares to explain to me how he loved the grey stones of Bradford, their strength, durability and handsome appearance, and that he was very sorry for Leeds which had altogether too many mean bricks.'

It's true that Bradford has indulged in architectural self-harm. A friend of mine who used to live in Bradford describes it as 'the town that bombed itself'. Between 2004 and 2014 there was a great crater in the centre of town where the building of a shopping centre had stalled, and I think the Bradford ambassador was trying to counterbalance this hole by taking me up to Undercliffe.

The demolition of many of its Italianate Victorian glories qualifies Bradford (along with Leeds) for Gavin Stamp's book, *Britain's Lost Cities*. 'It was certainly very different from its nearby rival Leeds,' he writes of the city. 'This was partly due to the large influx of German and German-Jewish merchants and manufacturers who created a remarkable philanthropic and artistic local culture: the composer Frederick Delius was a product of one of those families.' In *English Journey*, J. B. Priestley wrote of Bradford before the First World War as having 'a kind of regional self-sufficiency, not defying London but genuinely indifferent to it.' (This was the position in Halifax too, as far as I could tell from my historical researches. The local paper, the *Halifax Courier*, was as dense and money-oriented as the *Financial Times*. The local councillors became local celebrities; shops stayed open late; there were letterboxes on the trams, with a collection at midnight.)

North German merchants living in Bradford built Little Germany north of Leeds Road – a district of beautiful warehouses. Some mills were also highly distinguished, including Manningham Mills (for silk) by Samuel Cunliffe Lister, and the alpaca and mohair mills of Titus Salt, created as part of the model community, Saltaire, by Lockwood & Mawson, who had also designed the Wool Exchange and the Town Hall. All the above are, or have been, cosseted by schemes of regeneration (and the Wool Exchange is a Waterstone's), Bradford having repented of the demolitions of the 1950s and 1960s. Stamp describes how civic pride at the time was undermined by the increasing ascendancy of London and the faltering of the textile trade: 'the smoke-blackened nineteenth-century buildings of the city became a reproach, something to be ashamed of.' The way must be cleared for the motor car, and the plan was overseen by the

City Engineer and Surveyor, Stanley Wardley, who was born, it aggravates me to note, in Hendon. 'Many distinguished buildings were swept away,' writes Stamp. One particularly sad loss was the Swan Arcade, a large block of the 1870s next to the Wool Exchange containing four linked arcades with glazed iron roofs. Demolished in 1962, it was replaced by Arndale House, designed by the criminal architect John Poulson.*

I like Bradford, but do not know it well. I associate it with the dreamy Yorkshire tone, rather than the belligerent one. I hear the wistful voices of Rodney Bewes (from nearby Bingley) or David Hockney (from Bradford itself) when I think of the city. In an article for the *Guardian* of 2 March 2011, I wrote, 'If Leeds is a brash businessman in a pinstripe suit and too-pointy shoes, Bradford is a soulful public sector employee, wearing an anorak and reading a battered paperback book.' I first went there as a twelve-year-old boy – to go skating at the ice rink (now Bradford Ice Arena), which is on the top floor of a nondescript high rise building on Little Horton Lane – and the last thing you expect to see at the top of a high-rise is an ice rink. What compounds the surrealism is the different weather up there: it's colder. I say that I went to skate, but really it was to fall over a couple of times before sitting down with a cup of tea to watch other people skate. Loud pop music played: I remember the sound of Abba, reverberating on the ice. The rink was run by Mecca Leisure when I went there. In 1991, Mecca threatened to close it, and it was taken over by Krystyna Rogers, who had recently moved to Bradford from Poland, and whose daughter, Emily, loved to skate. Emily died in 2005, aged

---

* Poulson, who secured some commissions by bribery, was jailed for corruption in 1974.

twenty-six, and a skating trophy bearing her name is presented every year to the best skater in Bradford. A song that would sound good played during a quiet evening at the rink would be 'Sleeping Satellite', a danceable ballad about the American moon shots, co-written and performed by Tasmin Archer, who's from Bradford. ('Did we fly to the moon too soon?') The association arises partly from my thinking of Bradford as a quieter satellite of Leeds.

The last couple of times I've been to Bradford, I've stayed at the Midland Hotel, one of the few ex-railway hotels to maintain a railway connection, in that there's a walkway leading towards Forster Square Station. But when you arrive, there's almost nothing there – just a long platform, with a perfunctory shelter and an arcaded wall giving a poignant reminder of the old station. We have Mr Wardley of Hendon to thank for this: he also flattened Forster Square itself. And he bequeathed us the horrible, plasticky Bradford Exchange station, in place of the city's *other* Victorian train shed.

I can't say I've been into the Broadway Bradford shopping centre that was finally built on top of the above-mentioned crater. The statue of W. E. Forster, Victorian educationalist and MP for Bradford, seems to be beckoning people out of the place. I like to go to the National Media Museum, where you can watch a vast archive of old TV programmes for free; then I might sit down with a sandwich in Centenary Square, which provokes a positive note even in *Streets of Darkness*. George Simpson, a decent, if compromised, policeman, observes

the calmness of Centenary Square, Bradford's fightback against decay. It contained a 4,000-square-metre mirror pool with more than a hundred fountains, including

the tallest in the UK. Watching over it was the City
Hall clock tower, rising 220 feet above ground level
and inspired by the Palazzo Vecchio in Florence. It was
the old world watching the new and, for the briefest of
moments, Simpson found hope for Bradford.

In the New Beehive Inn, on Westgate, Bradford has one
of my favourite pubs, with a well-preserved Edwardian
interior, nicely low-lit; in fact, the main illumination in
winter comes from the roaring open fire. I once saw a man
eating a very large Indian takeaway in this pub, and when
he'd finished, he chucked all the cartons on the fire, which
consumed them instantly. I myself have eaten many excellent, cheap curries in Bradford, of course. I like Karachi,
probably the most famous curry house, where a waiter
once addressed me as 'Captain'. In another Bradford curry
house, I heard a white man say, 'I love yer chicken tikka
gravy, Iqbal, but I want it on t'meat,' which I thought a
nice bit of cross-cultural banter, of which Bradford could
do with more.

'It is partly so charming because it is so strange,' Angela
Carter wrote of Bradford in that *New Society* piece of 1970,
'the presence of so many Pakistanis creates not so much the
atmosphere of the melting pot for, at present, the disparate
ethnic elements are held in an uneasy suspension, but an
added dimension of the remarkable.'

But Bradford remains in uneasy suspension, a city largely
(outside the centre) segregated along racial lines. Certainly,
it does not seem to be as happily cosmopolitan as it was
in late Victorian times, but then a few decades before that
supposed golden age, Bradford had been a notorious slum.
Today, Bradford has areas of high deprivation, and areas
of the opposite. Its economy, now diversified into finance,

engineering, chemicals, electronics, and still with some textiles, is growing rapidly. Things change, as the hills look down.

Phyllis Bentley, novelist and non-fiction writer, was the child of a Halifax mill owner. She would write while sitting the hills above the town, the highest of which is Beacon Hill. Bentley wrote the script for *We of the West Riding – The Life of a Typical Yorkshire Family*, a British Council film of 1945. It was meant to be a post-war morale booster, but if I'd been watching it in a cinema in York or Hull at the time of its release, I'd have felt alienated from my own county, such is its partisanship to the hilly West Riding. About halfway through, Phyllis lets rip: 'Rough sweeping hills crowned with dark rocks and purple heather; miles and miles of lonely moor where the curlews dip and call and the great winds tear across the sky driving the clouds before them, bending even the stubborn heather – that's *our* country.'

The location is Halifax, although it's not named. The narration is from the perspective of a young boy who becomes a young man in the course of the film. His characterisation seems to me confused, although perhaps it just reflects the ambiguities of Yorkshire romanticism. On the one hand, he is anxious to 'get inside the mill where everything important seemed to be going on', and he is proud of learning about all the far destinations to which the wool is exported but, as he walks past a prison-like mill wall, he reflects that the West Riding is a 'grim and drab place'. He cheers up when, as a young man, he gains a half share in a tandem. 'We're great cyclists in the West Riding, you know,' he says, perkily. 'Every weekend in rain, wind or snow – and it's generally one or t'other – we get on our bikes and leave the smoke of the town behind.' These cycling scenes also made me feel guilty as a Yorkist, in that everyone seems to be enjoying even going uphill. The cycling scenes reminded me of a film made four years later, *A Boy, a Girl and a Bike*, which was filmed largely in Hebden Bridge, and featured a fledgling Honor Blackman. It's on YouTube, and one of the comments reads,

Honor Blackman spoke with a creditable Yorkshire accent and I particularly remember the scene when, after having a puncture, she asks John McCullum to 'pass the patches and solution'. Years later I met Miss Blackman when she was learning to fly at my flying club, Flairavia at Biggin Hill in 1964 after having just played the part of Pussy Galore in *Goldfinger* – she couldn't remember saying those (to me) immortal lines from the 1949 film![*]

The Brontës come into Bentley's film, of course: 'The wild novels of the Brontë sisters were born in these moorlands: *Wuthering Heights* and *Jane Eyre* were written about these lonely houses and the brooding loneliness of the West Riding hills,' loneliness being something of a key word in this supposed tribute to Northern togetherness. In *English Journey*, Priestley describes a trip out from Thornton, which is west – and up – from Bradford, to Top Withens, the ruined farmhouse that was supposedly the inspiration for Heathcliff's home: 'it stands on the brink of nothing but bog and wild weather. You feel that at any moment Heathcliff may be roaring in the doorway.'

The Brontë sisters were born in Thornton and lived there before the fatal move to unsanitary Haworth. Of all the

---

[*] *Variety* called the film 'Feeble ... valueless for the US market'.

Brontë productions, the most famous and successful was the most vertiginous, *Wuthering Heights*, in which the anti-hero's very name suggests altitude. For a short poignant interlude, the greatest expert on the sisters was the only one left alive, Charlotte, and she wrote a preface to the 1850 edition of her late sister's novel, which is a sort of apologia for the book's wildness. 'It is moorish,' she wrote (a word Microsoft keeps trying to capitalise on my screen), 'and wild, and knotty as the root of heath ... the author being herself a native and nursling of the moors.' Emily's native hills 'were far more to her than a spectacle; they were what she lived in'.

The best thing I have seen about the Brontës is Sally Wainwright's BBC film of 2016, *To Walk Invisible*, which focuses on the sisters' response to their unstable brother, Branwell. There are scenes of them sitting in that grey parsonage next to the graveyard, the house itself resembling another, larger, gravestone, and all silently writing, scratching away with fine nibbed pens on little pieces of paper, an apparently physical process, like detailed embroidery, rather than a mental one. In the film, Emily is portrayed (by Chloe Pirry) as a stroppy, stunted girl with dirty fingernails, ever likely to tell people to 'Fuck off' or 'Come here and say that.' She strides about with a knobbly stick. Her dog looks like the kind that gets put down after killing someone. Charlotte (Finn Atkins) says of Emily, 'It's a wonder how quiet they all think she is in the village, and how loud she is at home.' The Emily of the film rings true to me; she reminds me of Billy Casper – curdled, small, aggrieved – in that other escape-to-the-hills tale, *Kes*.

In *Wuthering Heights*, the hills are shown in good weather and bad. You might say that Emily was neutral about them, except for the fact that they give the tale its whole life force, energising an awkwardly structured novel. The nearest we come to an endorsement of their mystical wisdom comes in a remark by the level-headed housekeeper and main narrator, Nelly Dean: "'I certainly esteem myself a steady, reasonable kind of body," she said, "not exactly from living among the hills and seeing one series of actions, from year's end to year's end . . .'" But that is considered as a possibility.

Calderdale

As we descend south along the eastern side of the Pennines, it seems natural to go from the Brontës to Ted Hughes and Sylvia Plath. In *The Brontë Myth*, Lucasta Miller calls this almost mythological couple 'the Cathy and Heathcliff of their generation. There are shades of *Wuthering Heights* in their tempestuous relationship and separation, in her "madness" and early death and in his – and our – subsequent inability to escape her ghost.' In August 1956, two months after their marriage, Hughes and Plath made a pilgrimage to Haworth and Top Withens. Plath recalled the visit in her poem of 1961, 'Wuthering Heights', in which she imagines her bones being whitened among the heather. As Lucasta Miller writes, the poem has been taken 'as symptomatic of her pathology, her death wish, just as *Wuthering Heights* was taken to be Emily's suicide note'. But Miller counters the notion: 'In its tight control of language and imagery, it feels more like a literary exercise than a chaotic outpouring of emotion.' Certainly, the poem contains a virtuoso description of those supporting players in any moorland scene, the sheep, which are characterised as 'grandmotherly'.

Sylvia Plath was born in Boston, Massachusetts, Ted

Hughes in the industrial village of Mytholmroyd, in the Calder Valley, which many of his middle-class admirers (a disproportionate number of whom were female) couldn't pronounce. The correct way is 'My-thumb-royd.' At the time of the visit to Top Withens, Hughes and Plath were staying about 15 miles away, in the house of Hughes's parents in Heptonstall, a satellite village to the town of Hebden Bridge in the Calder Valley. In 1962, Hughes left Plath for Assia Wevill. In 1963, Plath committed suicide in Primrose Hill, London, by putting her head in a gas oven; she had sealed the kitchen door to protect the lives of Frieda and Nicholas, the children she'd had with Hughes. Nicholas would himself commit suicide as an adult. In 1969, Assia Wevill killed herself and Shura, the daughter she'd had with Hughes. Plath is buried in the churchyard at Heptonstall.

And now that we have arrived at a gravestone, we come, rather belatedly for a book on Yorkshire, to geology. In an essay of 1964, 'The Rock', published in *Writers on Themselves*, Ted Hughes wrote about Scout Rock, a cliff face that looms over Mytholmroyd. 'It was a darkening presence, like an over-evident cemetery.' He continues, about the West Yorkshire landscape generally, 'I suppose in some ways it was eerie, and maybe even unpleasant. Nothing ever quite escapes into happiness. The people are not detached enough from the stone, as if they were only half born from the earth, and the graves are too near the surface.' Hughes, frequently described as craggy, was an almost geological phenomenon himself, as adamantine and statuesque as any work by those West Yorkshire sculptors, Henry Moore and Barbara Hepworth.

If anybody ever produced a Yorkshire pocket diary, it ought to contain, along with standard things like the dates of the full moon and the shooting season, a geological

map. Most histories of Yorkshire begin with a paean to the
variegated geology underpinning the county. Yorkshire
is unusually high in the west, unusually low in the east.
Reading from left to right, there's limestone, sandstone,
then coal, then chalk. As far I understand it, one is entitled
to use a poetic term very redolent of Yorkshireness, 'millstone grit', to denote a particularly coarse-grained and dark
sandstone appearing on the Southern Pennines.

In 1971, Glyn Hughes, poet and painter, wrote a book
called *Millstone Grit* that has become a Yorkshire classic. It
was about his move from Greater Manchester to the Calder
Valley, where a view of Hardcastle Crags, near Hebden
Bridge, determined him on a literary career. So Glyn
Hughes seems to have been as much in thrall to geology
as his near namesake, Ted. In 1985, he produced a revised
version of the book, cumbersomely titled, *Glyn Hughes's
Yorkshire: Millstone Grit Revisited*, and this is the version I
own. At the time of writing, a second-hand copy of *Millstone
Grit* is available on Amazon for £760.00, which made me
interested to see how much the version I own might fetch.
The answer: £0.01. It's a beautiful book, nonetheless, full of
pictures of the Calder Valley under dark, rainy skies.

Millstone grit breaks out of the fields and slopes, as the
bones press through the flesh of a hungry cow ... The
stone is rough, dark purple, the colour of ripened black-
berries. Millstone grit oxidises to this dark tone even
without the help of the hundred-year plague of coal soot
that has only recently ceased to fall.

His summarizing words for this landscape are 'authentic' and 'real'. Of the Calder Valley, he writes: 'It splits the
Pennines, but links Lancashire with Yorkshire.' At the end

of the valley, at Todmorden, the division between the counties becomes subtle. There is 'something very Lancashire in the more sprightly, less dour cast of Todmorden humour, but its oldest and strongest tendencies are towards Yorkshire'. Hughes suggests that the town's 'natural allegiances' are expressed in a joke: 'A lady, uncertain which county she lived in, inquired at the post office, and when told she was in Yorkshire, replied, "Thank God for that! I believe they have terrible weather in Lancashire."'

I made my own pilgrimage to the Calder Valley, which is the southernmost part of the Dales, but outside the national park. And it seems fitting that Calderdale was not invited to that particular party, its millstone grit bestowing a dark, surly character, as against the creamy limestone of the national park.

The focus of Calderdale is the east Pennine hill town of Hebden Bridge. I had driven there over the moors along the A6033, or tried to, but a few minutes after it became apparent that mine was the only car on the moor, I came to a row of bollards and a sign reading 'Road Closed. Find Alternative Route.' That is perhaps standard Highways Agency language, but I detected in it a Yorkshire terseness. It was raining heavily, and the sky and the moors were dark blue-grey. The sign announcing the closure was one of those yellow, luminous ones, and its luminosity had come into play, such was the darkness of the day. I stepped out of the car to photograph the sign – or tried to. I had to push the car door with two hands to open it, and when I finally did take the shot, it came out blurred, not so much because the camera was unsteady, as because *I* was. I tried to think what I could do to remain upright, but there was nothing to hold onto. It was as though the wind and the rain were conspiring: 'We've got this guy on his own; there'll be no witnesses, let's do him in.'

Hebden Bridge is an artistic focal point, thanks partly to Hughes's association with the area. Any Yorkshire writer might expect to do a stint of teaching at the Arvon Centre at Lumb Bank, just outside the town, and they might aspire to give a reading in the town's Little Theatre. At the time of writing, I am signed up to do the former; I did the latter in 2004. If Hebden is known outside Yorkshire, it is probably as a hippy-ish haven. I recently read an article in the *Daily Mail* about the painter Lucian Freud's fourteen children. The following three facts about one of his sons seemed to flow quite naturally: that he lived in an artistic community; that it was in Hebden Bridge; that he was an expert whirling dervish.

Before setting off to write about Hebden for this book, I read *Hebden Bridge: A Sense of Belonging* (2012) by Paul Barker, who grew up in the town. When the mills closed in the 1970s, the first 'offcomers'* arrived, attracted by cheap houses in a beautiful location. Barker characterises them as 'leftist, arty-crafty, New Age ... Ill-paid lecturers at Manchester, Leeds, or Huddersfield polytechnics ... Instead of manufacturing cloth for cheap textiles, Hebden started to manufacture lifestyles.'

Barker confronts the idea that, alongside the moral strivings of the offcomers (peaceniks, eco-freaks), a persisting post-industrial lassitude has led to Hebden becoming 'Suicide Central'. The phrase is from the headline to an *Independent* article about a documentary film of 2009 depicting drug and alcohol abuse in Hebden, *Shed Your Tears and Walk Away*. 'So far as I can make out,' Barker writes, 'West Yorkshire has slightly worse suicide rates than the national figure; within West Yorkshire, the entire

---

* Or, to be even more Yorkshire about it: 'offcumdens'.

borough of Calderdale, including Halifax, is slightly worse than that; and the Upper Calder Valley (not just Hebden Bridge) is slightly worse again. The statistical differences are tiny.'

As I stepped out of my car on bustling Market Street, I bumped into a woman with dyed orange hair, who was carrying a bag of flour. I was reminded of John Morrison's satire, *View from the Bridge* (1998), in which Hebden is thinly disguised as Milltown. Among the Hebden-ites he depicts is Willow Woman: 'Her response to everyday calamities is to bake. Using the smoke detector as a food timer, she turns out mountainous batches of inedible stoneground bread. It's called "stoneground", incidentally, because its main ingredient is gravel.' Also featured is Wounded Man, 'a founder member of the Holistic Plumbers' Collective who, when called out, try to put plumbing problems into a more global context'. A satire of Hebden Bridge probably writes itself, but the book is funny nonetheless.

I walked past a shop called Spirals, which sells Fairtrade eco products and earth-friendly UK ones – *objets d'art*, clothes, toiletries. Its sister shop Earth Spirit is dedicated to the holistic and spiritual (crystals, tarot cards and so on): 'Our shop is a safe and sacred space for all.' A noticeboard advertised 'Indigo Scribbles: intuitive readings', 'Candlelit Gong Baths'. Over the road, Papa's Chicken, Pizza and Kebabs came as a welcome respite from this wholesomeness. A banner on Market Street read, 'Shop Local'. Earlier in the day, I'd seen the same legend on a small banner in nearby Todmorden, which is like Hebden, but less so. In a car park there, I had seen a man playing football with half a dozen border collies, all of which were good tacklers, even if their passing of the ball was haphazard.

I walked to the banks of the Rochdale Canal, which runs

through Hebden, and connects it to Todmorden. The houses on the waterside were almost barn-like in their rough stoniness, but their gardens were prettified by fairy lights and bunting. From the canal, I looked at the town, which is a matter of looking *up*. Hebden is tastefully constrained on its wooded hillside – no suburbs. The grey stone houses seemed older than the trees amid which they stood, which perhaps they were. I walked a little way along the sleepy canal. After a mile or so, I stopped to take a film of some cows plodding through a waterlogged field. A man on a rattly bike was coming along the towpath. Still filming, I stepped out of his way, but not far enough for his liking. 'Daft bugger!' he yelled as he passed. Now there, I thought, is a man who could have benefited from a candlelit gong bath.

I should say that everyone else I encountered in Hebden was pleasant, including the three people I asked directions to Heptonstall. I'd kept getting lost in the town's vertical terraced streets, one of which was called Palestine Road, and I was torturing my Audi's gears as I kept reversing and doubling back. Eventually, I was referred to a 'turning circle', a phenomenon I'd never heard of before. It's a semi-circular arrangement off the main road, allowing one to take a direct run at the hill leading to Heptonstall.

The ancient village has a huddled, Pyrenean aspect. There is a church, with an older – thirteenth-century – ruined church adjacent, and I began looking for Plath in the graveyard belonging to this ruin. I was aware of being observed by a long-haired man of indeterminate age who was lounging against a stone wall. He wore a grubby black moleskin suit and had the general air of a loitering poet. As I approached him, he was smirking somewhat because he knew what I was going to ask. He directed me to Plath's grave, which – surprisingly for such an eminent person – is in a nondescript overflow graveyard. Eventually, I found this death 'held in place by a stone'.

Plath's gravestone was regularly desecrated by feminists – often American ones – who objected to the reference to the poet's name being given as 'Sylvia Plath Hughes'. A Hebden stone mason kept a stock of letters to replace 'Hughes' whenever it was chiselled off. Today, the word 'Hughes' on the tombstone does look patched in. Numerous felt pens and biros had been stabbed into the grass of the grave, in writerly solidarity. Of course, I took a photograph.

The above-mentioned Lumb Bank is just below Heptonstall. It's an eighteenth-century mill owner's house bought by Ted Hughes in 1968. Hughes leased it to the Arvon Foundation, which now owns it, but what Hughes gave with one hand, he took away with the other, because over his writing career, and especially in *Remains of Elmet*, he cleaned out the Calder Valley of metaphors and similes.

I never met Ted Hughes, even though I overlapped with him for a dozen years as a Faber author. I believe he lived in Devon at the time, but his attitude towards publicity displayed an ongoing Yorkshireness. Mrs Gaskell's phrase 'exaggerated reserve' comes to mind. A woman who worked in the publicity office told me he sent them a crate of champagne at the end of every year in which they had not troubled him.

On Ilkley Moor

Insofar as anybody can be, Colin Speakman is an expert on Yorkshireness.

I was put in touch with him by the Ramblers, Britain's largest walking charity, which started life less generically named as the National Council of Ramblers Federations in 1931. Having qualified as a teacher, he worked as a transport consultant for the Yorkshire Dales, where he was involved in the campaign to save the Settle–Carlisle Railway. He is co-founder of the Dales Way long-distance footpath between Yorkshire and the Lakes, and he has written more than fifty books, mainly about Yorkshire, walking and the countryside, including the only book I am aware of that is exclusively devoted to the Yorkshire Wolds. Colin has written several position papers for the Yorkshire Society, a more inclusive descendant of the above-mentioned Society of Yorkshiremen in London, which fizzled out in the 1970s. The new one – 'the first Yorkshire society to be based in Yorkshire' – was founded in 1980 to promote the county. ('We strongly believe that the time has come for all parts of Yorkshire to start working together so that God's Own Country, post-Brexit and post-Covid, can begin to punch its weight in a world that is clearly changing.') Colin grew up in Salford, but he now lives (as he would have to, given all the foregoing) in Yorkshire, at Burley in Wharfedale, and he looks as you would expect: fit and wiry.

We had arranged to go for a walk on Ilkley Moor. I had briefed myself beforehand, by reading his book, *Walk! A Celebration of Striding Out*. The book paints a nuanced picture. Yorkshire, especially West Yorkshire, played an important role in the campaigns to secure access to the countryside, because of the sheer numbers of potential ramblers in the county, and the sheer number of acres potentially available to them. But Yorkshire was not quite as central to the story as I had chauvinistically hoped.

On the one hand were the 'highly motivated upper-middle-class people from professional backgrounds', such as the founders, in 1925, of the Campaign to Protect Rural England, whose first meeting was held at the offices of the Royal Institute of British Architects in London. But there was also 'a different, if complementary tradition of access campaigning, with its roots in the ordinary, urban lower middle class and working-class communities'. These had attachments to their own special bits of countryside – for example, Snowdonia for Liverpool, or the Dales for Leeds and Bradford. But when Speakman lists some Victorian and Edwardian rambling societies, the focus moves away from Yorkshire: the Manchester YMCA Rambling Club, the Midland Institute of Ramblers, the Liverpool YMCA Rambling Club. In 1905, sixteen rambling clubs in London formed the Federation of Rambling Clubs to negotiate cheap walkers' excursion tickets on the railways, and federations of Northern and Midlands Rambling Clubs formed in the 1920s and 1930s were 'following the London example'. By now rambling was beginning to be called 'hiking', an American term denoting a more working-class, less meditative kind of walking, hence the need for a country code. It represented a shift away from the 'muscular Christianity' that had helped propel the first walking boom, although Speakman notes that 'a love of plain living and high thinking ... permeates the rambling fraternity to the present day'. (It does so especially, I think, among those irritatingly determined middle-class people who walk with walking poles, as if they were cross-country skiers. The poles have given then an opportunity to spend money on walking above and beyond the acquisition of the optimal weatherproof gear, and by voluntarily encumbering themselves with the sticks, they can't possibly be swigging from a bottle or smoking a fag as they walk.)

A class conflict was shaping up: the 'right to roam' against the shooting fraternity that owned or controlled much of the moors, and the latter was a particularly strong force east of the Pennines. The conflict came to a head on Kinder Scout, in what is now the Peak District. Here, in 1932, the famous Trespass took place, organised by the Young Communist League. A group from Manchester were the main trespassers, but there was also a group from Sheffield. Speakman writes that 'the whole episode gave new input to the wider access movement and the growing campaign for the establishment of British National Parks.' In 1949, the National Parks and Access to the Countryside Act was passed, but the 'access' part was not delivered, many bureaucratic obstacles being thrown in the way by landowners and county councils. The watershed was the passing of the Countryside Rights of Way Act in 2000, or rather its full implementation in 2005, when access to, for example, the Yorkshire Dales went up from 4 per cent to 62 per cent.

Speakman reports that, 'As a mode of travel, walking is in decline ... But as a leisure activity it is in significant growth.' Unfortunately, rising car ownership has facilitated that growth, and I am reminded of a John Shuttleworth routine in which he agonises, in his plodding, conscientious way, about motorways. Yes, they blight the landscape, but on the other hand, 'They offer speedier access to sights of outstanding natural beauty.'

Colin Speakman and I walked onto Ilkley Moor, which is an urban common, owned by Bradford Council, so everybody has – and has always had – the right to roam on it. Bradford Council did let out parts of the Moor for shooting from 2008, but local protests brought this to a stop in 2018. The weather was temporarily fine; the heather rising up before us was as gloriously purple as the wrapper on the hazelnut and caramel Quality Street. Colin asked if it was my first time on the Moor. It wasn't, not by a long chalk. I've been on it in bright sun, horizontal rain and snow, all without really trying. I mean, the law of averages dictates that I've been on Ilkley Moor in all weathers and most emotional states, because I've been on it so often. I would have been about ten when somebody told me that 'On Ilkley Moor bar t'at' meant without one's hat. It would have been a couple of years later when somebody – probably a geography teacher – told me that the Cow and Calf rocks on the Moor were formed of millstone grit.

I spent a couple of days in Ilkley when researching my historical novel, *The Somme Stations*. The story begins and ends in the North Eastern Railwaymen's Convalescent Home that occupied one of the grand stone mansions on the fringes of the Moor, and is now flats. Ilkley generally has an air of well-heeled convalescence. In the seventeenth century, the White Wells Bath House was constructed on the Moor (it's still there) so that gullible people could drink and bathe in the waters of the spring there. Hydros began to be built, in which people could experience various water treatments at a price, but the clean air was free, and it lured the wool merchants from Halifax and Bradford.

In the late nineteenth century, a firm called Robinson's, located on Cowpasture Road, made the 'Ilkley Couch', in which a recumbent person could be slightly propped up. They also made commodes, self-propelling chairs, leg rests and crutches. The Moor must have presented a challenge to customers of Robinson's, just as it does to any obese folk who might be gazing up at it today. The Yorkshire and the Humber region has the highest levels of obesity after the North-East. But obesity goes with deprivation, and there isn't much of that in Ilkley, which is in a 'golden triangle' of Yorkshire property, with Harrogate, Leeds and York at the corners. (Ilkley has a Bettys, of course, just like York and Harrogate.)

Colin and I talked about the Yorkshire Society, and its hopes for the county. The key word was green. He envisaged a 'green future for Yorkshire', involving its 'tough, intelligent workforce' in environmental technologies, which are, conveniently, 'labour-intensive'. He would like Yorkshire to make things again, and he would like Yorkshire people to consume Yorkshire products, hence the idea of a 'Made-in-Yorkshire' kitemark. He believes in regionalism, fostering a sense of pride in one's area, but he is liberal and progressive with it. The trick is to banish the old arrogance and xenophobia.

I quote from a position paper that Speakman wrote for the Yorkshire Society:

Yorkshire is about a sense of belonging. 'Being Yorkshire' is as much about having a shared living, open culture as it is about a sense of place, although this latter is extremely important. It is not about accident of birth, race (whatever that term might be chosen to mean), parental background, skin colour or politics. It is also inclusive of other heritages – you can be Jewish, Sikh, Muslim or Christian, or be African, Afro-Caribbean, French, Latvian, Chinese or Indian heritage, yet still belong to Yorkshire, the region where you live and work, and be proud of your dual identity.

Of course, Sadiq Khan might say much the same about London, but I take Speakman's statement to be a refutation of the chauvinism sometimes associated with Yorkshire.

Our fellow ramblers, courteously waiting for us to pick our way through the ferns and heather (or we waited for them), tended to be middle-class, white and getting on in years. Colin admits the problem, although he sees promising signs in the cycling boom among the young. 'They'll be ramblers one day,' he said. As for the whiteness of Yorkshire ramblers, Colin told me about the Mosaic Partnership, an initiative by the Campaign for National Parks to encourage ethnic minority walking.

That evening, I was sipping a good Chablis in the forecourt of Martinez Wine, which is either a wine bar or a wine merchant's but definitely not an off-licence. It is located on the Grove, which is the high street of Ilkley. The trees all along the Grove had fairy lights in them; the pinkish evening air was faintly aromatic with the scent of the heather on the moor.

I was thinking of something Colin Speakman had said about heather – a revelation akin to my discovering that drystone walls arose from enclosures. Heather, he told me, appears on Yorkshire moorland because of shooting. It has been a feature of the landscape for about 150 years, deliberately planted because grouse thrive on young heather plants: 'Otherwise, the landscape would be different – scrub and trees.' I have no personal experience of the Yorkshire shooting set, but a friend of mine knows the scene. She lives in London but has a second home in North Lincolnshire. She sometimes crosses the border to go shooting in Yorkshire.

'Well,' she told me, 'the social scene is shooting and hunting, and it's quite feudal. They'll chat to their butlers, gamekeepers, gardeners, make a cake for their birthdays – all quite easy and informal. But their radars are always out for people who aren't quite right, who are a bit *nouveau*. People who play golf, say. The grand and pretty grand people all have family money. They're what they call "naturally rich". They all know each other, and they drive miles to see each other. They might say, "Oh, nobody lives around here," meaning nobody like them.'

Did these people ever go to London?

'Yes; it's important to see a play now and then, and they might have a place there. But they don't like it: "It's so dirty. How can people possibly live there!"'

I asked my friend what these people would make of me, if I ever made enough money to buy an old house with a few acres.

'Well, if you were clever and funny enough – which you are* – you'd probably be invited to dinner, but it's unlikely you'd be invited to a shoot or a hunt.'

And are these people particularly proud of being from Yorkshire, I wondered?

'Yes, insofar as it's big, so it's got a lot of countryside, and they really do love the countryside.'

---

* She dutifully added.

The Camping Club

In 2019, a cousin sent me a batch of letters written to her mother by *my* mother, who had died in 1971 when she was thirty-three and I was nine. My mother was in and out of hospital at the time and looking for reasons to be cheerful about the future. One of these was the recent acquisition of a new (albeit second-hand) car, an Austin A40, which replaced our family's first car, a Morris Minor, acquired a couple of years before, and driven exclusively by my mother. My father would not learn to drive until after her death, and very terrible at it he was. The front and back house doors and all the windows had to be closed as he over-revved while backing our third car – absurdly named a Singer Gazelle – out of the garage amid gouts of black smoke.

My mother was a graceful driver. Being small, she sat on a cushion that she'd made herself, and the steering wheel of the Morris seemed more like a ship's wheel in proportion to her size. But she held the wheel lightly, and you seldom noticed her gear changes, whereas every one of my father's was a minor crisis; he would begin sweating after a few particularly crunching ones. My mother's letters are so enthusiastic about the A40 and its liberating possibilities – since it promised to be more reliable than the Morris – that

I felt quite ashamed of having devoted so much time to writing about trains.

As soon as we acquired the Morris, we headed for the hills, ignoring any such rural attractions as the Vale of York might have presented. Our default excursion was to the Kilburn White Horse on the southern edge of the North York Moors, which indeed lie about 25 miles north of York, and which I always considered '*the* Moors'. The ascent to the car park below the Horse was steep, and on one occasion the Morris Minor hadn't made it, and we'd had to stop to let the engine cool, before turning round and coming back. The failure imported a tension into subsequent ascents, and my father would snap at my sister and me if we spoke as our mother negotiated the climbing bends – although our talking bothered him rather than her. I was never quite sure if it was worth it, because when you stood on the Horse (which had been cut in 1857 by a schoolteacher and some of his pupils), it seemed rather like a car park itself.

It is the largest and most northerly hillside white horse in Britain (on a clear day, you can see it from Leeds) but it's more grey than white, the rock of the hillside being limestone, which is not as white as chalk, from which the majority of hillside white horses in England are cut. The journey back would be more relaxed, and my father would ask my mother to stop if there was a large amount of horse manure on a country road. He'd scoop it up with a seaside spade he kept in the boot for that reason. It was 'good for the garden', and collecting it gave him a role to perform in the car, making up for his inability to drive.

Sometimes, we'd drive onto the Moors proper, perhaps for a desultory stroll around the rim of the Hole of Horcum, that great, heathery amphitheatre that is part of the valley made by the Levisham Beck (heroic work, given the piddling size of the Beck). If it was raining, we might just park in the adjacent layby, where the bays are arranged so that the cars face the Hole. We'd keep the windscreen wipers going, to maintain the view while we ate ice creams from the van that always seemed to be in the layby.

'Hole' is a good, unpretentious Yorkshire word for a landscape feature. Also on the Moors is the idyllic village of Beck Hole, north-west of Goathland. The village pub, the Birch Hall Inn, has a 'Big Bar' (which is tiny) and an even smaller 'Little Bar'. There is also a counter selling sweets. I used to like the way the soot from the fireplace in the Big Bar had slightly stained the wallpaper over the mantle, which depicted huntsmen on horses. The Birch Hall Inn was one of those heavenly spots that I believed could only be found in Yorkshire; another was the village of Hutton-le-Hole, whose rurality was very concentrated, in that the sheep grazed on grass banks *within* the village.

On the subject of holes, incidentally, there are surely far more in Yorkshire than in Blackburn, Lancashire, and an article about Yorkshire holes was written by Roy Mason in the *Dalesman* of August 1968. 'To my knowledge', wrote Mason, 'no student of Yorkshire dialect has ever accorded full and due recognition to the simple word "hole". Pronounced "hoil" or perhaps better still "oil" without the aspirate, it is one of the most popular and widely adapted words in the West Riding.' A lift shaft in the West Riding is, apparently, or was in 1968, 't'lift hoil', and Mason quotes the characteristic Yorkshire injunction 'Shut thi cayak hoil' ('Shut your cake hole'). But it is time I admitted that I have never heard anybody in Yorkshire say 'thee' and 'thou' except in self-parody.

On other occasions, we'd visit the market towns of the Moors or the Dales, and these memories are confused in my mind. Whether it was Pickering, Thirsk or Helmsley there'd be a castle, a stream and market square, although we had to take the existence of the actual market on trust, since it was never held on the day of our visit, which was always Sunday. The drive back would be slightly melancholic, with Monday school looming, and sometimes the fumes in the Singer Gazelle would bring on one of my migraines. I also associated the beautiful purple flowers of moorland heather – of which you got more on the Moors than the Dales – with a certain wistfulness, because they came out in late summer, when the holidays were coming to an end, and the ferns growing alongside the heather were brown and dying at that point. In my mind's eye, I see purple heather under a low, very orange sun.

After my mother's death, a lovely family down the road – the Walkers – took my sister and me under their wing. They gave us unofficial part shares in their Border Terrier and took us camping with them on many summer weekends. We have already met Paul Walker – he was my golf partner in the opening section. His father, Malcolm, is a very entertaining, slightly built, bronzed man. He leads guided walks around central York and is a keen amateur actor: he's a good mimic, like his son.* Malcolm worked at Ben Johnson's, a York printing firm, but he was and is a countryman at heart. As a young man, he'd been a member of York Mountaineering Club, which sounds a surreal concept, given York's flatness.

In August 1955, Malcolm and some of his fellow mountaineers read a challenge laid down in the *Dalesman* by Bill Cowley, who farmed at Swainby, south of Middlesbrough,

---

* Paul likes to demonstrate the difference between the York and Leeds accents (the Leeds one is slightly more droney), and then – *the pièce de résistance* – he'll do you a Tadcaster accent, Tadcaster being halfway between Leeds and York.

and had founded a Yorkshire Society at Cambridge University. The idea of the challenge had come to Cowley when he was standing on Glaisdale Rigg, the ridge between Glaisdale and Fryupdale (which is indeed pronounced 'fry-up dale'). The challenge was to cross the North York Moors from west to east – a distance of about 40 miles from Osmotherley to Ravenscar on the sea – in less than twenty-four hours. Malcolm and a dozen friends took up the challenge and completed what would be christened the Lyke Wake Walk within the twenty-four hours, an effort described by Bill Cowley in the *Dalesman* of December 1955.

The walk became a camp cult, steeped in morbid and deathly language. If you did the walk seven times, you qualified as a 'Doctor of Dolefulness'; all women who completed it were 'Witches'. 'Lyke' is the Northern equivalent of 'lych', meaning corpse, as in the lych gate of a churchyard, and a wake ... well, everybody knows what that is. People who complete the walk are entitled to wear a little black badge in the shape of a coffin. It is often assumed that the walk follows one of the medieval coffin trails or corpse roads, along which coffins were carried from settlements to burial grounds, but that's not actually the case. The walk was characterised as funereal by Cowley almost on a whim because it passes some stone crosses and a Bronze Age burial mound near Westerdale. On 1 August 2015, Mike Parker, author and self-declared 'wanderer', wrote a very amusing entry on his Map Addict blog called 'Whatever Happened to the Lyke Wake Walk?' (a piece deriving from an account in his book, *The Wild Rover*):

In the early days it was almost entirely local: the first log books of the walk, which were kept in cafés at either end for people to sign in their times and experiences, are full of entries by groups from places such as York Technical College, Middlesbrough GPO Telephones Division, a Stockton-on-Tees scout pack, Selby Round Table and Darlington Young Liberals ... The few southerners who took it on fared dismally, none more guaranteed to make a Yorkshireman crack a thin smile than a party from the London Region of the Youth Hostel Association who, in 1961, curtly confessed to the log book that they 'did not take magnetic variation into account – ended up in Middlesbrough'.

By the 1970s, the walk was a national attraction, and even though it followed recognised rights of way, conservationists of the moors feared its destructive effects, especially the summertime danger of dropped cigarettes. Parker characterises the walkers as 'a curious mix of grizzled Yorkshire farmers, a few bald bank managers taking a walk on the wild side, some wiry fell runners and a generous sprinkling of bearded prog rock pagans'. The boom has passed, but the walk endures.

I did the walk with Malcolm, Paul and others about fifteen years ago. We started at 10 p.m., to get the walking-in-the-dark out of the way first. I recall the ceaseless, metronomic shuffling noise made by a friend of Malcolm's, a scrawny, super-fit sixty-something whose clean white ankle socks rubbed together as he walked. At some point we looked south, to see the twinkling lights, a sort of multi-coloured Milky Way, of the great ICI works south of Middlesbrough – the view that apparently inspired Ridley Scott, who's from South Shields, to create the opening scenes of *Blade Runner*. We would have been at about Westerdale when the sun began to come up – a great red parturition above the black moor – and after twenty-five miles of walking, another day seemed almost unwelcome.

I keep my coffin-badge in my desk drawer. If I was the kind of person who wore badges on his jacket lapels, this is the one I'd sport. Any stranger considering taking liberties with me might find it salutary and think twice.

The Walkers (I am referring now to Malcolm's family) were members of a camping club that had been an outgrowth of the York branch of the Cyclists Touring Club, which had been founded in 1878, and is today Cycling UK. The members of the camping club had outgrown cycling, and some of them had outgrown tents as well, so they had trailer tents or even caravans. The Walkers just had a tent. The locations have tended to blur into one in my memory, but they included Grinton, Clapham and Appletreewick in the Dales, and Rosedale in the Moors – a great valley with the ruin of an ironstone line running along the top of one bank. In the valley bottom is the sleepy village of Rosedale Abbey, named after a religious institution that went down with the dissolution, and of which no ruin is left.

The Rosedale memory does remain distinct. It was 1976 – that scorching summer. I was apprehensive about what was for me a return to Rosedale, because I'd been there the week before on a school trip, and a long hot walk down a road of dazzling white limestone had brought on one of my migraines. I'd had to sit down on a bank of heather in the care of Mrs Marcroft, the French teacher. Much to my embarrassment – but not to Mrs Marcroft's – I was sick, after which I could continue.

As it turned out, I was sick again in Rosedale on my return with the Walkers, because for the first of what has turned out to be many times, I got drunk. It happened at the camp barbecue, at the culmination of a glorious day of shooting rapids on the little River Seven, which runs alongside the campsite, and is not to be confused with the much bigger River Severn. Malcolm and Edna Walker were in no way to blame, since Paul and I crept under a trailer tent to snaffle some cans of beer that had been stored there in a cooler bag. And it was well worth it. Before being sick, I had my first smooch – to 'Fool to Cry' by the Rolling Stones – and my first snog, with a pretty girl who was about three years older than me.

If I catch the whiff of toothpaste outdoors, floating on the air during a summer's evening, I recall those camping days, because people would clean their teeth at the sinks of the toilet blocks, some of which were attached to the buildings' exteriors. I also recalled my camping days when sitting shivering in a pub garden during semi-lockdown, because the evenings of our *al fresco* campsite suppers were often cool.

I have continued to visit the Moors and the Dales ever since. On the Moors, my focus is usually Pickering, ideally on a Monday (market day), when the steam trains of the North York Moors Railway are running. I like to ride in the oldest carriages, the teaks (because that's what they're made of), which have mellow, tawny interiors, made pinkish by a setting summer sun. Even better is to be on the train in winter, when the steep passing hills, coming and going amid swirling clouds, look dangerous. I like to disembark at Grosmont, which until the 1890s was that very Yorkshire thing: an industrial village. It had an ironworks for the local ironstone, and a hill made of a million tons of slag. The station buildings of the NYMR at Grosmont are particularly pretty: the Oriental Blue and ivory of North Eastern Region of BR. (The stations of the NYMR all have different colours, for historical–educational purposes.) I evoked the railway in a book about heritage lines, *Steam Trains Today*, which I then sent to the chairman of the NYMR, Andrew Scott. He replied that he had enjoyed the book, but that I had missed an important element of the line's theatre: 'The view of the train as an object – or even a performance – in the landscape.'

My visits to the Dales have usually been more strenuous. I will tend to hike, and I've done the circular 24-mile Three Peaks walk half a dozen times. The walk – which you are supposed to complete within twelve hours – can be under-taken clockwise (Ingleborough, Whernside, Pen-y-ghent) or anti–clockwise. I once did it on a day of blazing heat with my oldest son when he was ten years old. I was very proud of him, and he seemed to relish the experience, but when, that evening, we were having an Indian meal at the excel-lent Royal Spice restaurant in Settle, he politely excused himself, walked out of the front door and was neatly sick in the street, like a cat.* I should not have introduced him to long-distance walking and exotic food on the same day. When doing the walk, I usually base myself in the town of Settle, where the viaduct carrying the Settle–Carlisle line through the town seems hardly any more dramatic than the viaducts carrying railways through Leeds. But when, at the halfway stage of the Three Peaks walk, you reach Ribblehead, the line has had to make a more dramatic accommodation to the countryside, and the viaduct is 104 feet high (and when you're on a train riding over it, your ears pop, as on an aeroplane).

Here is an article I wrote about the Three Peaks for the *New Statesman*. It appeared on 27 May 2002, and 'the Vicar'

---

*   Sorry, by the way, for all the vomiting in this section.

is my friend Paul Walker, who was ordained before becoming an NHS chaplain.

Last week, I went up to the Yorkshire Dales to walk the Three Peaks — Pen-y-ghent, Whernside and Ingleborough — with my friend the vicar and my friend the builder. Beautiful countryside always takes me in the same way, and halfway up Pen-y-ghent, I turned to my friends and said: 'You know, I wish I was a drystone waller. I heard a man talking about it on the radio. He said it was the greatest job ever.' The vicar nodded. 'Real sense of achievement, too. You can see exactly what you've done every day.'

'It's a bit tricky, though,' said the builder. 'You, in effect, build two parallel walls with linking stones, so you have to be able to think in three dimensions.' Taking heart from the fact that he had not said that this was beyond me, I walked on, thoughtfully.

Later, our path took us through a pretty farmyard. 'Be a great life to be a farmer, wouldn't it?' I said, as we edged past some geese. 'But I suppose it's very difficult to get started.'

'Not if you go to Scotland,' said the builder. 'They're desperate for people to take on the crofts.'

'But what would I farm?' I wondered.

'Sheep,' said the vicar, promptly.

'But there's no money in that,' I said.

'Specialist sheep,' said the vicar, who then told me an encouraging story of a friend of his who'd done well with a breed called Jacob sheep, which are brownish.

Further on we came to the Ribblehead Viaduct, which is part of the anachronistic Settle–Carlisle Railway. There was a signal box close to the viaduct, with a signalman inside it, warming himself before a real fire, judging by the smoke rising from his chimney. 'Now, that's the life,' I said.

'Yup,' said the vicar. 'Total tranquillity. And he's in charge of those beautiful old semaphore signals.'

'Your dad was on the railways, wasn't he?' said the builder. 'You'd probably find you had an aptitude for it.'

By evening, we were walking – or hobbling, really – through Giggleswick churchyard, where Russell Harty is buried. My friends the vicar and the builder suggested I be photographed next to the headstone.

'Why?' I asked, rather defensively.

'Well, you're a media sort like him,' they chorused. Doomed to stay one, too, their tone strongly suggested.

RESORTS

Scarborough Fair

There is a theory that to ascend the Yorkshire coast from south to north is also to make a social ascent. In *Goodbye to Yorkshire*, Roy Hattersley writes about how his family had first holidayed in Bridlington. But as his family became better off, after the war, 'our summer holidays began slowly to move up the coast. The further north we got the higher we had risen in the world, for Yorkshire resorts gained social status with latitude.'

Hattersley places southerly Withernsea at the bottom of the social pile, 'with the lighthouse on its main street as its only distinction'. He places Scarborough – which his family graduated to in 1952 – at the top of the social pile. Trouble is, it's not at top of the geographical one: that's humble Redcar, a resort that seems entangled with the remains of Teesside industry, what with the rusty-looking wind turbines in the sea, and the occasional light-industrial concern along the front. Saltburn and Whitby are also north of Scarborough, and Hattersley does address the Whitby objection, contending that the town is 'quaint and quirky ... too complicated and confused to be allocated a very precise place in the seaside social register'.

Hattersley was concerned with the 1940s and 1950s, the

golden age of the Yorkshire seaside. Back then, the hierarchy
would have held true for Scarborough down to Withernsea,
and Hattersley's recollections remind us that, whereas the
Scarborough of today is not usually considered smart (self-
deprecating locals will joke that the last five letters of the
town's name are the telling ones), it used to be a place you
might dress up for.

Scarborough has always been the most important resort
on the Yorkshire coast. It is by far the biggest, being built
on the elemental Yorkshire scale. An Edwardian poster
promoting the 'cheap tourist tickets' of the North Eastern
Railway showed a cherubic boy skipping a along a beach
with the slogan, 'Scarborough Braces You Up.' It also tires
you out. It's very hilly, hence the need for funicular railways
between the town and the bays, and there's officially a ravine
between the South Cliff and the central St Nicholas Cliff.
If you walk along St Nicholas Street, you are level with
the rooftop domes of the twelve-storey Grand Hotel. If,
on family visits in the 1970s, we walked along the Marine
Drive from the North Bay to the South Bay, we certainly
wouldn't walk *back*, but would take a bus, ideally an open-
topped one.

Scarborough was big enough to incorporate a social
range. In his book, *Pavilions by the Sea*, Tom Laughton, a
Scarborough hotelier, and brother of the actor, Charles,
describes Edwardian Scarborough as 'a very class-conscious
town. "The best people" resided on the South Cliff, trades-
men and shopkeepers lived and worked in the centre of the
town, the lodgings and boarding houses were mostly on the
North Side.'

Laughton's parents originally ran the relatively modest
Victoria Hotel, which still stands – with a plaque announcing it as the birthplace of Charles Laughton – in the middle

of town on Westborough. But in 1908 they acquired the more prestigious Pavilion Hotel, which resembled a French chateau overlooking the railway station. The Laughtons were among the 'best people', and Laughton's memoir interests me as a chronicle of Yorkshire seaside poshness, a commodity almost lost to memory:

> Sometimes when we left the hotel we would set our course for the sands; two little boys in sailor suits, equipped with buckets, spades and shrimping nets. Through the station yard with the horse-drawn waggon-ettes and the sweet smell of horse dung, down the valley and along the valley road to the sea; passing a line of one-horse phaetons drawn by horses driven by postillions dressed in faded jockey costumes, on to the sands below the walls of the Spa promenade, to our destination, the Children's Corner, the place where the so-called 'best children' played.

Scarborough was cast in a smart mould by its importance as a spa. In the 1620s, two mineral springs were discovered at the base of cliffs south of the town. Scarborough was highly rated by the contemporary chroniclers of spas, who read today like so many verbose quacks, and snobbish ones at that. A Dr Robert Wittie of Hull was chief publicist of the Scarborough waters, which he said were efficacious for a range of ills from 'wind to leprosy'. In 1660, he noted of the Scarborough 'Spaw' that 'it hath of late years been well known to the citizens of York, and the gentry of the county, who do constantly frequent it; yea and to several person of quality in the nation.' Wittie also talked up the virtues of sea bathing, an activity unavailable in the inland Yorkshire spas at Harrogate and Knaresborough.

In the early eighteenth century, buildings were constructed to institutionalise the spa. Gradually the 'spa season' became a holiday in a more modern sense. As one visitor to Scarborough wrote, in 1769, 'health is the pretence, but dissipation the end.' But the specious alchemical tone lingers in a book called *The Spas of England, Vol 1: Northern* (1841), by A. B. Granville, who wrote that the air at Scarborough is 'more genial and elastic, and purer than that of the moors, which are then charged with moisture'. Elsewhere, he was more touristic:

> I am enchanted with Scarborough . . . I was not prepared to find a bay of Naples on the north-east coast of England; nor so picturesque a place perched on lofty cliffs, reminding an old and experienced traveller of some of those romantic sea views which he beheld abroad, particularly in Adriatic and Grecian seas.

(He also liked Filey: 'And what a lovely and curiously seated fishing village this very Filey is, with its beautiful and ample bay, displaying at low water the finest sands on this coast, to the extent of nearly three miles! Even here a mineral spring is found, and there is one also at Bridlington . . .')

The Spa building of today dates from 1880, its predecessor, built in 1839, having been destroyed by fire in 1876, an event rendered picturesque by Atkinson Grimshaw. Today, the Spa is an entertainment complex. In style it's Italianate, like Scarborough railway station, and that's what it looks like: a station too close to the sea. It sits just above that select part of the beach called Children's Corner, and alongside the South Cliff funicular that takes people up to the equally select white stucco houses of the Esplanade.

In my childhood visits to the town, the Spa was the

epicentre of South Side poshness, by virtue of the genteel entertainments it offered. Nightly concerts were given there by the violinist Max Jaffa and his Palm Court Orchestra. Posters of Max Jaffa, holding his violin and dressed in white tuxedo, were all over town. We never went to see him, even on those special occasions when we overnighted at a guest house.

I lobbied for us to see Jaffa, but in a way, it was not necessary to go: you could just extrapolate from the posters. It would probably be warm in the Grand Hall of the Spa; the 2,000-strong audience (it was always a sell-out) would be in their Sunday best, although not as smart as the Palm Court musicians. The air would be full of the heady smell of the flowers at the front of the stage, which might fleetingly engage my hay fever. By the time Jaffa got around to his signature tune, 'Dark Eyes' (after selections from the great waltzes, some Rossini and Ballade Number 1 in G Minor by Chopin) a certain percentage of the audience would be asleep, because Scarborough does wear you out. A couple of years ago, on a rainy day in Blaenau Ffestiniog, I saw a copy of Jaffa's autobiography, *A Life on the Fiddle*, mouldering away in a charity shop. My own charitable instincts were aroused, this seeming such a wrong setting for the urbane Jaffa (there are no palm courts in Blaenau) that I bought it.

Reading the book, I felt it was magnanimous of Jaffa – born into a Jewish family who lived at Langham Street in the West End – to give up his racy life in London to play at the Spa and live in the sedate Scarborough suburb of Scalby Mills. Max Jaffa had learnt his trade, and learnt about life, playing in one of the orchestras of the luxurious Piccadilly Hotel in London, where he lunched every day on two sandwiches: one caviar, one smoked salmon. He learned about opera from the Italian waiters, and about other things from

the waitresses. He writes that hotels 'don't have that seduc-
tive aura of assignation and *affaires* about them for nothing,
and in the fashionable slang of the day, the Piccadilly was
rather "fast". We used to call it a bit of a knocking shop –
though naturally a very high class one.' Jaffa was persuaded
to go to Scarborough by his wife, Jean, who had done a
stint as guest pianist at the Spa. 'She promised me beautiful
countryside and scenery, historic houses, old ruins, fresh air;
and the best fish and chips.'

His orchestra played two shows a day, seven days a week,
over a seventeen-week season for twenty-seven years.
Nothing in the programme was repeated within three
weeks, because Jaffa knew that some people came to his
show every night during a holiday that might well be as
long as three weeks.

There were many regulars in his audience: 'We made personal contact with so many of them, and they really became
good friends.' Jaffa became an honorary Yorkshireman.
He enjoyed horse racing at York, Thirsk and Beverley
('an absolute gem of a country course'), where the Max
Jaffa Sprint Stakes was named after him. In 1987, his final
year at the Spa, he was given the freedom of the Borough
of Scarborough, 'along with Alan Ayckbourn, the town's
famous international playwright and director. Following
the ceremony at the Town Hall the council gave us both a
wonderful party at the Royal Hotel.'

It is instructive to read Jaffa's assessment of his first season,
1960: 'I sensed that Scarborough was pushing the boat out
to attract a bigger public for the summer; the Spa ballroom
had been completely redecorated, Dickie Valentine would
be leading the stars with a show called *Make it Tonight*; the
Black and White Minstrels were booked into the Futurist
Theatre . . .' Reading that made me think that perhaps Jaffa

did not symbolise the poshness of old Scarborough so much as the emerging populism of the new one.

Whereas some resorts capitulated to the crowds as soon as the railways came, Scarborough had remained stand-offish. As John Heywood writes in *Beside the Seaside: A History of Yorkshire's Seaside Resor*ts, 'there was an initial reluctance to encourage the "Day Tripper" . . . a reluctance to offend the wealthy and middle classes upon whom it had depended for so long.' The most desirable visitors would have stayed at the Grand Hotel . . .

In the early eighteenth century, a clifftop bench would have been as likely to face away from the sea as towards it. The sea was a regarded as a watery wilderness, inclined to violence. Then the Romantic Movement declared it beautiful, hence the seaside holiday, and the Grand at Scarborough is testament – in Belle Epoque style – to the absolute conviction that the seaside was where people would want to be. When it opened in 1867, it was the largest hotel and the largest brick-built structure in Europe. On opening, the Grand had thirty lounges and public rooms. Dinner could be taken in various of them, and balls were not necessarily held in the ballroom; they could easily be accommodated elsewhere. The triple-height main hall is surrounded by stately arches; the majestic staircase is wide enough to allow two ladies to pass in ballgowns with their escorts by their sides. The landing runs around the hall, and, according to Bryan Perrett, in *A Sense of Style: a Brief History of the Grand Hotel, Scarborough*, the arrangement was designed to allow a lady on the landing to monitor the hall below so she could 'choose her moment to make a memorable entrance'.

The Grand Hotel takes its place within a Yorkshire nexus. It was designed by Cuthbert Brodrick, who was also the architect of (in descending order of importance) the

Town Hall and Corn Exchange in Leeds,* the Wells House Hydro in Ilkley, and the lodges and gates of the General Cemetery in Hull, where Brodrick was born. On its completion, Brodrick painted a picture of the Grand, which was accepted by the Royal Academy. Atkinson Grimshaw, who was born in Leeds and painted many Leeds scenes, also depicted the Grand in a work called *Scarborough Lights*, one of Grimshaw's 'moonlights', for which he was famous – highly atmospheric and photographically detailed depictions of scenes that were either inherently beautiful (like the Grand) or made to seem so by Grimshaw, as in the case of Hull Docks, or Boar Lane, Leeds. *Scarborough Lights* appears to depict a town infested by mellow glow-worms. These points of light trace a path from the Grand, over the Cliff Bridge to the Esplanade and the Spa: the track of the town's social elite on their Sunday promenades. The painting is sometimes viewable in Scarborough Art Gallery.

But the Grand Hotel transcends Yorkshire – or it did once. It is said that several wars were started by international types firing off telegrams from the Hotel. Adolf Hitler earmarked the Grand for his Northern headquarters if (he would have said 'when') Britain fell to him. There is a whiff of Paris about the Hotel, not only in its looks. The first manager, M. Augustus Fricour, was late of the Hotel Mirabeau in Paris, and Cuthbert Brodrick would retire to Paris aged only forty-seven when the commissions for his particularly monumental statements ran out. In an article about Brodrick in the *Yorkshire Journal* (Summer, 1993), Lynn F. Pearson writes, 'as clients began to demand attention to detail and clarity of function, Brodrick gave them only castles in the air.'

---

* There's a Wetherspoon's pub in Leeds called the Cuthbert Brodrick.

Bryan Perrett describes how M. Fricour knew that, besides the gentry, he would be catering to Northern manufacturers, who might lack a certain refinement, so 'he imposed standards that were to be maintained for the next century, insisting that they should always be smart at meals.' Ladies were not to wear bonnets at dinner, and gentlemen were to wear black frock coats or dress coats. These standards weren't *quite* maintained for the next century, because in the 1950s lounge suits were tolerated if a man did not possess a dinner jacket. But Perrett writes that, in 1967, the hotel's centenary year, it 'continued to function as a seaside Savoy'. It would have been at around this time that I first saw the Grand, and when I began to realise its importance, I complacently thought I would get around to staying there eventually, which I did, as we will be seeing.

After the passing of the Bank Holiday Act in 1871, the numbers of railway-borne day trippers and excursionists arriving in Scarborough began to increase. In 1883, two new platforms were added to the station, one of which featured the longest railway bench in the world, a quarter of a mile long. In 1908 a sister station, Scarborough Londesborough Road, opened especially for excursion trains. But not all the visitors deemed vulgar came by train. *Triple Fugue* (1924), by Osbert Sitwell, includes a short story called 'Low Tide', which concerns two genteel spinsters of Scarborough. They regard motor cars as 'fast' in every sense and 'so trippery'.

Only slowly did Scarborough accommodate the masses. In 1877 a vast underground aquarium was constructed on the South Bay. This was an attempt to rival the popular Brighton Aquarium, which had opened five years before, and it was built by the same architect, Eugenius Birch. The Stories from Scarborough website quotes a description of the Scarborough Aquarium from *People's Palaces: Britain's Seaside Pleasure Buildings*, by Lynn F. Pearson:

> Red, buff and black encaustic tiles with a central haw-thorn blossom pattern ornamented the dados; while those used on the floor were patterned with shells, sea-weed, starfish and dolphins. Amid this colourful mass of international motifs, English pastoral scenes in oils were intended to add light and interest to the concert hall.

If the Aquarium was aimed at day trippers, it missed its mark. The price of admission was high, and as an entertain-ment it was considered fey, with its 'Mohamedan-Indian' theme, a pedagogic slant to the presentation of the fish, the addition of a luxurious dining room and a grotto that incorporated a waterfall and an orchestra. The Aquarium was sold to a William Morgan who, as the manager of the Winter Gardens at Blackpool, understood the excursionist market. His rule of thumb was that 'visitors would rather see a juggler than an uncooked lobster', and he proceeded to give them jugglers in that underground space, as well as many other music-hall types. He introduced alligators to the aquaria; he set up a gallery of optical illusions and installed a swimming pool, in which Ada Webb and her Champion Troupe of Lady Swimmers regularly performed; the cross-Channel swimmer Captain Webb (no relation) also made an appearance there in 1880. What had been the Aquarium was now the People's Palace and Aquarium. As John Heywood puts it, 'A Blackpool man had turned the aquarium into Scarborough's Blackpool Tower.'

But the Aquarium went bust again in 1925, when it was taken over by the council, who renamed it Gala Land, com-mitted to 'Melody, Mirth and Merriment', and continuing

Sergeant Peppery strangeness. It became home to Evelyn Hardy and her All British Ladies' Band. There was Decar's Circus with performing monkeys, geese and ponies, and Cyclon, the kicking mule. There was Professor Frederick and his Mouse Circus, and Madam Jan, clairvoyant. Gala Land was known as 'the umbrella' because people went there on a rainy day – or night, since it stayed open until eleven. There was further unbuttoning on the part of strait-laced Scarborough in 1911, when beach huts were provided on the North and South Sides. These were a more risqué alternative to the traditional bathing machines for changing, which stood in the shallows of the sea, in that the swimmer would have to walk semi-naked from the beach huts to the sea.

And so a balancing act was underway, but accounts of Scarborough in the first five or six decades of the twentieth century still emphasise the upmarket strain. On 1 September 2009, Margaret Drabble told the *Yorkshire Post*, 'I used to love Filey and Scarborough as a child. We'd go to posh Scarborough for a lunch or a tea, and stay in a bed and breakfast in Filey.' Drabble was born in Sheffield in 1939, so this is presumably Scarborough in the 1940s and 1950s. The novelist Susan Hill, who was born in Scarborough in 1942, has written on her website that, when she was growing up in Scarborough, 'it was a very genteel resort, full of retired and older people.'

In *Pavilions by the Sea*, Tom Laughton alludes to the balancing act. On the one hand, his guests included Sir George and Lady Ida Sitwell, who would stay at the Pavilion while their large house on Scarborough Crescent was prepared for them. (Today the house, Woodend, offers 'creative workspaces'.) On the other hand, increasing numbers of 'substantial down-to-earth' folk would come to stay, including a Leeds factory-owner who, in 1924, reduced Laughton to tears when he summoned him to his bedroom to complain about a tough pheasant served at dinner: 'It won't do, mi lad, it won't do.'

Laughton, a connoisseur of wine, food and art, installed small paintings in the bedrooms, 'such things as Landseer sketches, eighteenth- and nineteenth-century pastels, Gaudier-Brzeska drawings', and today some of these are in the Tom Laughton Collection at Scarborough Art Gallery. His taste was not always appreciated. One guest complained about a sketch by Duncan Grant of a swan-necked woman: 'Did you ever see a woman with a neck like that?' He was given another room. But the impression the reader has is of a sybaritic and sophisticated hotel world. Themed fetes were held in the Pavilion ballroom: 'the band dressed in special costumes, and elaborate paper favours, imported from Paris, were distributed to the guests.'

In 1935, Laughton took over the Royal Hotel, which was twice as big as the Pavilion and located on the South Side seafront. His head chef was called Tognoli. He specialised in souffles, and 'He distilled his own liquors and used them to flavour water and biscuit ices.' After the War, Laughton refurbished the hotel, acquiring the principal chandelier from Bath House, Piccadilly (among many other chandeliers). In 1947, he gave a party for the Ballet Rambert company, during which one of the male dancers whirled Madame Rambert around his head. In the early 1950s, he named one suite the Churchill Suite, another the Sitwell Suite. Osbert and Edith Sitwell, son and daughter of Sir George and Lady Ida, came to inspect it. Osbert was particularly taken with 'a small painting by Sir John Armstrong of a monastery above Amalfi'.

In 1965, Laughton sold the hotel and retired to Antibes,

where he continued to enjoy the finer things in life. There is no hint in his book that these things were becoming more elusive in Scarborough, but the town was entering its decline. In *Goodbye to Yorkshire*, Roy Hattersley mentions the Royal Hotel as it was in the mid-Seventies. He grumbles that the white-painted balustrades of the galleries are now 'paralleled by high glass screens in case adolescents should plunge to their death as they giggle down to Monday night's teenage disco in the Neptune Ballroom'. He adds, 'Critics might argue that Scarborough has gone down in the world. Scarborough will insist that the world has gone down around it.'

In 2021, I spent a night at the Royal Hotel, which now offers rooms at about the same budget rate as the adjacent Grand Hotel: thirty quid. So what had been the two smartest hotels in Scarborough are now the two cheapest. The Royal retains its galleries and chandeliers and looks less battered than the Grand; apparently some of the original art introduced into the hotel by Tom Laughton remains, but throughout my stay a broken umbrella remained undisturbed on the side of the main staircase. My room had once been half of a bigger room, but at least there was a bathtub, a rare commodity in budget hotels, the tyranny of temperamental showers usually being imposed. After a day of walking around Scarborough in rain and wind (strong enough to have closed the Ferris wheel on the front), I was ready for a bath, and had undressed and started to run the water when I realised there was no bath plug. I got dressed and went down to reception, where I was told, 'We can certainly get you a bath plug, sir, but not until the morning.' It was 7 p.m. at the time.

The bathtub had a showerhead above, but I managed a few minutes of immersion, using the rubber bathmat to block the plughole. An hour later, when I was sitting in the Leeds Arms in the Old Town, I had an inspiration. Scarborough is one of those places – all of them in Yorkshire or Lancashire – that has a Boyes. These are essentially hardware stores that stock such Yorkshire requisites as knitting needles, dog leads, spades, bird baths, paddling pools and, surely, bath plugs. After finishing my drink, I walked to the Scarborough Boyes's and saw that it would be opening at nine in the morning, which would give me the best part of an hour in which to have a proper bath, check-out time at the Royal being 10 a.m. (which seems fairly draconian when you consider that the earliest check-*in* time is 4 p.m.).

I arrived at Boyes's at five to nine and was first one in, together with a woman with a child in a pushchair, who said to the kid, as she was admitted to the shop, 'Right. Now let's get some grease!' It's a cavernous store on three floors, and the manager directed me to the third floor for bath plugs. I bought one for 50p and paused to look out of the window, which on this sparkling morning gave a good view of the Castle, framed by a display of mops and brooms. As I was exiting the store, the manager said, 'Did you manage to get one?', which a manager in a London hardware store probably wouldn't have done.

The bath plug fitted the plughole perfectly, and I had an enjoyable half hour's soak. As I was quitting my room, I considered whether the memory of Tom Laughton would be best served by leaving the bath plug in the bathroom – allowing other guests the luxury of a bath – or taking it home with me. I decided to take it home. The Royal Hotel clearly was not geared up for baths, presumably to save on hot water. Somebody might misuse the plug, filling the bath to overflow and causing a flood. The owners, secure in the knowledge that there were no bath plugs in the hotel, might not be insured against this eventuality, and I might be blamed, and sued, in which case, all my happy memories of Scarborough would be erased.

When my mother was alive, we walked around the many gardens: the South Cliff Gardens, for example, incorporate the Rose Garden, the Italian Gardens, the Sunken Garden and Holbeck Gardens ('offering the best views from a putting green anywhere in England'). Somebody once commended Scarborough to me: 'It's got a bloody good public parks department.' My mother, a lover of flowers, liked to walk the whimsical zigzag path up through the South Cliff Gardens from Spa to Esplanade, whereas I preferred the funicular, which resembled a creaking, creosote-smelling cricket pavilion that would slowly levitate. The slogan, written on the roof of the bottom station, so you could see it from the cliff top, was, 'Two hundred and twenty-four steps avoided for 1d.' Today, it's £1.20. Two of the original five funiculars in Scarborough survive: the other, the Central Tramway, is at St Nicholas Cliff next to the Grand Hotel. The station at the top is beautiful in cream and maroon, with a hexagonal ticket booth in front of which stands – and stood throughout my childhood – a figurine of a pretty boy with half-closed eyes. He holds a collecting tin on behalf of local blind people, and I generally do contribute. It's very poignant that the boy is facing away from the lovely view down to the Harbour.

We were conscious of the poshness of the South Bay and liked to look smart for it. Dad would wear a cravat on our day trips to Scarborough, with a jumper draped neatly over his shoulders. The town brought out my own nascent dandyism. On Newborough near the station there was a men's and boys' clothes shop called Anthony Gordon, the name

written in fountain pen–effect on a candy-striped background. I bought a terrycloth yellow V–necked T-shirt there
with the collar fastened by an imitation gold chain, and an
anchor motif on the breast pocket. That was my seaside shirt
until a combination of it shrinking and me growing made
it unviable.

I wore the shirt in combination with a pair of red
Bermuda shorts, and with these clothes I was insisting that
the weather in Scarborough was good. But in practice, the
sea was always too cold for us to swim in, and you had to be
careful about getting cold at 3 p.m. because you wouldn't be
allowed access to your boarding house, and its hot bath – in
the sinister, high–ceilinged, clanking bathroom – until six.
(I believe it is easier to formally establish a boarding house
now, hence greater competition between them; hence, in
turn, the demise of this sort of lockout.) We did swim in
the North Bay Bathing Pool, a huge and unheated lido
opened in 1938 that might leave me still shivering on the
train back to York.

I don't remember swimming in the South Bay Pool,
which had opened in 1915 and was, according to the Stories
from Scarborough website, 'a glamorous hotspot'. It used
seawater and was refreshed by every incoming tide. On a
hot day there'd be as many people spectating from the high
banks of seats as in the water. The South Bay Pool featured
on a London and North Eastern Railway Poster in the 1920s
('It's Quicker by Rail'): in the foreground a blazered man
is chatting up three flapper–ish women, while somebody is
doing a swan dive from the high board in the background,
appearing as a mere minnow against the summer sky.

The north end of the South Bay does incorporate the
slightly raucous Foreshore Road, where the amusement
arcades and fish and chip shops overlook the harbour. They

occupy quaint premises that really belong to the Old Town –
effectively a fishing village – that rises above and behind. In
this sense, the brashness of Scarborough is only skin deep.

The climax of our Scarborough days came at about five
o'clock when my sister and I were given money to spend in
the Foreshore amusements. Once, aged eight or so, I put a
coin in a slot to see 'the Haunted House' become animated.
A cupboard door opened, and a skeleton jerked out. From
that point on, I slept with the wardrobe door in my bedroom open, to ward off such surprises.

In a glass booth outside one of the arcades, Gilly's
Amusements – which I think was there in my childhood – stands, or sits, a fortune-telling robot called Zoltar,
a turbaned oracle with a Fu Manchu moustache (except
that Zoltar's goes *up*). There are Zoltars in America, and
one of them plays an important role in the film *Big*. But
when you put your pound into the one outside Gilly's you
do seem to be getting a very personal service, as Zoltar
shifts position to stare at you with his surprisingly blue and
shrewd eyes, which is especially disconcerting on a stormy
evening. When Zoltar speaks, however, it's one long dis-
claimer – 'Life is what you make it' etc. – and the actual
fortune, which emerges on a printed ticket, is disappoint-
ingly generic: 'Look to the future . . . Your hard work will
be rewarded,' and so on.

The Joke Shop on Eastborough, just up from Foreshore,
was certainly present during my boyhood, and this too I
found slightly unsettling. With its itching powder, fake
cigarette burns, soap that washes black, it had a slightly
malicious streak that clashed with the South Cliff floral
displays. The shop survives, and long may it, but I do feel
its wares are more in tune with the harsher tone of modern
Scarborough.

I always found the North Bay front bleak – not enough there. The enormous beach seemed empty and bereft, as though still missing the pier that had been destroyed in a storm of 1905. Instead of the cluster of cosy eateries available on the South Bay, there was one huge place on the front called the Corner Café. It was self-service, and I remember being deputised to walk up from our table to the counter to buy some tea and cakes. Once at the counter I forgot some detail of the order, but I couldn't be bothered to walk all the way back to the table to double check on it, so I just improvised. When I had moved to London in the late 1980s, I returned to the Corner Café, which exemplified the difference in the scale of living space between Yorkshire and London. Peeing in the gents there, I counted about forty stalls in the urinals. (The Corner Café was demolished in the 1990s, replaced by flats with retail on the ground floor – shops and bars of sensible size.)

On the North Bay, there was – and is – the narrow-gauge North Bay Railway, billed as 'a railway for pleasure since 1931'. It uses diesel engines designed to look like steam engines. Ignorant commentators decry this as a swizz, but the 'steam outline' diesels supplied to the railway on its opening by Hudswell Clarke of Leeds are historically significant, being among the very earliest diesels. Any persistent complainer is told that the oldest of the engines, *Typhoon* (which looks like *Flying Scotsman* but one-third the size) was the world's first ever diesel hydraulic locomotive when it was built in 1931. 'That usually shuts them up,' a guard on the line once told me. The trains run past the Scarborough Open Air Theatre, which opened in 1927, with a production called 'Merrie England'; then comes a crazy golf course reverting to nature, followed by rusty sea railings with empty beach beyond. People alighting at the Scalby Mills terminus are warned to check the tide before walking along the base of the cliffs to the north.

Peasholm Park – also on the North Bay – has some of the floral charm I associated with the South Bay, and indeed it was planned by Harry W. Smith, the Scarborough Borough engineer who had been responsible for the South Cliff Gardens and the South Bay Pool. As Dad would regularly inform me, the Park had been created within 'a natural glen' (whatever that was). When you walk next to the park stream, in its wooded valley, you might almost be in the Dales, except for the occasional palm tree. The park is known for its exotic planting and its oriental theme, with waterfalls, bamboo bridges and pagodas, inspired by the design of a willow-pattern plate.

Yet this restful theme is undermined every few days in summer by an entertainment called *Naval Warfare*. A man sitting in the park bandstand (a pagoda on the boating lake) breaks off from playing light classical music on an organ to announce 'a jolly good battle'. Coffin-sized battleships lumber into view from around the other side of the artificial island, with council employees lying down inside them (think *corpses* in coffins). The employees wiggle their fingers through the portholes of their ships by way of greeting to the crowd. They then trigger pyrotechnical effects mimicking torpedoes, while the man in the pagoda commentates. In my boyhood, the antagonists were brazenly described as Britain against 'the Germans', but when Scarborough began to benefit from European Union funding (including a major refurbishment of Peasholm Park) it became Britain against 'the enemy'.

I once interviewed a Mr Kevin Barrand of Scarborough Council, who told me that 'The origins of Naval Warfare are a bit grey,' but he believed it had started in 1927, which, he contended, made it the longest running entertainment *in the world*. I learned that the technical supremo was a Scarborough Council electrician who worked from what he called a 'control point' on one of the boating lake islands, but which his colleagues referred to as 'the shed'. The climax of the show is the sinking of an unmanned submarine, after which the organist cheerfully announces that 'Everyone lives to fight another day,' a sentiment undermined by the smell of cordite drifting across the lake.

I still visit Scarborough about three times a year. Sometimes I drive, in which case I park in the South Side underground car park. It's interesting to be there alone, because it occupies the site of the old Gala Land, which was demolished in 1968. I sense the afterglow of Captain Webb, Unthan the Armless Violinist, the Clock-Eyed Lady, Evelyn Hardy and her All British Ladies, Mr Walter Wode, female impersonator, or Miss Flo Everette (and her Clever Canine Pets). But I usually travel by train, and the station always seems quiet. There is never anyone sitting on the long excursionists' bench that can accommodate a couple of hundred. But then I don't recall seeing anyone sitting on it even in my childhood. The bench was refurbished in 2020 – I assume to preserve a Grade II monument rather than to maintain a passenger facility.

When I step out of the station, the soaring sound of gulls – that 'far cry', as James Joyce put it – always lifts my spirits. I think they would be lifted even higher if the Pavilion Hotel were still across the road from the station, but it was demolished in 1973 to make way for a block called Pavilion House. The private bowling green that was in the square alongside is now a car park. 'Perhaps the starkest contrast between beautiful old buildings and the ugly ones which replaced them', wrote Dave Barry in the *Scarborough Review* on 10 November 2017, 'is provided by the Pavilion Hotel and Pavilion House.' In a way, it's a shame I ever read Tom Laughton's book evoking the hotel. If I hadn't, I might never have missed it. I certainly don't recall its being demolished, even though I would certainly have visited the town in the summer of 1973. If I did notice the demolition, I probably assumed it was for the best; that Scarborough knew what it was doing. I would not have appreciated the true significance of the demolition, which was that it symptomised the town's malaise just as surely as did the amplified, urbane tones of the bingo callers down on Foreshore Road.

The Anthony Gordon shop, where I bought my seaside shirt, closed in 2020, as I read in *Scarborough News*. Its owner, Gordon Kipps, was in for an active retirement, it seemed. He is chair of the Scarborough Rifle Association and the Bridlington Canine Society, and he owns ten golden retrievers.

I usually set off walking along Valley Bridge Parade, heading snobbishly for the South Side. If I'm in funds, I'll check into the four-star Crown Spa Hotel on my favourite street, Esplanade. (No definite article – very classy.) If I have a sea view, I will be looking towards the Spa and the site of the South Bay Pool, which was closed in 1988 and stood derelict, becoming flooded (odd thing to happen to a swimming pool) until its demolition in 2003. There is now a star map, illuminated at night, on the site. (The essentially downmarket nature of the *North* Bay Bathing Pool was confirmed when it became in quick succession, Waterscene, Water Splash World, then Atlantis. It closed in 2007.)

The reputation of Esplanade took a knock after Jimmy Savile was outed as a predatory sex offender. Savile, who died in 2011, had owned a flat there. He is pictured sitting in it – on a horrible white leather armchair – on the cover of *In Plain Sight: The Life and Lies of Jimmy Savile*, by Dan Davies. The book – which was originally going to be called by what became the title of the first chapter, 'Apocalypse Now Then' – includes the revelation that Savile was born on Halloween. In the cover photograph, he totes a cigar. The light in the room is made murky by the brightness of the scene beyond the window. On the wall behind Savile are a couple of framed certificates bearing crests and seals and no doubt testifying to his great worth as a person.

In September 2012, a gold plaque was put up on the building that incorporated this flat. A month later, it was taken down. What had happened in the meantime was that a TV documentary had disclosed the truth about Savile. The black memorial stone on his grave at the Woodlands Cemetery in Scarborough was also removed and a South Bay footpath called Savile's View was renamed. Most of the seafront benches in Scarborough bear memorial plaques, and Savile, in his confident and cocky way, commissioned one commemorating a still-living person, i.e. himself. It was on St Nicholas Cliff, near the Grand Hotel, and it read, 'Sir Jimmy Savile: But Not Just Yet.' That's gone now as well. Savile's main base was Leeds, and he would cycle from there to Scarborough. Like Cuthbert Brodrick and Atkinson Grimshaw, he epitomises the connection between Scarborough and Leeds, those twin poles of Yorkshire, the one representing work, the other leisure. In *Yorkshire Tour*, Ella Pontefract and Maria Hartley write, 'South Yorkshire and the coal district choose Bridlington while Leeds gravitates to Scarborough.'

If feeling not so rich, I stay at the Grand Hotel, where I once upgraded to a sea view for five pounds. I might as well let Bryan Perrett, chronicler of the Grand, make the pivotal statement about Scarborough, and indeed the entire British seaside. We last heard from Perrett when he was being chipper about the hotel in 1967 ('still a seaside Savoy'), but this confidence was short-lived and illusory: 'Year by year, cheap air travel and the package tour to the Mediterranean combined to attract more and more people away from traditional British resorts.

'The Grand Hotel is, to quote Charlotte Oliver, writing in the *Dalesman* in August 2020, 'now firmly located at the most economical end of the holiday accommodation market'. I've walked into that triple-height main hall to a variety of undignified soundtracks: bingo calling, karaoke singing, the beeping of a fruit machine bearing a picture of Noel Edmonds. On a couple of occasions, I've been required to sanitise my hands on entering, and this was a pre-pandemic stricture, necessitated by the hotel's own private health crises. I once stayed on the top floor with a sea view, and it was as if the hotel had become part of the cliff it sits upon; certainly, the gulls roosting on the window ledge seemed not to know the difference. That sea-facing side is covered in guano; on the landward side, buddleia and other weeds sprout amid the decorative stone seashells.

From St Nicholas Gardens, I look up at the side wall of the Grand, which is frighteningly vertiginous, and half covered with green slime, as if the hotel were occasionally overwhelmed by the sea. There are just too many bricks – an entirely unreasonable number – and I am reminded of the Irish ghost story writer, Sheridan Le Fanu, who was morbidly obsessed by the huge Georgian houses of Dublin, one of which he inhabited. His perpetual fear was that the bricks of his house were insupportably stacked, and that one night they'd come tumbling down as he slept. When he was found dead in bed of a heart attack, apparently having been scared to death, his doctor said, 'That house fell at last.' In a sense the problem with the Grand today is not that it's no longer Grand, but that it's *too* Grand – too big to be easily managed. The upper floors are particularly ghostly, with their framed and faded black and white photographs of Yorkshire cricketers. Up there, Geoff Boycott is always thirty years old.

I like to wander around the cobbled streets of the Old Town, where no two houses are the same, except for some local authority ones, and where Alan Ayckbourn lives in a Georgian mansion, whose grounds I once tried to enter, having taken them for a public park. I might drift up towards the cemeteries connected to Scarborough Parish Church, which are like small meadows with a few graves in them. Anne Brontë is buried hereabouts, but for years I could ever find the grave. I was wandering about in one of the cemeteries on a cold early summer's evening in 2021 when a young girl sitting on a brick wall and sucking a popsicle suddenly turned to me and said, 'Where have *you* come from?' That being a hard question to answer, I said, 'I'm looking for Anne Brontë's grave.' 'You'll find her up there,' she said, using the popsicle to point up a grassy bank towards a broken brick wall. 'Go through the hole in the wall; she's on the right.'

There's a case for saying that at least two of the Brontë sisters – Anne and Charlotte – were much keener on the sea than the moors with which they are associated. Charlotte had a moment of epiphany in Bridlington, as we will be seeing. Anne had always liked Scarborough, and she would often visit it with the Robinson family, to whom she was governess. She came to Scarborough in her final year, 1849, partly to relive happy memories, and partly to 'take the waters' in the hope of mitigating her tuberculosis. In the sense that she would go to the Spa both to listen to music and to take the waters, she experienced Scarborough when it was on the cusp of becoming a tourist town. It is poignant to think of emaciated Anne walking with difficulty between the Spa and Wood's Lodgings, where she stayed when in town, and where the Grand Hotel now stands. The Grand is decent enough to commemorate Anne with a blue plaque, but as the hotel has gone down market, I assume that fewer and fewer of its guests would know who she is.

Scarborough features in her two novels, *Agnes Grey* and *The Tenant of Wildfell Hall* (limpid, unshowy books with a Jane Austen-like deftness), although it is not named as such. The climax of *Agnes Grey* occurs on the headland just above where Anne is buried:

> I shall never forget that glorious summer evening, and I will remember with delight that steep hill, and the edge of the precipice where we stood together watching the splendid sunset mirrored in the restless world of waters at our feet – with hearts filled with gratitude to Heaven, and happiness, and love – almost too full for speech.

Further up that same hill from the churchyard, there's a Victorian folly resembling a house-sized castle. This is called the Towers, and it was owned by Thomas Jarvis, retired brewer and patron of Atkinson Grimshaw. Behind it is another, smaller folly, also resembling a castle and commanding (if you step out of its front door and turn right) a stunning view of the North Bay. This was known as Castle-by-the-Sea, and Atkinson Grimshaw lived there from 1878–9. Little is known of his life, but he might have wanted to escape his native Leeds because three of his children had died there of diphtheria. Today it's a guest house, with a plaque commemorating Grimshaw and (every time I've walked up there) a 'No Vacancies' sign propped in the window, so that I imagine a conclave of 'Grimmy'* fans permanently in session. Towering above both these joke castles is the real Scarborough Castle on its headland, or what's left of it.

I have quite often visited Scarborough to write an article with the theme 'Scarborough's on the up', and I am always on the lookout for supporting evidence: signs that modern Scarborough is not merely, as a council employee once told me off the record, 'a great place to be unemployed'. Unfortunately, the peg for those pieces has usually been quite slender. The cue for one of them – about twenty years ago – was the opening of a new Ask Italian pasta restaurant near the Harbour; another coincided with the refurbishment of the Spa in 2006. At around the same time, I attempted to put my money where my mouth was. I made an offer for a small flat on Esplanade, envisaging it as a base for my operations as a Professional Yorkshireman. I withdrew the offer after a long conversation-cum-shouting-match with my wife: 'We can barely afford the mortgage on our first home let alone acquiring a second one!'

As I write, in spring 2021, the needle does seem to be pointing strongly up. EasyJet's loss – through Covid – might be Scarborough's gain. I have a friend who lives in the town, and who styles himself my 'Scarborough correspondent'. He and his wife moved there from Bradford, so he is what's called a 'Wessie' in Scarborough (meaning somebody from West Yorkshire). 'We moved,' he told me, 'because we love the sea, and we go and worship it every day.' A typical email might begin, 'We just had a splendid Scarborough walk on "our" side

---

* As he was known to his friends.

of town, in bright sun and with a high-kicking sea responding to the command, "Bring on the dancing girls."'

His recent enthusiasms include a new hotel, the Chapel House ('very classy restaurant'), and a venture called Seagrown. This is a seaweed farm operating in tandem with a boat in the harbour which is a combined café and shop selling seaweed products. The South Cliff Gardens are being made over at the time of writing, following a purge of dead vegetation described by my correspondent as 'a sort of *Chainsaw Massacre*'.

There are cautionary notes from my correspondent: much of the centre of the town remains 'shabby' and, while Scarborough has a high percentage of self-employed young people working in IT, 'there is also deprivation'. An Index of Deprivation Report for North Yorkshire, compiled by the Department for Communities and Local Government and covering the year 2015, disclosed that 'North Yorkshire is among the least deprived local authorities in England', but Scarborough is the most deprived district within it, and some areas of the town are among the most deprived 1 per cent in England.

On the South Side front, the cavernous Futurist Theatre, which had been closed since 2014, and hadn't looked futuristic for decades, was demolished in 2018. The demolition was controversial because the Futurist was architecturally significant, having been one of the palatial 'super cinemas' when it opened in 1921, hence the bold name. Plans to create a funfair on the site were also controversial. In my boyhood, the Futurist would be offering Ken Dodd, Les Dawson, Cilla Black or the Black and White Minstrels as a breezier alternative to Max Jaffa at the Spa. Its doom was sealed when the council decided to concentrate on the Spa as the town's leading live venue. The Scarborough Spa Orchestra remains in residence as 'the only remaining professional seaside orchestra', and if you do see anyone in a suit and tie in Scarborough, it is towards this orchestra that the gentleman will be heading. But the Spa bill-topper on any given summer evening is likely to be a tribute band, or an act like Showaddywaddy, who might as well be a tribute band. Bigger names play at the Open-Air Theatre, which closed in 1986 but reopened in 2016, the re-opening being performed by a very big name: Her Majesty the Queen. Regality is fitting since Scarborough (along with Brighton) always did call itself the 'Queen of the Watering Places'.

I will conclude about Scarborough by quoting – with apologies for dubious punctuation – from the most recent 'fortune' supplied to me by Zoltar: 'You worry too much about the past, travel forward and excel in the future, it is waiting for you. August is a lucky month.' I commend those words to the town of Scarborough.

Further Shores

Before Covid, I had a telephone chat with a spokesperson from Discover Yorkshire Coast (formerly Scarborough Borough Council Department of Tourism and Leisure Services), which promotes Whitby and Filey as well as Scarborough itself. She was optimistic, as I suppose she would have to be. Overnight stays were up, and the average stay had risen to four nights, during which people tend to move up and down the coast. The area had benefited from the fall of the pound (and the rise of the 'staycation') since Brexit, and from the establishment of the annual Tour de Yorkshire, the legacy race of the Tour de France's visit to Yorkshire in 2015. The spokesperson described the various regeneration initiatives in Scarborough as 'kissing Sleeping Beauty'.

But what is the state of consciousness of the other resorts?

Historically speaking, where Scarborough led, the other resorts followed, or tried to. Bridlington, Filey and Whitby all attempted to get in on the medicinal water racket, but most had to await the coming of the railways for touristic success. The most brazenly railway-made place was the clifftop resort of Saltburn-by-the-Sea, which did not even exist until the railways came. What *had* existed was the village of Saltburn, devoted to fishing and smuggling. The heart of the smuggling operation was the Ship Inn, where the whispered phrase, 'William's cow has calved', meant that a load of contraband had been landed. The more respectable Saltburn-by-the-Sea was the creation of Henry Pease, an ironstone magnate of Middlesbrough, who'd had a vision of a beautiful resort – a haven for those working in Teesside industries – while walking along the cliff above Saltburn village in 1858. To facilitate it, he persuaded the Stockton & Darlington Railway to extend its line from Middlesbrough to Redcar further south and to build the Zetland Hotel adjacent to the station. Pease laid out a town plan, with the streets named after jewels.

Saltburn-by-the-Sea flourished gently until the First World War, the main attractions being the pier (which survives, but now traverses only the beach) and public gardens. But Saltburn-by-the-Sea never made the big time. In 1939, Ella Pontefract and Maria Hartley wrote in *Yorkshire Tour* that the place 'seems to require another genius to rise up and finish its planning'. The beachfront still looks ripe for development. There's very little there, except half a dozen sleepy pavilions. From the town, you can see the last remaining blast furnace – now cold and defunct – of what remains of the Teesside Steelworks. Today, Saltburn looks north, towards the bright green meadows on the high cliffs that start with Hunt Cliff. The Zetland Hotel overlooked these fields, with the railway station behind and connected to the hotel by a glass canopy. The building (converted to flats in 1989) has a central turret, and a telescope was kept at the top of this, for guests to look out over the cliffs and sea.

But what was given by the railways could also be taken away. Dr Beeching, the railway 'axeman' of the 1960s, seemed to have had it in for Whitby, in particular. He closed two of the three lines serving the town: the one running south along the coast to Scarborough, which also served Robin Hood's Bay, and the one connecting Whitby to York via Pickering. (The line running north along the coast to Middlesbrough had already closed in the 1950s, stultifying the commercial development of Sandsend, Staithes, Saltburn and Redcar.)

Beeching ensured that, as a boy growing up in York, I hardly ever went to Whitby, because the only way of getting there by train from York was via Middlesbrough, which took nearly four hours; and so Whitby was denied my holiday money – a modest sum, admittedly, but if we multiply it by a few millions we see the effect of a highly attractive coastal town being cut off from major local centres of population. I did not actually make a railway arrival at Whitby Station until the summer of 2018, and that was via the North York Moors Railway, the preserved line that re-connected Pickering to Whitby in 2007. The journey over the beautiful sunlit Moors culminated in arrival at the graceful, classical station, built by George Andrews in 1854. It's right on the water, like Santa Lucia Station in Venice, and that photographer of Victorian Whitby, Frank Meadow Sutcliffe, once took a picture of a tall-masted sailing ship framed by two pillars of the station portico.

We did not visit Whitby as a family until we acquired a car, which was in 1969, when I was seven. We went perhaps twice, since it was a long haul for our temperamental Morris Minor; I remember the Abbey coming into view as we descended from the Moors, and smoke rising from the chimneys of the town, creating a sense of coming upon some remote encampment. As a teenager, I sometimes went by bus to Whitby. Once, I was driven there by a friend of

mine in his motorcycle sidecar. It was winter and I nearly
froze to death. I could barely see out from that rattling pod,
but I think, going by some sudden swerves and outbursts
of swearing from my begoggled friend, that we also came
close to a more violent death on a couple of occasions. If
we *had* fatally crashed, two more would have been added
to the thousands killed, in effect, by Dr Beeching.

To the south, Beeching's closure of lines running
through the Yorkshire Wolds cut Bridlington off from its
tourist clientele in south and west Yorkshire; he also closed
the railways to Hornsea and Withernsea. Scarborough
retained the lifeline of its railway to York, and this is the
way it has tended to work among the Yorkshire resorts:
Scarborough comes out on top. It also did most things first.

Scarborough and Filey both have elegant early Victorian
streets called Crescents. The one in Filey is actually the
Royal Crescent, and it was the focus of the town's appeal to
the upper classes, but it was not built until 1835, whereas
the one in Scarborough dates from 1833. Whitby has
two Crescents (East and Royal), both of which post-date
Scarborough's. Scarborough's Esplanade also came before
the ones at Whitby and Bridlington. Bridlington gained
its own Spa in 1896, thirty years after Scarborough's. It
was an entertainment venue, like the one in Scarborough,
and with Herr Lutz, ex of both Vienna and Scarborough,
as conductor of the orchestra. Whereas Scarborough's first
Spa was destroyed by fire in 1876, Bridlington Spa did not
get around to being burnt down until 1906, a new one
being immediately built.

The Assembly Rooms in Saltburn-by-the-Sea, opened
in 1885, were renamed the Spa Pavilion in 1935; it is now
the Spa Hotel. And on the West Cliff at Whitby there is
this little historical and terminological thicket . . . In 1879

a theatre called the West Cliff Saloon was opened. In 1915, its name was changed to the Spa Theatre. In 1924, a second theatre – conservatory-like and dedicated to chamber concerts rather than plays and films – was built alongside. It was called the Floral Hall, but later on (possibly in 1953) its name was changed to the Spa Pavilion. In 1989 it was demolished and replaced by something called simply The Pavilion, which is now known as the Northern Lights Suite. It and the original theatre are – at the time of writing – jointly referred to as Whitby Pavilion.

All the resorts have similarly named public gardens. For example, Saltburn, like Scarborough, has Italian Gardens, but Scarborough's came first. A chamber concert venue in Bridlington that opened in 1904 was later decorated with hanging baskets and renamed the Floral Pavilion after the one in Scarborough. The Floral Hall at Hornsea opened in 1913.

Scarborough had the first pier on the Yorkshire coast (1869), but the North Sea is very intolerant of piers, and all the resorts that had them have them no longer, except Saltburn. The pier at Hornsea lasted only six months: opened in May 1880, most of it was destroyed by a ship (well, a storm was the real culprit) in October. Withernsea retains two towers that once formed the entrance to the pier. The first funicular railway at Scarborough – the one from the Spa up to the Esplanade – was also the first funicular railway in Britain; it opened in 1875. Saltburn got its funicular in 1884.

Given all this overlapping, I think it more profitable to focus on what differentiates the resorts.

Filey, Bridlington and Scarborough all have huge sandy beaches, but the beach is a more remarked-on feature at

Bridlington and Filey, since there is less happening inland at those places. Whereas you sense that Bridlington would like *more* to be happening, the town being an aspirant Scarborough, Filey has settled for being quiet and small. If you step outside the railway station, which has a sleepy, rustic aspect, like a Victorian barn, there's a noticeboard about the town's history. It begins, 'In the eighteenth century, Filey was a fishing village with a population of just 500,' which creates a narrative tension, the expectation of great subsequent expansion, but Filey only has about 6,000 people today, compared to over 100,000 in Scarborough.

Filey has always been more sedate than Scarborough, and in the 1830s it was also considered more refined. In that decade, John Wilkes Unett – who was to Filey what Henry Pease was to Saltburn-by-the-Sea, and whose family made their money, I'm afraid, from the slave trade – built the above-mentioned Royal Crescent: six stuccoed blocks which stand in the centre of the town like a white cliff. In *Yorkshire Coast Path*, Andrew Vine describes the Royal Crescent as 'the most fully-realised dream of grandeur the Yorkshire coast ever achieved'.

Natural features also lend Filey an elevated tone, and you do focus on the sea and the sky, the light of each perpetually redoubling that of the other. In *Yorkshire Life* magazine of September 2011, Margaret Drabble described Filey as 'the most numinous place on earth'. To the south of the bay, the brown clay cliffs gradually rise and become the chalk cliffs of Bempton, Speeton and Flamborough Head which, viewed from the beach, seem to resemble the massed, grubby-white sails of a fleet of tall ships. On the north side of the Bay is the Brigg, a rocky promontory incorporating many rock pools and so facilitating the pursuit of 'rock pooling' with its genteel accessories like shrimping nets, adapted jam jars, floppy sun hats and the *Observer's Book of Sea and Seashore*. Rock pooling was eminently civilised, unless you happened to be a shrimp or starfish rudely transported in one of those jam jars back to the boarding house sink for further study. The rock pools of the Brigg today seem to hold fewer darting, scuttling things than in my childhood. They seem more like still lifes. In her memoir, *The Child in the Crystal*, published in 1939, S. M. Lubbock (Lady Sybil Lubbock), recalls Filey Brigg:

> In the pools were whole aquariums of crabs and prawns and little crayfish, shells and sea anemones and seaweeds; the beauty of the underwater world was so marvellous that we would sometimes ... lie for half an hour just gazing at the changing kaleidoscope of life and colour.

In my childhood, the drag on Filey's claims to social smartness was provided by the Butlin's holiday camp just outside the town. We were not quite working-class enough to have had that *Hi-De-Hi* experience of communal forced jollity. Indeed, we Martins did our bit to scupper the Yorkshire resorts by being early adopters of the Continental package tour. We didn't go by the newly fashionable charter flights to Italy or Spain, but by train, since Dad was a member of the British Railwaymen's Touring Club, with the lapel badge on his summer blazer to prove it. With our foreign holiday booked, I would sadistically quiz my contemporaries about where they were off to, and if they said — as they often did — 'Oh, just Filey Butlin's', they would be slightly shamefaced about it, much to the satisfaction of my snobbish ten-year-old self. 'I've heard that's really nice,' I would patronisingly respond. But Billy Butlin got his own back. When I was in the throes of trying to make a living from freelance journalism, I was offered a lucrative commission by the *Sunday Times* Magazine: 'We'd like a piece on holiday camps, Andrew, and we're assuming that, since you're from Yorkshire *and a bit of an oik* [that part was not actually spoken], you must have gone to the Butlin's at Filey. We can offer eighteen hundred quid for a personal and nostalgic reminiscence.' Having no such memories to draw upon, I was forced to decline the commission, and my relationship with the magazine never recovered.

Filey Butlin's closed in 1984.

The central focus of Filey ought to have been the Royal Crescent, but in my childhood, it seemed to be the big red, customised tractor parked on the Coble Landing, on standby for dragging the fishing boats called cobles across the beach and into the sea. It had enormous rear wheels, like a dragster, to elevate the engine above the water. Cobles are peculiar to Yorkshire: their flat bottoms allow them to be hauled over the sandy beaches of the county, and their high prows afford protection against North Sea waves. The fishermen have long contributed to the picturesqueness of Filey. Here is Lady Sybil Lubbock again: 'Go we did to the harbour, in the cool gleam of the evening after supper, and indeed it was a sight worth seeing. Every boat in the place had its crew, old men and boys were pressed into service that evening; and as the sun set they sailed, a noble sight as they swayed towards the horizon over the malachite sea.' In 2003, I began a piece about Filey for the *New Statesman* with the speculation that, whereas most Londoners have heard of Scarborough, even if they're a bit hazy about which county it's in, only about half of them have heard of Filey. In the piece, I misspelled 'coble' as 'cobble', thereby perhaps proving my point about the relative obscurity of Filey, because nobody wrote in to complain.

When I was last in Filey, in 2020, the customised tractor had been replaced by something less bizarrely amphibious – an ordinary, if old-fashioned, tractor, and it was blue, not red. It still seemed to be the centre of attention though, and as I took a photograph of it another man was doing the same. A more modest tractor suits the more modest fishing fleet. 'Until three or four years ago', a Filey native told me during that visit, 'there were eighteen cobles on the landing; now there are half a dozen.' Until the 1970s, Yorkshire was the most important fishing territory in the UK, largely thanks to the scale of operations in Hull. Today, it lags behind Scotland, Devon and Cornwall, and the steep decline of fishing was cruelly co-terminous with that of tourist overnighting. In both cases, you could say, Europe is to blame. As far as fishermen were concerned, the loss of fishing grounds resulting from the Cod Wars with Iceland in the 1960s and 1970s was compounded by the too-generous terms offered our partners when we entered the European Union. So most fishermen voted 'Leave'.

'We were promised that control of our waters, zero to two hundred miles, would be non-negotiable,' Andrew Locker, a career fisherman at Whitby, and Chair of the National Federation of Fishermen's Organisations, told me. It didn't turn out like that. 'Brexit has been an absolute disaster for everyone associated with fishing. We were shafted, big time.' It's not just about territory; there are also the newfound difficulties of exporting fresh produce to Europe. Today, that produce is shellfish rather than what fishermen call 'finfish'. Or they speak of 'static gear' – lobster pots, for example – rather than 'mobile gear', such as trawling nets. The number of trawlers operating off the Yorkshire coast is in the low single figures, whereas once there were hundreds operating from Hull alone. The

former users of 'mobile gear' have diversified quite success-
fully into fixed gear, so the situation is not as apocalyptic
as it might sound; and this is why you will still see fishing
boats where you would expect to see them, for example in
the harbours at Scarborough and Bridlington (the largest
shellfish port in Europe), and also, albeit in small numbers,
in those places you'd *hope* to see them, such as Filey, Robin
Hood's Bay, Staithes, Flamborough, Redcar – which is just
as well for the tourist industry. 'People have always wanted
to see a catch being landed,' said Andrew Locker, and at
busy times the landing places have to be roped off from
gawping tourists.

I asked Mr Locker whether Yorkshire fishermen could be
compared to Yorkshire miners, in the sense of being hard
men doing a hard job that they were proud of in a way, but
also disliked. He said there was a difference, arising from a
sense of excitement. 'Fishermen are the last of the explor-
ers. We are what's called "co-venturers", and when you see
that full lobster pot pulled up there's a sense of euphoria,
because you know it's payday.'

During that 2020 visit to Filey, there were perhaps a few
hundred people on the beach, but there was still far more
beach than people. Everyone seemed to be pursuing con-
sciously old-fashioned seaside tropes: paddling thoughtfully,
making sandcastles, trying to catch the drips of melting ice
creams. I ate a delicious crab sandwich in the gardens on
the front, then walked up to the other garden in front of the
Royal Crescent, where little notices credited the organisations that had sponsored that particular bed: 'Filey Ladies'
Monday Club', 'Filey Lions Club'. The wishing well, a notice
apologetically informed me, was 'Under Refurbishment'.

Until the local government reorganisation of 1974, Filey

ran itself, and it was determined to keep Filey unspoilt.
Even today, fish and chip shops don't proliferate in the
town, since they are, in municipal terms, 'obnoxious
trades'. Today, the town council is merely a parish council, and Scarborough Borough Council calls the shots,
and there is a slight suggestion that Scarborough had
attempted to re-make Filey in its own brasher image. For
many years there was only one amusement arcade in Filey:
Holdsworth's on the Coble Landing, and it was long stip-
uated that any other amusement arcade would also have to
be on the Coble Landing. But another Holdsworth's has
now opened, on the principal street, Belle View Road.
'They had an uphill struggle to get that in,' I was told, by
George Cairncross, a shopkeeper on that same road, 'but
it's no trouble to anyone.'

Mr Cairncross's shop is fascinating, somehow epit-
omising the retrospective style of Filey. It is in part an
old-fashioned gent's outfitter, in that Mr Cairncross
sells fancy handkerchiefs for display in one's top pocket
(I bought a couple of green- and white-spotted ones to
serve as anti-Covid masks), but there is also a fancy-dress
element, in the form of old Naval tunics, regimental dress-
wear and other militaria, together with items suitable for
a rainy day in the boarding house, such as slightly risqué
playing cards featuring pin-ups from yesteryear. He opened
his shop in 1962, and he's been behind the counter ever
since, smartly besuited, and available for discussions about
Filey that are historically informed but free of undue nos-
talgia and lachrymosity. 'Day-trippers keep the numbers
up,' he told me.

As a child, I went to Bridlington perhaps half a dozen
times, sometimes staying overnight, but not regularly

enough to refer to it as familiarly as 'Brid', which is how it's known to habitués. Trouble was that, to get to Bridlington from York, you had to change at Seamer. The journey took at least eighty minutes, compared to half that for Scarborough.

Bridlington struck me as a dilute version of Scarborough, committed to the formula 'fresh air and fun', but with more of the former than the latter, and my persistent thought during my most recent visit, made in that brief window of summer freedom in the locked-down year of 2020, was 'There'll be no problem with social distancing here.' I parked in the huge, almost-empty car park next to the railway station and walked down a battered avenue of guest houses towards the sea. ('Purely Victorian building never seems so bad in seaside places as it does inland,' write Ella Pontefract and Maria Hartley in *Yorkshire Tour*, 'perhaps because the high bay-windowed houses are associated in the mind with the joys of seaside holidays.') In my childhood, the guest houses would boast 'Colour TV' or 'Tea and coffee-making facilities in all rooms'. On my walk to the Bridlington front, one guest house was still advertising '22-inch flat-screen TV', but more common was 'Free Wi-Fi'. A couple of notices proclaimed, 'Contractors welcome', which was code for something – perhaps 'East Europeans welcome'. One guest house ambiguously advertised 'Separate Bathrooms'. Most of the guest houses announced 'Vacancies'. When I visited Scarborough or Bridlington as a boy, I found it very satisfying to watch the landlady sweep aside the lace curtain of the front room in order to reverse the 'Vacancies' sign so that it read 'No Vacancies'. You didn't really want to be in a guest house that still had vacancies; that suggested you had come to the wrong place.

I came to the front, on what's called South Cliff, but really there are no cliffs in Bridlington proper. As a 1970s tourism leaflet had it, 'Bridlington is perfectly level with no tiring steep hills' – a dig at Scarborough, of course, and the reason Brid is attractive to retirees. But the town does have *horizontal* scale, and I recalled one early testament to it as I stood looking out to sea.

In September 1839, Charlotte Brontë, aged twenty-three, made her first trip to the coast; her whole life up to then had been spent in the West Riding. She had been staying at Easton, near Bridlington, with her old schoolfriend, Ellen Nussey, whom she had met at Roe Head School in Mirfield, and whose brother, Henry, a curate at the Wolds village of Burton Agnes (whose rector was Charles Henry Lutwidge, uncle of Lewis Carroll), had proposed to Charlotte earlier in the year.

On the day Charlotte and Ellen took a coach to Bridlington, Charlotte was without her glasses, which she had lost at Easton, so she did not see the sea properly until she was right on the quayside. I own a pamphlet that describes what happened next. *Charlotte Brontë on the East Yorkshire Coast* is attributed (in slightly ghostly fashion) to 'the late F. R. Pearson BA, formerly senior history master at Bridlington School'. 'When she caught sight of the magnificent bay', he writes,

> bounded on the one side by the white cliffs of Flamborough, and on the other by the wasting, sandy shores of Holderness, Charlotte found it impossible to control her emotion. Begging her friend to leave her alone for a while, she was discovered some time later, her eyes red with weeping and her hands trembling – so intense was the effect upon her sensitive spirit of that

element which she had never seen before but of which she had dreamt so long and ardently.

'Even a year afterwards', Pearson continues,

when the wind is whistling round the dark stone walls of Haworth Parsonage, it only serves to awaken once again within her mind that first and unforgettable impression of the sea. 'From what quarter the wind blows I cannot tell, for I never could in my life,' she writes, 'but I should very much like to know how the great brewing-tub of Bridlington Bay works, and what sort of yeasty froth rises just now on the waves.'

'Would *Jane Eyre*, *Shirley* and *Villette* have had different settings,' wonders Harry J. Scott in *Portrait of Yorkshire*, 'or, indeed, have appeared at all if Charlotte had married Henry and moved from Haworth to the east coast?'

The posh end of Bridlington was the North Side, if only because the South Side was largely undeveloped until the building of the Spa in 1896. On the North Side, a funfair now squats on the Princes Parade, so it's as though the authorities had been trying to make the scales balance. The Floral Pavilion survives as a place of various entertainments but has been smothered by 1960s extensions. It now includes a 'Continental Café' and a 'Pirates of Penzance Shooting Gallery'. I find the Bridlington North Side a bit tonally 'off'. For example, speed boats can be hired 'for weddings, ashes scattering and any type of party'. The truly posh part of Bridlington is the Old Town, which lies a mile inland and is separated from what used to be described as Burlington Quay by the Scarborough–Hull railway line. The Old Town, which grew up around the Augustinian Priory, is really just a lovely Georgian street, quaint enough to have been used as the main street in the recent *Dad's Army* film. It has many old curiosity shops, the Old Globe Inn, the Black Lion (formerly a music hall, in the days when music halls *were* pubs) and a former convent called the Scriptorium.

At both ends of the street are little road signs indicating 'Yorkshire Wolds', as though by way of inviting the right kind of motorists, certainly not drivers of four-by-fours, to sample those scenic delights. The Wolds are Bridlington's backyard: villages with ponds and somnolent market towns, all within a crescent of lowish chalk hills that touch the sea at Flamborough Head and stretch down to the Humber. It is as though someone has thrown a protective arm around the old East Riding. Until 2015 David Hockney had a house in Bridlington – a surprisingly unartistic suburban one – formerly owned by his mother. He was in Brid because of the Wolds, where he had worked as a boy, stoking corn, and which he liked to paint, or to depict by some process I don't understand on an iPad, or to record, perhaps with nine video cameras strapped to the side of a Jeep, to make installations. A *Times* leader of 29 October 2013 elided Bridlington and the Wolds:

> The David Hockney show at the Royal Academy revealed that the great man of Bradford had to go away to appreciate the glory of what he had left behind. In his later work, the shadows of East Yorkshire's glacial valleys are suddenly radiated with light. It is as if Hockney had to go to California to understand the majesty of Bridlington.

In the catalogue to his exhibition of 2012, Hockney entertainingly described his set-up in Bridlington.

The large studio, he wrote, is organised by Jean-Pierre Goncalves de Lima, 'the only Parisian living in Bridlington', while Hockney's computer expert, Jonathan Wilkinson, lives in Bridlington on weekdays, but returns to Harrogate ('the Baden-Baden of the north of England') at weekends.

His Wolds paintings have hallucinogenic colours – trees might be purple or blue – and they are joyful despite being devoid of people, or perhaps for that very reason. I've seen the Wolds mainly from a car, and they always look lonely to me. You're travelling over hills and through farmland, so this is not a space claimed by cagouled, yomping folk. It's enjoyable to drive through the Wolds because of the sinewy roads – and if you don't feel obliged to stop, since the Wolds, unlike the Dales and the Moors, is not a National Park. It is the forgotten landscape of Yorkshire, and my edition of the *Rough Guide to England* makes no mention of it. According to Fleur and Colin Speakman, authors of *The Yorkshire Wolds: a Journey of Discovery*, one of the few books devoted exclusively to the Wolds, 'The landscape of rolling chalk hills, dry grassy valleys, scattered woodland, dramatic coastline and ancient tracks has been described as a little bit of southern England in the North, as its character has much in common with the Wiltshire or South Downs.'

When it does feature in books, it is described as 'timeless', 'peaceful', 'old world'. I do associate a mood of regret with the Wolds. My stepmother lived in the Wolds village of Saxton, early in her first marriage. She loved it there, and when she married my father she spent years trying to persuade him to move from York to the Wolds, but he had a different sort of Yorkshire romanticism, that could be satisfied by regular visits to the racecourses of the county. When I was writing this book, my stepmother urged me to drive from York to the coast via the Wolds, using the A166 to Driffield rather than the more northerly A64, and she drew a map for me, with points of interest along the way.

The Wolds featured disproportionately in a book I wrote about British ghosts. There is the deserted medieval village of Wharram Percy; the memorial to the seven crew of the Halifax bomber that crashed on Garrowby Hill in 1944; the apparently very haunted Elizabethan mansion, Burton Agnes Hall, near Driffield, or the Iron Age chariot burial at Wetwang Slack. (The elegant Wolds villages have lovely old Norse Old English names like Thwing, Foxholes, Octon, Thixendale.) Here is the entry from my book, *Ghoul Britannia*, about Burton Agnes Hall:

This was built for three aristocratic sisters called Griffith, who observed the completion of their fine Jacobean mansion from premises over the road. When the house was nearly finished, in about 1628, Anne Griffith was attacked by robbers. As she lay dying, she insisted her head be kept at all times within the new house – a morbid wish commonly accounted for by her death delirium, and one ignored by her family, who buried her body, including the head, outside the house. Cue much banging of doors and unprovoked rearing of horses etc. The head – now a skull – was detached from the body and placed inside the house. It is, perhaps, walled up behind a panel in one of the bedrooms. The owners know, but will not say, or at least they say they do. Even so, the ghost of Anne Griffith – fawn in colour – still walks the house, along with many tourists, since Burton Agnes Hall is open to the public. Besides the house, there's a gift shop and garden shop, an ice cream parlour and a children's playground with guinea pigs.

My mother's family were oriented east, and she had an aunt called Nora, who lived on a farm near Wetwang with her husband, Ernest. Nora chain-smoked, apparently with impunity, because she lived to a good age, and left me £6,000 when she died. But all the time I knew him, Ernest sat wheezing in a kitchen chair from emphysema – something to do with breathing in corn dust – so Nora ran the farm along with a couple of young blokes from Wetwang. That kitchen had a stone floor, with a couple of greasy sheepskins on it. There was a parrot in a cage that would bite you if you put your finger through the bars. It would address you with a Yorkshire severity, saying things like 'Simmer down, now.' Once or twice when my mother was dying, I stayed overnight in the farmhouse. The beds were very high, and the floors were stone, albeit with the sheepskins on them. Only one room in the house had a fitted carpet, along with soft furnishings and ornaments on the mantlepiece, but that room was never used, and might have belonged to a different house. When I visited Wetwang, it always did seem to be wet – grey and rain-ing – but the barn, where I spent a lot of time leaping from high to low hay bales and which sometimes accommodated cows, was always very hot, as a result of too much nature imprisoned indoors.

Despite Hockney's patronage, Bridlington, according to another *Times* article (a property piece of 23 October 2020 by Jayne Dowle), 'awaits its moment in the sun ... Average sold house prices here are just £146,256 compared with £197,348 in the second-home capital of picturesque Whitby, a mere 30-odd miles up the coast.' In lockdown, I kept reading about the desirability of Whitby. In June 2020, it attracted more property searches than any other coastal town, and property prices had already risen by 5 per cent in the previous year. I learned this from the *Evening Standard*, so here were Londoners being invited to fantasise about a move to Yorkshire. Of course, the word 'quaint' came up.

Whitby is quaint. It looks good on those hand-drawn illustrated maps, with all that great wash of green to the right, and even more blue to the left. The tall, narrow houses are shown clustered on their cliff like a quiver full of arrows, surmounted by the gaunt ruined Abbey, trademark of the town. On those sorts of maps, there is usually a big, elaborately decorated 'North' arrow somewhere in the sea, and Whitby has always had its mind on points further north than Yorkshire. The hunting grounds of the Whitby whalers were towards the Arctic Circle. William Scoresby, whaler of the town (and scientist and later clergyman of Bradford), published his *Journal of a Voyage to Greenland* in 1822. Scoresby's father invented the crow's nest, and Whitby does seem high-minded and far-seeing. 'Whitby had a stronger sense of companionship with places like Edinburgh, Newcastle and London than it did with York or the West Riding,' writes Richard Morris in *Yorkshire: A Lyrical History of England's Greatest County*. 'The wide moorland plateau at its back could not be crossed at speed.' And when you *have* crossed it, Whitby is not particularly pleased to see you: it is looking the other way, out to sea. In the past it might have been waiting to greet smugglers, or celebrate the return of whalers or fishermen, or watching the departure of a fledgling collier, built in the town and going off to carry coals from Newcastle to London.

The leisure craft and more localised fishing boats that come and go from the harbour today do not require such an intense gaze. Whitby is primarily a tourist town, but it is still sea-facing, and the chirruping gizmos in the four amusement arcades on the harbour seem marginal to its true concerns.

Whitby is a no-nonsense place – the whale jawbone arch on the West Cliff says so, as do the memorials to lost fishermen in St Mary's Church – and it commands respect in the county. I have never heard a word of criticism of Whitby from any Yorkshire person; I have always wanted to live there. I once cut out from a national newspaper an advertisement for a property on the West Cliff. It showed a big Georgian house, one of those formerly owned by a ship's captain with a flagpole in the garden, the garden facing inland, towards serene Pannett Park, where the premises of Whitby Museum – offspring of the Whitby Literary and Philosophical Society (the *brain* of Whitby) – are located. About a week later, a friend of mine from university days sent me the same cutting with a note: 'I bet you'd like to live here.'

Whitby has been promoted as quaint for well over a hundred years. A booklet published in 1904 by the North Eastern Railway, *The Yorkshire Coast: Its Advantages and Attractions*, speaks of the town's 'ancient and picturesque character'. The focus of the quaintness was the Old Town on the East Cliff, with its narrow streets and higgledy-piggledy houses ascending towards the Abbey. George Hudson, the Railway King, was involved in the development of the West Cliff – with its East Crescent, Royal Crescent, Esplanade – as a sort of amphitheatre, from which the new, prosperous railway-borne travellers might view the East Cliff, with the harbour below and the Abbey above forming salutary sights.

I suspect most people subconsciously see the Abbey as a giant tombstone, while the masts and spars of any sailing ships berthed in the harbour still seem like thin crucifixes, especially when Whitby is shrouded in a sea mist or other Atkinson Grimshaw-like effects. The quaintness of Whitby – which is a dark quaintness – has not always been as highly prized as you would think. Under the heading 'How Things have Changed', the Summer 1993 edition of the *Yorkshire Journal* ran a photograph, taken in 1957, of Tin Ghaut, an alleyway dating from 1426, and leading down to the sea from Grape Lane in the Old Town. 'It was quite usual to see one or more artists at work in this alley with its natural composition of old walls and flags leading to the tiled cottage in the centre with its overhang, and, beyond, a framed view of the upper harbour.' Below this was a photograph taken of the same spot in 1993. It shows a car park – a 'utilitarian' car park, as the *Journal* has it, as if there is any other kind.

You're liable to notice utilitarian things, letting the side down, in such a romantic place as Whitby. Michel Faber's novella, *The Hundred and Ninety-Nine Steps* (a reference to the ascent from Old Town to Abbey) compares the ascetic life of the medieval monastery with the more quotidian modern day. 'What was it doing here,' asks the central character, observing the car park by the Abbey ruin, 'littering a sacred space with automotive junk?' In A. S. Byatt's novel *Possession* (1990), two modern-day academics visit Whitby on the trail of a Victorian poet they are investigating. Whereas the poet had noted the Abbey soaring over 'a moving sphere of masts and smoking chimneys', the academics observe 'general signs of unemployment and purposelessness'. *Possession* was written at a low period for Whitby. But the book's success, and the inclusion of Whitby scenes in the TV drama *Heartbeat* (Whitby became commodified as part of '*Heartbeat* Country') helped make the town fashionable again. The connection to the North York

Moors Railway has also been highly beneficial. Whitby remains basically working–class, but with a gilding of glamour, hence the high house prices. 'Whenever we see another colour supplement article about Whitby', one resident told me, 'we go, "Oh, no!"' Then again, another local told me he had sold his house in the centre of town for a good price to a purchaser who wanted it as a second home. He had then moved to the outskirts of town, a more practical place to live: 'Central Whitby isn't much good for anything except walking around with a bag of chips in your hand.'

Michel Faber and A. S. Byatt join a long list of writers associated with Whitby. *Whitby Writers* by Marion Keighley (1954) lists about 400, one of whom is Leo Walmsley. He wrote a couple of non–fiction books about Whitby but is best known for his trilogy of novels set in the imaginary fishing village of Bramblewick, which is really Robin Hood's Bay, where he had grown up. The inscription to one of them, *Three Fevers*, reads, 'If you're born to be drowned, worrying about it won't help.' The book was filmed in 1935 as *The Turn of the Tide*. It tells the story of a pair of lovers who (as in *Romeo and Juliet*) belong to rival families, and these are fishing families whose professional practices are shown in detail – for instance, the cutting of hazel twigs to make lobster pots. Graham Greene called the film (the first produced by J. Arthur Rank) 'unpretentious and truthful'. It was shot – in moonlit black–and–white – in Robin Hood's Bay and Whitby. Both places look too close to the sea.

Robin Hood's Bay manages to retain a gritty image even though its fishing industry was displaced by tourism before the Second World War (it didn't help that it has no harbour), and most of its houses are second homes. In his book of 1906, *Yorkshire Dales and Fells*, Gordon Home

wrote that in the town 'one is obliged to walk warily
during the painter's season ... for fear of obstructing the
view of the man behind the easel you have just passed.'
In the equally quaint fishing village of Staithes (ten miles
north of Whitby), he wrote, fishermen would demand 'an
afternoon's baccy' in return for sitting for a photograph,
and I bet it would have taken more than that for them to
smile at the camera.

From Whitby, I usually walk along the West Cliff beach
to the small town of Sandsend, which perhaps would have
been less small if the clifftop railway serving it hadn't been
closed in the 1950s. Its beach is depicted on the cover of
a beautifully illustrated booklet produced by the North
Eastern Railway in 1914: *Alice in Holidayland,* 'a parody in
prose, verse and pictures', in which Alice travels along the
Yorkshire coast in magical circumstances. On the cover,
the Walrus and the Carpenter are shown looking cheerful
(which they never are in Carroll's poem), and the caption
reads, 'They cheered like anything to see such quantities of sand,' whereas in the original book they 'wept'
like anything.

Perhaps the makers of the booklet were aware of Lewis
Carroll's association with Whitby. He visited the town in
1854 with a reading party from Oxford University. He
would apparently sit on a low rock on West Cliff beach and
tell stories to the children of strangers, which wouldn't be
allowed today, especially in his case.

The best-known literary evocation of Whitby is by Bram
Stoker in *Dracula.* Chapters Six to Eight are set in Whitby,
and they're the only readable ones, if you ask me. The
Count, having sailed from Transylvania, comes ashore in
the form of a dog, loping up to the Abbey Church from a
shipwreck on Tate Hill Beach. Consider the impossibility

of the Count landing at Scarborough or Blackpool. The section presaging his arrival suggests the dual nature of Whitby: a tourist town, but never wholly jolly: 'Shortly before ten o'clock the stillness of the air grew quite oppressive . . . the band on the pier, with its lively French air, was like a discord in the great harmony of nature's silence.'

Stoker never went to Transylvania, but he did go to Whitby on holiday, staying at Mrs Veazey's guest house, at 6 Royal Crescent, in July 1890. In Whitby subscription library, he discovered *An Account of the Princes of Wallachia and Moldavia* (1820) by William Wilkinson, which refers, on page 19, to a historical Romanian ruler called Dracula, and I think this fortuitous moment should be cited in all promotions of public libraries. ('You never know what, or who, you will find in a library.') Stoker recorded the shelf mark, 0.1097, but the book itself has been lost. However, the London Library (a private library, of which I'm a member) has a copy. In an article for the Library's website, Philip Spedding reports that 'The corner of page 18, directly opposite the all-important Dracula reference, has been turned down.' It seems likely that the vandal in question was Bram Stoker himself, who was a member of the London Library. 'Did Stoker come back to the book when he returned to London from Whitby?' Spedding wonders. 'Did he turn the page down as a reminder to himself of his interest in the name? Was it another reader noting the similarity, or just someone marking a page?'

Stoker researched his Whitby scenes by ingratiating himself with fishermen of the town. They liked to relax by smoking their pipes in the graveyard of St Mary's Church, which lies in the shadow of the Abbey, compounding the morbidity of the East Cliff. Stoker would stroll up there to extract their best Whitby tales, so he really got his money's worth out of Whitby, but then he returned the favour, making the town famous, and bringing all those Goths in his wake. (And anyhow, *all* novelists are vampiric if not actually vampires. I myself once researched a novel in Whitby, interrogating a dozen locals, and asking a fisherman in an Old Town pub – the most authentically 'grizzled' person I have ever met – how he would get rid of a body in the sea off Whitby. He replied with alarming fluency: 'Steal a herring boat off Tate Hill beach, wait till late at night, slip through t' gap in t' harbour wall . . .')

In *Dracula*, Mina Murray has a fleeting glimpse of the monstrous Count ('something dark') on the East Cliff as a narrow band of moonlight, 'as sharp as a sword cut', swoops over the Abbey.

For years, the Abbey was the top English Heritage attraction in Yorkshire, but in 2019 the 'visitor offer' was improved, with the aim of nudging it into the national top five, along with Stonehenge, Osborne House, Dover Castle and Tintagel. The main project was the refurbishment of the Visitor Centre, located in a seventeenth-century mansion that, in my boyhood, was a gap-toothed ruin itself, adding to the generally haunted air of the headland. I seem to remember smoking a cigarette on the grass next to the Abbey ruin while looking down on the town late one night, as though the Abbey were as casually accessible to me as it had been to some grazing cows in a famous photograph by that chronicler of Victorian Whitby, Frank Meadow Sutcliffe. But this must be a false memory; the ruin has long been walled off. (It's possible I climbed over the wall, though.)

As remodelled, the Visitor Centre gives visitors 'a sense of this depth of history on the headland'. They will have no excuse for not knowing that the current ruin is of the third monastery to have been built on the headland.

The first was founded in the seventh century by the King of Northumbria, Oswiu, who appointed Lady Hild (St Hilda) as abbess. This monastery – the focal point of Christianity in Northumbria and home to the poet Caedmon (the first of those 'Whitby writers') – was laid waste by Viking invaders. In the early twelfth century, a Romanesque Benedictine monastery arose from those ruins, and a century later its church was rebuilt along fashionable Gothic lines. After the Dissolution of the Monasteries, the whole Abbey site was acquired by the up-and-coming Cholmley family. They demolished the monastery buildings, but the shell of the church was allowed to remain, perhaps as a navigational aid to seafarers.

In 1670, the Cholmleys built the mansion, and the ruined Abbey church was a kind of folly in their garden. By the early nineteenth century, Whitby was becoming a magnet for genteel tourists attracted by geology (fossil hunting or Whitby jet), and the relatively new and romantic notion of the 'picturesque'. The word might have been invented for the Abbey ruin, which would have been slightly less appealing to the romantic taste had not the stolid central tower obligingly fallen down one summer's day in 1830.

The new Visitor Centre is atmospherically lit, with a backdrop formed by gently glowing friezes of the 'ten key characters' associated with the site. One is Bram Stoker. The ruin gives Whitby its tone, which is a tone of darkness. It's there in the memories of whaling, almost as dangerous to the whalers as the whales; in the literal blackness of the coal once carried by the Whitby colliers, or in the blackness of the jet, which is found in nearby seams of shale. In the 1870s, jet jewellery (frequently worn at funerals) began to be produced on an industrial scale in Whitby.

Jet is a variant of coal, and I think of it as holiday coal, it being a standard purchase by visitors to the town, including the Goths, whose first Whitby festival occurred in 1994. (There are now two, in April and October.) It occurs to me that the Goths, decked out in their subfusc and jet, do what the equally dandified Victorian visitors to the Yorkshire seaside used to do: they promenade.

An Inland Resort: Harrogate

Like York, Harrogate has a Bettys tea rooms (actually two of them) and an expanse of greenery at its heart – a Stray – to mitigate any sense of urban intensity. Also like York, it has elegant Georgian architecture (*Bridgerton* could have been filmed in Harrogate) and that daintiest of industries: sweet-making, although Harrogate's was never on the scale of York's. In fact, Harrogate makes York look like proper Yorkshire. It is prosperous and contented, with none of the melancholic undertow caused by involvement in heavy industry.

What put Harrogate on the map was water. From 1596, when a Captain William Slingsby discovered a chalybeate spring on the heath that became the Stray, to the Second World War, Harrogate became an inland spa. The above-mentioned snooty chronicler of Northern spas, A. B. Granville, visited the town for his book of 1841. 'Harrogate has the very air of a watering place,' he writes. But it was important to go at the right time. A friend of Granville's who lived in Harrogate warned him that in July the place was full of 'clothiers from Leeds, and cutlers from Sheffield, besides all the red noses and faces in England collected together'. The people of 'gentle blood' came at the end of July, and stayed until 'Doncaster races', which I think means the St Leger in September. Harrogate was still flourishing as a spa in the 1930s, when Ella Pontefract and Maria Hartley visited: 'It was prophesied that it would never compete with Scarborough as a spa, yet Scarborough has one little kiosk to compare with the vast amenities here.'

Harrogate's famous confection, Farrah's Toffee, was developed to take away the foul taste of the sulphurous if supposedly beneficial waters. Talk about having your cake and eating it. Farrah's also used to make sweets called Fairy Cushions, and that, combined with the fact that Dunlopillo mattresses used to be made in the town, has always made me think of Harrogate as a place of soft landings. If you do well in Leeds or Bradford, you might well end up in Harrogate, which is only fifteen miles from the one, and nineteen from the other.

I have written half a dozen articles about Harrogate; it's usually just a matter of rounding up some of the recent accolades. In any given year, Harrogate will have won a best-place-to-live competition or a Britain in Bloom or received some strikingly good review. In the lockdown year of 2020, *The Times* reported that a panel of experts had voted it 'best place to work from home', judging by criteria including broadband speed, availability of green space, clean air, quality of local schools. At the time of writing (July 2021) the *Tatler* has just called it 'the Belgravia of North Yorkshire'. The magazine was particularly impressed that the Cork Street gallery Messums has set up there, and apparently 'Lady Georgina Anderson (better known as Lady G), a Cordon Bleu-trained chef and the daughter of the Marquess of Downshire, will cater for your dinner parties,' although how you get hold of her, the article didn't say.

The journalist's task is made easier still by the way that everyone in Harrogate seems to be in love with the place. For a piece that appeared in the *Daily Telegraph* on 21 July 2007, a taxi driver gave me a free tour of the best outlying streets, including Fulwith Mill Lane, which is the most expensive street in Yorkshire, and reminded me of Beverly Hills. (And I have *been* to Beverly Hills, incidentally.) The driver also showed me Duchy Road and Kent Road, where every house is a mansion. He mentioned several footballers who lived nearby, including David O'Leary and Jimmy Floyd Hasselbaink. (Today, Gareth Southgate lives in a Grade 1-listed manor house near Harrogate.) We drove past the frontage of Harrogate Ladies College, which took a while, and from which hung a banner reading, 'Congratulations Everyone, We Are a Top 12 School'. I tried on the driver the one consistent criticism I'd heard of Harrogate: that the traffic was bad. 'Not as bad as York, where you're from,' he said. ('York is seen as smart but partly industrial,' a Harrogate estate agent once told me, 'whereas Harrogate represents moneyed leisure.')

Here are three things that people who live in Harrogate have told me about Harrogate. 'We don't *have* litter or dog fouling.' 'I used to live in Kent; in Kent, people scurry, whereas in Harrogate, they stroll.' 'The crime rate is so low, I have to remind myself to lock the door when I go out.' And here are three things I saw in Harrogate in 2020: a man with a baby in a sling waiting to use the baby change facility in the gents at Waitrose, which was being used by another father; a man cleaning a grille in the railway station with a pink duster of the Ken Dodd 'tickling stick' variety; plastic flowers in the bus station.

In Harrogate, hydrotherapy has faded (except for the palatial Turkish Baths), although the sandstone rotunda of the Royal Pump Room is still the fulcrum around which the elegant wheel revolves, and the Royal Baths still looks magnificent even if it is now a Chinese restaurant. By the 1960s or so, the town had wanted rid of the valetudinarian image. The treatments of the town – galvanic paths, violent massages – are sinisterly depicted in the film, *Agatha*, in which Vanessa Redgrave stars as Agatha Christie. In 1926, Christie had a sort of nervous breakdown, on learning that her husband intended to leave her. She 'disappeared' for eleven days, most of which she spent in Harrogate, staying at the hotel still known at the time as the Harrogate Hydro, but which had recently changed its name to the Old Swan. Despite a huge police womanhunt, Christie lived openly in Harrogate, and Laura Thompson's stylish biography of her, *Agatha Christie, an English Mystery,* has interesting speculations about her state of mind during this episode. Why did she choose Harrogate? Well, Christie was born into a wealthy, upper-middle-class family in Torquay and, according to Thompson, 'Harrogate was the Torquay of the north. It was where "people like us" went; even when they disappeared.'

Another form of sociability has superseded hydrotherapy, in that Harrogate is a leading conference and convention centre, a role it has taken over from Scarborough, just as it superseded Scarborough as a spa. The result is that now, as in the days of hydrotherapy, Harrogate is full of people who are not from Yorkshire.

Because of the need to accommodate all those hypochondriacs, and the conventioneers of today, Harrogate is a town full of hotels. (And the annual Harrogate Crime Writing Festival occurs in the Old Swan precisely because Christie stayed there, although the authors attending that event are doing the opposite of trying to disappear.)[*]

---

[*] If readers detect a jaundiced tone, it's because I have never been invited to this event in thirty years of writing crime fiction, most of it set in Yorkshire.

On my regular visits, I like to stay at the Hotel du Vin, whose rooms have names. My wife and I once stayed in a room called Peter Lehmann. 'I think he's a literary agent,' my wife suggested, and that wasn't inconceivable in the context of Harrogate, but in fact, he was a leading wine maker. The Hotel du Vin has what it describes as 'serious' showers; there's a full-sized purple snooker table off the lobby and a walk-in humidor. When it was legal to smoke in public buildings, I used to buy a Havana and take it to the oldest pub in town, Hale's Bar, where I would light up from one of the gas jets burning on the bar.

In 1988, Alan Bennett wrote and narrated a TV documentary, *Dinner at Noon*, about what is possibly Harrogate's poshest hotel, and certainly its most refined, the Crown. The film is reminiscent of John Betjeman's documentary of fifteen years before, *Metroland*, because here is this apparent teddy bear being sarcastic at the expense of the excessively genteel. Having noted that the chamber maid has pleated the end of the toilet roll in his room, he says, 'It's a good job they didn't do this when I was a child or I'd have imagined this was standard practice throughout the land, our family's toilet roll unique in its ragged and inconsequent termination.' Everybody in the Crown seems to be performing an Alan Bennett script, saying things like, 'Have you had a slice?' and declining another chocolate: 'That's a record for me already.' He observes Mrs Baker and Miss Wood taking tea.

I like Mrs Baker and Miss Wood – and I don't think of them as old people. Just as Paris is geared to thirty-five-year-old career women, so is the North to women like these. In London, they'd be displaced and fearful; here, accomplished pianists and stylish ballroom dancers, they still help rule the roost.

He observes a function held in the Brontë Room. 'There must be Brontë rooms all over Yorkshire – venues for discos and parades of beachwear, demonstrations of firefighting equipment and new lines in toiletries, all brought under the grim umbrella of those three ailing and unconvivial sisters.'

That there should be a Brontë Room in the Crown suggests that Harrogate is proud of its Yorkshireness. Harrogate is in the very centre of the county, after all, and it is the home of Yorkshire Tea (a brand of Bettys and Taylors Group Limited, who also own the tea rooms), and the Farrah's range includes boiled sweets called Yorkshire Mixture. It's touching that Harrogate should want to align itself with a county that it has, in a way, transcended, like those multi-millionaires who still insist they are working class.

EDGELANDS

EDGELANDS

Larkinland: Hull

Yorkshire is proud of being 'the Broad Acres', but the size of the county means that some of its settlements are far flung, and so the notion of Yorkshireness is stretched. I want to consider three places – two cities and a town – located on the edges of the county, to the east, south and north. Anyone visiting these places from London would be strongly aware of their Yorkshire qualities, but they are Yorkshire in different ways, and to some extent their geographical marginality brings into question their allegiance to the county.

We begin in Hull, in 1971.

I was nine years old and my mother was very ill, so my sister and I were sent to stay with our uncle and aunt, who lived just outside Hull. My mother was dying, which I never guessed at the time, but I knew things were going out of control at home, and now I had come to the very edge of Yorkshire. Whatever happened next was likely to be dramatic.

I remember going on a shopping expedition to Hull, late one dark afternoon with my aunt, who was pushing her own young son in a pushchair. As we approached what I now know to be Whitefriargate, we passed a dock. The water was black, and the wind seemed to be picking up parts of it and flinging them towards us. It amazed me that my nephew remained asleep in the pushchair, and I remember shouting (I had to shout against the wind), 'Will he be all right?' as my aunt and I walked fast, with heads down and collars up, towards Hull Marks & Spencer's, whose parapet was decorated with stone waves and a ship's prow. I remember the sense of entering a sudden haven: the warmth, light and cosiness of the interior of that most consoling of shops.

The dock we passed was Prince's Dock, and I do not remember there being any ships in it. My memory is of bleakness, and photographs of Prince's Dock from the time show only floating rubbish on water overlooked by a giant, rotting warehouse. Hull, like my mother, was becoming ill at the time, and after my mother died, Hull also died a kind of death with the loss of much of its fishing industry. In subsequent years, I equated Hull with depression. The very word Hull – a glum monosyllable it is impossible to pronounce cheerfully – suggested a bad end, although it is actually the name of the river on which the city stands. Edward I, having taken a liking to what was then the hamlet called Wyke (which he discovered while chasing a hare), christened the place Kingston upon Hull, and I bet the city authorities have often contemplated banishing those last two words in favour of the grandiose and regal one.

I was aware from geography lessons that the Humber, the wide estuary on whose north bank the city sits, was that not very glamorous thing: a drain. I knew Philip Larkin was living there, and he himself was a byword for gloom. He seemed professionally connected to Hull in the way undertakers are professionally connected to dead bodies. In about 1998, I returned to Hull – to give a talk at the Carnegie Library (now the Carnegie Heritage Centre) in West Park to some of my readers. Well, that was the idea. In fact, the only people present were the three organisers of the event and myself. The organisers diplomatically blamed the weather, it being another black day of wind and rain. In 2013, *The Idler Book of Crap Towns: The Fifty Worst Places to Live in the UK* was published: 'The fifty towns we've selected for this book are the places that have been nominated the most often by the public on the website and made us laugh the most.' Hull stands at number one in the book; the ribaldry gets underway with sentences like, 'Unemployment rates are high, as are crime and addiction levels.' By many indices, in the first decade of the twenty-first century Hull was the poorest city in UK, and when I returned to Hull in September 2020 I was braced for depression.

But this time, everything was different, especially the weather. The city has a flickering beauty that comes and goes with the sun, and is more evident the nearer you are to the sea. Prince's Dock had become Princes Quay; the water was glittering; the rotting warehouse had been replaced by a conservatory-like shopping centre.

The streets of the Old Town looked new as well as old, with their well-scrubbed red bricks and pristine cobbles. The buckled pink and white mansions of the Museums Quarter are among the jewels in Hull's crown. A lot of heavy treasure chests must have been humped in and out of those handsome doorways. Museums aside – and the principal one is Wilberforce House, birthplace of the leading anti-slaver, William Wilberforce – the residents are suitably patrician: architects, ship's chandlers, solicitors.

There is a continuation of quaintness as the Old Town becomes the Fruit Market, which is Hull's cultural quarter, a sector boosted by Hull's stint as City of Culture in 2017:

'Whether it's new businesses popping up, exciting art and events coming to town or thrilling developments in the local tech community, there's much to talk about.' The food and drink is equally artistic, and there is still fruit in the Fruit Dock, albeit mainly in the form of lemon slices in botanical gin. Nearby are what used to be Railway Dock and Humber Dock; they are now jointly Hull Marina, which has a holiday aspect on any decent day – a complete change of mood from the 1880s, when Atkinson Grimshaw depicted Humber Dock one rainy evening, with the twin domes of the Dock Office (now the Maritime Museum) in the background. The mood in that painting is one of melancholic tiredness at the end of a long working day. A man emerging from dockside building is in the act of raising his umbrella. You feel he has a long trudge home ahead of him. A couple of loaded wagons are rolling away, fading into the gloom.

These two small inner docks were closed in the late 1960s. Containerisation required rangier outlying spaces and didn't require the dockers. Activity at, say, Alexandra Dock, where Siemens created a service hub for North Sea wind farms in 2016, seems to be conducted discreetly. My reading had assured me prior to my visit that Hull remains an important port for the trading and servicing of goods, but I had to take that on trust. Until the mid-1970s you knew where you were with Hull. You were in a city of dockers and fishermen, especially the latter. Whereas York had a chocolatey aroma, Hull stank of fish. J. B. Priestley celebrated the fishiness of 1930s Hull in *English Journey*. 'Most of us still think of Grimsby as pre-eminently the fishy place, but now Hull beats Grimsby – for sheer quantity if not for quality.'

He visited Hull over a couple of days of heavy, sleeting

rain and during the Depression, but 'It has not the usual down-and-out look, nor any suggestion of stagnation in the docks. Something of the outward character of the Scandinavian and Baltic countries with which it trades has crept into the appearance of Hull. It has a cleanish, red-brick look.' And he found in Hull none of the 'terrifying murk' of London and Liverpool docks.

'By 1955, the tide had gone out,' writes Roy Hattersley, who attended Hull University in the early 1950s, in *Goodbye to Yorkshire*, and no doubt this perception influenced his notion of the Yorkshire coast hierarchy, with Hull at the bottom both geographically and socially. What happened between Priestley and Hattersley was the war, in which Hull was the most heavily blitzed city after London, but at least the bombs dropped on London were meant for London. In the case of Hull, insult was added to injury by the fact that some of the bombs were dropped by way of afterthought from German planes getting rid of surplus on their way home from bombing Liverpool. (And Bridlington suffered an even more demeaning fate, in that it got the bombs left over after Hull.)

'In 1951,' writes Hattersley, 'when I stepped out of Paragon Station, there were still great gaping holes in what had been the town centre. They were filled, during the next ten years, by a strange combination of concrete and a revival of the Regency classical revival.' Hattersley's recollection of Hull seems rather jaundiced. The notorious post-war 'planners' never really got their hands on it, and Hull still stank healthily of fish in the 1950s. It was the net effect of another conflict that would bring the fatal purgation: the Cod Wars. We will be coming back to Hull fishing, or the memory of it.

After the Old Town, I walked to Paragon Station, which

was looking pristine, living up to its boastful name. On the concourse is a statue of Philip Larkin, who came to Hull in 1955 to take up the post of Hull University Librarian. The statue shows him looking rather balletic and windswept. Inscribed at his feet is the typically downbeat first line of 'The Whitsun Weddings' ('That Whitsun I was late getting away'). Next door to the station is the Royal Hull Hotel and, as I approached it, I was entering Larkinland, a term that will be explained. A plaque outside the hotel announced itself as being part of the 'Larkin Trail', since Larkin was a regular at the hotel: he often 'lunched in the Brigantine Room'. In his poem 'Friday Night at the Royal Station Hotel', the salesmen have all returned to Leeds, suggesting that Hull is a workaday place and no venue for fun, and the last four words compound that notion, by evoking the empty hinterland of Hull: 'Waves fold behind villages.'

I was curious to see inside a Larkin haunt. A sign on the wall read, 'Boozy Afternoon Tea, £23.00. Tea with a tipsy twist', but this jollity seemed contradicted by heavy net curtains at the windows and apparently locked doors. Was this Covid-related? We were in lockdown-lite; hotels were still open. I had checked into one myself that morning. I indignantly knocked on one of the doors that ought to have given access to the lobby. A security guard opened the door a crack. 'You can't come in; it's closed.'

'Why?'

He shook his head and closed the door.

At the adjacent taxi rank, I asked a driver what was going on, and he gave a twisted grin. 'It closed when Covid first hit,' he said, 'and it's never properly re-opened. Now it's a Home Office hostel for illegal immigrants. Well, the council calls them asylum seekers, but it's pissed off with the Home Office for putting them in such a prime spot.'

Hull prides itself on having long been a 'city of sanctuary' for refugees. But let us revisit that piece about the North–South divide by the *Times* columnist Robert Crampton who grew up in Hull. Alongside the 'London versus the rest of the country divide', he wrote, there was also 'The east-west divide as revealed in the Brexit referendum – the nearer you lived to continental Europe, the further away you wished it was.'

Would Larkin have called the people in the hotel illegal immigrants or asylum seekers? Discussion of his moral character keeps him – and Hull – in the literary pages. The evidence about Larkin, as mustered in Andrew Motion's biography, can be used to depict a racist and sexist boor, a man apparently conforming to the unacceptable face of traditional Yorkshire bigotry (even though he came from Coventry), or you can discover a sunnier personality. Larkin's colleague and lover, Maeve Brennan, is quoted by Motion as describing 'a staid figure who appeared at Senate and Faculty boards wearing a dark suit, with a pocket watch ... which he consulted frequently and in doing so conferred on himself a gravity that could not be questioned'. But her impressions began to change when she glimpsed him in town wearing 'a bow tie and a highly coloured shirt' and discovered his 'devastating gift for mimicry'.

A friend of mine came from London to attend Hull University in the mid-1980s. She loved the city – but not Larkin. 'Anyone who used the library saw Larkin all the time, but we'd all been told not to approach him.' Aspirant poets in particular were warned off, but then again Larkin had, in 1982, written the foreword to *A Rumoured City: New Poets from Hull*, a volume that perpetuated the poetic reputation of the city – a reputation extending back to Andrew Marvell. When he was a student at Hull, the pop maverick

Genesis P. Orridge won a poetry competition judged by
Larkin, although he was Neil Megson at that point. The
author Stuart Cosgrove, who attended Hull University,
found inspiration in the collection of books about African-
American music that Larkin, a jazz fan, had assembled.
Cosgrove would go on to edit *NME* and the *Face*.

Larkin was often rude about Hull. Soon after his arrival,
he wrote to his friend, D. J. Enright, 'I wish I could think of
one nice thing I could tell you about Hull. Oh yes, it's very
nice and flat for cycling.' But, according to Andrew Motion,
he 'settled into the habit of praising Hull – not least for its
remoteness'. The poem 'Here' is taken to be his love letter
to Hull. It's like 'The Whitsun Weddings' in reverse, in that
it describes a train-borne arrival at what we can take to be
Hull rather than a departure from it, and this town, where
'domes and statues, spires and cranes cluster', might almost
be Venice, except for the cranes. Larkin describes the locals
as 'A cut-price crowd, urban yet simple' – but you wouldn't
expect fulsomeness in the context of Hull. In this place, the
narrator finds 'unfenced existence', 'Facing the sun, untal-
kative, out of reach'.

Insofar as Larkin has been adopted by Hull, so he has also
by Yorkshire. Andrew Motion finds in him 'a very English,
glum accuracy', which sounds to me like a Yorkshire quality. Surely it might also be used to describe the work of
Alan Bennett?

My mention of 'Larkinland' was by way of quoting the
title of a very enjoyable novel by Jonathan Tulloch. It joins
the dots of Larkin's poetry to relate the misadventures of
a Larkin-like poet in a Hull-like town referred to satiri-
cally as 'fishtown' or 'fishville'. The poet is called Arthur
Merryweather – the surname echoing Larkin's, being
surprisingly vernal compared to the plodding first name.

Merryweather is trapped in drab 1950s provincialism, a world of train compartments, bread vans, telephone conversations cut short by 'the pips', kippers for breakfast and heavy smoking (Merryweather's brand is Park Drive). The plot is simple and surprisingly tense. Will Merryweather get his leg over? It seems unlikely. After all, sexual intercourse (according to Larkin in his poem 'Annus Mirabilis') didn't begin until 1963. Tulloch was born in Cumbria but lives in North Yorkshire. As with Larkin, I detect a Yorkshireness in the glumness of Merryweather. When his lady friend asks what he makes of 'fishtown', he replies, 'Truth is, the whole place is spectacularly dreadful.'

'So you like it then?' she replies.

'Larkin glamorised [Hull],' Tulloch told the *Guardian* on 30 May 2017, 'made it his Venice. I think he was lucky to have Hull and Hull was lucky to have him. A lot of people take Hull out of his poetry and that's a great loss.'

So far, I'd been pushing my bike. Now I began riding it. In Larkin's day, everybody cycled in Hull, it being so horizontal. Apparently, Larkin's bike was enormous, and old-fashioned even by the standards of the time. (I knew *Larkinland* was a good book by the detail of Merryweather's cycle clips – 'two omegas' – being hung on his crossbar when not in use, which is how it was done in 1970s York.)

Hull, unlike York, is not one of those few towns where cycling remains a mass activity. The notion of a bike's utility needs to be buttressed by a belief in its moral superiority over the car, a kind of inverted snobbery, which could also be described as middle-class priggishness. Hull is too working-class for that, and I felt slightly iconoclastic as I pedalled north along a busy road, with lines of redbrick terraces radiating off to either side.

I came to another outpost of Larkinland: Pearson Park. It's overlooked by Edwardian villas, and Larkin lived in an attic flat in one of these between 1956 and 1974. The house bears a commemorative plaque. It's not one of the usual dinner plate-sized blue ones, but something more saucer-sized in green. The property, with its half-timbered gables, ornate iron gate and slightly overgrown garden, is pretty enough for a painting of it to be reproduced on a greetings card offered for sale by the Larkin Society. Pearson Park, and the view from this window, inspired 'The Trees', described as 'unresting castles' that 'thresh'. It is from the collection called *High Windows*, and if the title refers to the dormer window of Larkin's flat, then you have to conclude that the windows are only *relatively* high, being third-storey, and the trees facing the flat don't seem heroic enough for all that threshing. It just shows what a real writer can do with a limited resource.

The park dates from 1860, when it was called the People's Park. It's very municipal, floral rather than flowery. The dome from the top of Hull's Victorian Town Hall – which was built by Cuthbert Brodrick and didn't survive the Victorian era – is displayed in the park and does rather resemble something left over in a builder's yard. There's a duck pond – officially a 'lake' – with a flagging fountain, and unconvincing-looking imitation stones, as if they were made from *papier maché*, but the park is restful and redolent of past times.

I bought a cup of tea and a Kit-Kat from a kiosk near the pond. The total cost was £1.30; very reasonable given that it was a four-finger Kit-Kat.

'Pearson Park exercises a fascination over me,' Larkin wrote to his mother, 'and I always enjoy an hour in it.' In 'Toads Revisited', he depicts habitués of the park: 'Palsied old step-takers', and it is specified that you will see them in the afternoon.

I cycled around a few corners, and came to mouldering Spring Bank Cemetery, whose lodges and chapels were also by our old friend Cuthbert Brodrick. Larkin was a regular visitor here, on his bike with camera in hand. In 1964, he was interviewed by John Betjeman for an episode of the TV arts series, *Monitor*. As they sit in the long grass of the overgrown cemetery, each seems to be sending himself up. Betjeman, in his battered hat, says, 'I'd rather it were like this, than that sort of neat, ordered housing estate of a new cemetery.' Larkin, looking a bit jittery in suit and tight tie, says, 'I find that when I come here on a wet Sunday afternoon in December . . . when it isn't at all romantic . . . It gets my worries into perspective.'

I cycled on, passing one of Hull's white phone boxes – in fact they're off-white, described by Jonathan Tulloch in *Larkinland* as 'wheat-coloured'. They signify Hull's independent telephone network, and therefore symbolise the town's independence. My friend who'd been at Hull University found

a grandeur and a great self-sufficiency about Hull, and I found the people really interesting. They'd put their arms around you without you really knowing it. If you went into a laundrette, they'd say, 'You're a student, aren't you? You're obviously not going to understand these machines – here, let me show you.' They knew lots of people had never heard of Hull, and they didn't mind.

Another friend of mine, who spent time in Hull during its City of Culture year, said, 'The people there think of themselves as being from Hull – the idea of Yorkshire is a distant second.'

You get this partisanship, this emphasis on home, in the city's pop music. The Housemartins were formed in Hull, and their debut album was called *London 0 Hull 4*. The focus of the band was a terraced house in Grafton Street, Hull, near the university. In *Hit Factory: A Journey Through the Industrial Cities of British Pop*, Karl Whitney writes that the leader of the group, Paul Heaton, who was born in Cheshire, but had enjoyed a period of living in Sheffield, found in Grafton Street 'a milieu suited to [his] vision of working-class solidarity and droll bar-room observation'. Apparently, 'the door was always open and anyone could wander in.' In *The Old Grey Whistle Test* Housemartins special, broadcast in 1986, the band are shown miming their songs in the front room of the Grafton Street house. Important band decisions were made while the members sat on a climbing frame in a playground behind Grafton Street. Tracy Thorn and Ben Watt formed Everything but the Girl while students at Hull University; they received journalists in their bedsit near Pearson Park. 'In her memoir, Thorn mentions that few bands came to Hull,' writes Whitney. 'The city's geographical isolation – and the university's relative unfashionability – gave them a blank canvas. There was no scene to fit into. And because there was no scene, you had to create your own.'

I was now on the Cottingham Road, passing the buildings of the university: red-brick, yes, but ivy-clad. I was starting to think Larkin must have had a pretty nice time of it in Hull, that a lot of his moaning must have been 'put on'. I arrived at the pretty suburb, formerly the village, of Cottingham. When he first arrived in Hull, Larkin lodged at Cottingham, where the university has halls of residence. He was in Holtby House, where the parents of Winifred

Holtby, author of *South Riding*, had lived. It seems obliga-
tory, in books about Yorkshire, to discuss that novel, which
is widely loved. But I couldn't get on with it – about which I
felt guilty, given that Holtby wrote it while dying of kidney
disease. In the preface to the Virago Press edition of 2010,
Shirley Williams guilt-trips the reader, describing how, as
Holtby fought to complete the book, 'she also cared for her
sick niece Anne, for her mother, and for my brother John
and me when my mother (Vera Brittain), Winifred's dearest
friend, was coping with my father's serious illness and her
own father's suicide.'

South Riding was published in 1936 and concerns local
government in depression-era East Yorkshire – not the
most enticing premise, but it has two interesting women at
its heart: Mrs Beddows, 'an Alderman' (based on Holtby's
mother, who was also an alderman), and Miss Sarah Burton,
a headmistress. But there are about 140 other characters
in total, which I thought too many, and too contrivedly
reflecting a social range. The best things about the novel
are the evocations of landscape. The setting is Holderness –
the East Riding towards and including the coast south from
Bridlington to Spurn Point. The land is much more dramat-
ically flat even than the Vale of York, and ghostly with it,
since many of its former coastal settlements have fallen into
the sea: 'a Dutch landscape', Holtby writes,

> haunted by larks and sea-birds, roofed by immense
> pavilions of windy cloud; the brownish-purple shining
> mud, pocked and hummocked by water and fringed by
> heath-like herbs; the indented banks where the high
> tides sucked and gurgled; the great ships gliding up to
> Kingsport, seen from low-lying windows as though they
> moved across the fields.

Kingsport in the novel is Hull. Here is a description of a bus ride through Hull near the docks:

The walls of this street were powdered from the fine white dust of flour mills and cement works. Tall cranes swung towering to heaven. It's better than an inland industrial town, thought Sarah, and wished the bus were roofless so that she might sniff the salty tarry fishy smell of docks instead of the petrol-soaked stuffiness of her glass-and-metal cage.

I cycled to the King George's Playing Fields, Cottingham, which, according to the Larkin Trail website, provided the inspiration for his poem 'Afternoons'. 'In the hollows of afternoons', young mothers become old as they watch their children play. Note the frequency with which the word 'afternoon' is coming up. 'Have a lovely afternoon,' the man to whom I'd paid my toll on the Humber Bridge had said. I associate afternoons with Yorkshire, probably because of the generally slower pace of life, and the recollections of the long, somnolent Sundays of my childhood.

The light was turning golden in the trees as this present afternoon faded. Rugby practice for some junior school kids was coming to an end. The peremptory barks of the teacher in charge reminded me of Brian Glover playing the in-your-face games teacher Mr Sugden in *Kes*: 'And again, Tommy ... Keep working, Tommy ... Tommy, what's your plan?' A seagull stood on the grass nearby, like an emissary from a foreign land. Cottingham seems well insulated from the bleakness of the Humber.

On my bike ride, I kept coming to railway level crossings, which was surprising, given how many railway lines around Hull have closed. There is no longer a railway connection to the coastal resorts of Hornsea and Withernsea, which at one time were recreational annexes of Hull, the latter especially, and the direct access over the Wolds from York to Hull via Beverley has also gone.

At one time, according to *The Oxford Companion to British Railway History*, Hull, along with Burton-on-Trent and Lincoln, was 'notorious for the abundance of level crossings'; they are a function of flatness, of course, but Hull is not the flattest-seeming place I have been: that is Goole, 30 miles inland along the river Ouse, headwater of the Humber; and let us leave Hull for a moment, to visit it.

As though to illustrate the absurdity of local government designations in Yorkshire, Goole is today part of the new-made East Riding of Yorkshire, whereas for the previous 900 years it was in the West Riding.

Since 1826, Goole has been an inland port, which is something of a Yorkshire speciality. You do keep coming across the accoutrements of ports: docks, cranes, ships, sailors, apparently in the middle of fields – as at Selby, for instance. 'It is curious that a county like Yorkshire, with so long a coastline, should have so few ports,' writes Harry Scott in his *Portrait of Yorkshire*, 'and those few so far from the sea. Middlesbrough is several miles from the open sea at Teesmouth. Hull is almost halfway along the Humber from Spurn Point. And Goole is still further inland along the same river.' In the late 1820s Goole became the focus of the Yorkshire navigation and canal system. Three hundred years beforehand, Goole had arisen where a diversion of the River Don (the Dutch River) met the Ouse. When, in the 1820s, the Aire and Calder Navigation was diverted from Knottingley to Goole, the town prospered on the back of the coal trade. Today, the docks at Goole trade in timber, steel and a variety of containerised items. Siemens is building a train factory at Goole, where it will build the new generation of London Tube trains, ludicrously called Inspiro London. Somebody should write a book about the importance of the North to the London Underground, what with the above-mentioned Yorkist, Frank Pick, being its second-in-command in the inter-war period; his chief architect being Charles Holden, from Bolton; unemployed men from the North having travelled south to build the Tube's various extensions, and most of the seat coverings (moquettes) having been woven in Halifax.

I visited Goole a couple of times to research a historical novel. At one point, I climbed from a pathway up a low grassy bank to see an expanse of water (whether dock, river or canal I can't recall) that was actually above the level of the path I'd been on. Seeking to create the atmosphere of a waterlogged world, I was listening during that period of writing to *The Sinking of the Titanic*, by the experimental composer and double bassist, Gavin Bryars. The band on the *Titanic* reputedly kept playing as the ship went down, and Bryars' piece imagines the subsequent diffusion of the music through the waves. Only when I'd finished my book did I discover that Bryars had been born in Goole. Incidentally, the Spa at Bridlington carries a plaque reading

James Wallace Hartley
1878–1912
Band Leader RMS *Titanic*
Played Here During His Residence at Bridlington
1902–1904

Hartley was a violinist; his violin was recovered intact from the sea, albeit looking rather blanched like a piece of driftwood. It was in the hands of the Bridlington Salvation Army for a while before being sold at auction for £900,000.

As I rode back towards my hotel In Hull, I passed the Larkin flat again. Lights were burning orange in that dormer window. I hope the present occupant doesn't have literary aspirations. He or she must be feeling the pressure, if so.

That night, I got talking to a couple of blokes in a Hull pub. One of them was slightly suspicious of me. 'You're living in London but you're writing a book about Yorkshire?' I said I wouldn't be the first to do that. As I walked away at the end of the conversation, I overheard the less suspicious one saying, 'He was a nice guy,' which I was naturally pleased to hear, but then it occurred to me that the emphasis might have been on the 'nice', to counter some other epithet used by the other. In any case, they had been helpful, especially the less suspicious one, tipping me off about where to see the old fishing sights. 'You want St Andrew's Quay, but there's not much to see.' Apparently, St Andrew's Quay was on the west side of the docks, but the directions seemed a bit complicated, so I asked if I could get there by biking along the waterfront from the Old Town, which I *did* know how to get to. There seemed some doubt about this, and the next day I saw why.

To reach St Andrew's Quay, I had to traverse Albert Dock, then William Wright Dock, on their seaward sides. This involved a bit of cycling along a narrow path, and a lot of carrying my bike up stairs leading to walkways, then down again. The day was sunny, and the wide Humber glinted. On the opposite bank I saw – in a delicate blue haze – some cranes and silos, apparently about 5 millimetres high. All along the fringes of the water were broken and ghostly wooden spars. There was little sign of life in the docks I was passing. High, blank walls matched the wide, blank water. Sometimes, there'd be a big warehouse, with a sliding door pulled back, but only darkness discernible within. There were mysterious bales, mounds of sand, specialist cranes and earth movers, all stationary. Every so often, I saw a lonely-looking man in a high-vis vest.

I came to St Andrew's Quay, which is a rangy shopping centre with a large car park as the forecourt. On the seaward edge of this car park are signs advertising the shops, which are somewhat reminiscent of a ship's masts and sails. But my eye seemed to alight on those brands representing home comforts, as opposed to the wild waves of the North Sea: Furniture Village, B&Q, Sofa Store, Pets at Home. St Andrew's Quay used to be St Andrew's Dock. It was named after the patron saint of fishermen because it was built, in 1883, as a dock to accommodate the Hull fishing fleet, which was mainly a distant water fleet: that is, a fleet of trawlers.

In *English Journey*, J. B. Priestley describes seeing at St Andrew's Dock 'a misty and pleasing confusion of masts and funnels, finely tangled in the silvery mesh of the morning', and on the dockside, open wooden barrels full of fish ('it did not look as if there could be a cod left in the Northern seas'). At the time, about 350 trawlers were based at Hull. Photographs of them in the dock suggest an industrial city on the water, with the funnels in place of chimneys. Priestley was taken around the fish market and adjacent offices. Notwithstanding the Hampstead mansion he inhabited, he professed to find the idea of working in those offices attractive:

To set out for work in the very black of the night, to see the dawn break over the cash-book, to be finishing when other fellows are just settling down to the day's grind; all this would please me, give the job an urgency and romantic flavour; you would always feel you were working somewhere between Christmas and a declaration of war; and, not least, these must be jobs at which you would be sustained by frequent cups of tea.

Priestley spoke to a trawler owner who told him that the trawlermen were 'still a race apart, perhaps the last of the wild men in this tamed island of ours'. Andrew Locker, of Whitby and the National Federation of Fishermen's Organisations, had opined similarly to me about the modern-day fixed-gear men of Yorkshire, but whereas they go out in the early morning and are back by 4 p.m. on the same day, the trawlermen of Priestley's time would be at sea for three weeks at a time. At sea, they wore guernseys colour-coded so their home port could be identified if they were found drowned. On land, they were dandified, favouring high-waisted flared trousers and jackets of perhaps sky blue or pink. But you would be well-advised not to take the mickey. They were hard men; I once read the calculation that their job was seventeen times more dangerous than that of coal miner. In 150 years of Hull fishing, 6,000 men were lost. Every January or February the St Andrew's Dock Heritage Park Action Group organises a Lost Trawlermen's Memorial Day, and it plans to erect a memorial at the Quay. There is also a Hull Fish Trail, featuring forty-one sculptures of fish.

According to an article of 2015 in *Fishing News* in the 'Ports of the Past' series, 'Hull's heyday was probably in the 1950s, when stocks were still abundant in the distant water grounds.' (Iceland, Norway, Greenland, Labrador, and Bear Island off the Russian coast.) 'A major change came in 1960,

when Hull's first freezer trawler, *Lord Nelson*, heralded a
new era.' The freezer boats needed a bigger dock, so in 1975
William Wright Dock became the fish dock, by which time

Hull's decline began, as all the countries where the
Hull fleet fished imposed limits, culminating with the
Icelandic 'cod wars' which ended with Iceland's 200-mile
limit in 1976. Hull's distant water fleet had nowhere to
fish, and Britain also joined the EU at this time, adding
to the industry's woes.

Those woes were supposed to be cured by Brexit. As we
have seen further up the Yorkshire coast, they were not.
At the time of writing (May, 2001) the future for the one
trawler left at Hull, the state-of-the-art *Kirkella* – which
has a crew of a hundred and has been catching 10 per cent
of the cod sold in British fish and chip shops – looks grim.
After Britain's departure from the Common Fisheries Policy
of the EU, replacement agreements were supposed to have
been reached with the fishing nations covered by the CFP.
As I write, the failure to reach an agreement with Norway is
in the news. This failure cuts *Kirkella* off from the vast stocks
of Norwegian cod, and the vessel is tied up in King George
Dock, Hull. (I was told there are some smaller boats, fishing
'intermittently in and off the Humber', but apart from them,
Kirkella is all that remains of Hull fishing.)

To the east of the Quay is an area of scrub that is the old
Dock, silted up. It is frowned over by the huge crumbling
offices of the old Lord Line trawler company, and this is
dereliction on a scale you might expect in Detroit rather
than the UK. On the nearby waterside, a family were clustered around a boy with a fishing rod. A friendly policeman
had walked up to have a look. The boy had caught a fish,

which he had just put into a small bucket. The mother said to the policeman: 'He's so excited! He wants to go home and eat it now!'

As I cycled back to my hotel, along the quiet terraced streets off Hessle Road, which is where the fishermen used to live, I passed an NHS building: Hull Memory Clinic.

*

On my way home, I called in at Beverley, the comely Georgian market town eight miles from Hull. Its picturesque streets were packed with shops and shoppers. Beverley is a bolthole from Hull. Larkin cycled regularly to Beverley, seeking light relief, and people who find success in Hull tend to go and live there. The ideal trajectory for a successful Hull media person would be: Hull, Beverley, Beverly Hills, which is named after Beverley, in a roundabout way, and without the third 'e'.

Beverley used to be one of those characteristically Yorkshire inland ports and from the 1900s to the 1960s there was a shipyard in the town, on the River Hull, where trawlers were built and launched broadside, there not being much room on the river. In *Yorkshire: A Lyrical History of England's Greatest County*, Richard Morris writes that 'The Minster of red-roofed Beverley is one of the most calming places you can enter.' The Gothic Minster – a building of great verticality whose twin towers are like two rockets waiting to be launched – is the amusingly disproportionate parish church of the town, but then Holderness is full of churches too big for present requirements, and the flatness of the landscape gives them an additional, salutary prominence. The Minster was closed when I visited, but it was quite calming enough to watch the verger cutting the churchyard lawn on that sunny afternoon.

The Unknown City: Sheffield

It's hard to make any definite statement about Sheffield, except that it's enigmatic, elusive. It's only just in Yorkshire and is peculiarly ill-defined administratively. The Sheffield City Region includes the entire Metropolitan County of South Yorkshire as well as a North-East Derbyshire District and the Derbyshire Dales District, among other un-Yorkshire entities. 'In the late sixties only eight organisations had a "Yorkshire" name and a Sheffield telephone number,' writes Michael Bradford in *The Fight for Yorkshire*: 'in Leeds there were fifty-two.' He had in mind, for example, Yorkshire Television, the *Yorkshire Post*, and Yorkshire Chemicals Plc. 'Twenty years later', he adds, 'the comparison was nineteen and seventy-one.' In *Pies and Prejudice*, Stuart Maconie calls Sheffield a 'curio'. In *Hit Factory: A Journey Through the Industrial Cities of British Pop*, Karl Whitney asks, 'How do the Human League, Def Leppard and Pulp fit together?' In *Goodbye to Yorkshire,* Roy Hattersley wrote of Sheffield, 'It is still the unknown city, the name on the knife blade and no more.' He attributes this state of affairs to Sheffield being 'an industrial city where people work, not a commercial city which people visit'.

It was easier to be definite about Sheffield in the past when that industry was still blazing away. George Orwell is widely quoted on the subject, which is impressive given that he only spent three days there, in 1936. Here is what he wrote in *The Road to Wigan Pier*:

Sheffield, I suppose, could justly claim to be called the ugliest town in the Old World: its inhabitants, who want it to be pre-eminent in everything, very likely do make that claim for it. It has a population of half a million and it contains fewer decent buildings than the average East Anglian village of five hundred. And the stench! If at rare moments you stop smelling sulphur it is because you have begun smelling gas. Even the shallow river that runs through the town is usually bright yellow with some chemical or other.

On the other hand, he quite liked it:

At night, when you cannot see the hideous shapes of the houses and the blackness of everything, a town like Sheffield assumes a kind of sinister magnificence. Sometimes the drifts of smoke are rosy with sulphur, and serrated flames, like circular saws, squeeze themselves out from beneath the cowls of the foundry chimneys. Through the open doors of foundries you see firey serpents of iron bring hauled to and fro by redlit boys, and you hear the whizz and thump of steam hammers and the scream of iron under the blow.

The only reason he could apprehend this 'sinister magnificence' is that Sheffield is set on and amid hills – from which comes the millstone grit that made its grindstones and the running water that turned them – and if you perch yourself at a high point on one of those hills, you can see most of the city. Perhaps this is why Sheffield was chosen for *Threads* (1984), a powerfully depressing film written by Barry Hines about the effects of nuclear war on working- and lower-middle-class families. As the war is brewing up, with news bulletins becoming increasingly ominous, the entirety of Sheffield is regularly seen in long-shot. I wondered whether I was being invited to think that Sheffield people deserved comeuppance for being so presumptuous as to create a city in the beauty of those hills. Sheffield is a major city, like Glasgow, Leeds or Liverpool, yet it likes to call itself 'the largest village in England', and it has more trees per person than any city in Europe. The city is widely intersected by countryside, and green suburbs lying in the confusing valleys created by the Don and its tributaries, which are not household names even in Sheffield.

In 1961, John Betjeman wrote a piece about Sheffield for a *Daily Telegraph* series called 'Men and Buildings'. The article is uncharacteristically all over the place. It begins on a dark and wet Saturday afternoon, with Betjeman in 'an industrial part of straight, two-storey brick streets wedged along the tall walls of silent factories'. There is no grass in sight. Faint smells of gas and chemicals fill the air. His thoughts then turn to the leafy suburb of Broomhill in the west, and the 'handsome mansions of the Victorian industrialists who had made their pile from steel and cutlery in the crowded mills and slums below'. For Betjeman, Broomhill is 'the prettiest suburb in England', so Sheffield exhibits 'the best and worst of Victorian England'. He rapturises about the hills, as complemented by the public parks, but he laments that some of the hills have been covered with suburbs less attractive than Broomhill.

He turns his attention to the Park Hill blocks of council flats, then recently completed. These rear up behind the railway station and are now the most famous example of Northern Brutalism. At first sight, Betjeman dislikes them, as you would expect: 'tier on tier of concrete with ugly "contemprikit" detail'. But when he ascends to one of the 'decks' and looks out at the 'magnificent moorland', he decides the planning is 'thoughtful and ingenious'. But it is not so much that he likes Park Hill as that he likes the countryside it has spared. (At about the same time as I read this, I gave an online talk about John Betjeman's documentary of 1973, *Metroland*, which concerns the huge suburb built to the north-west of London by the Metropolitan Railway. Betjeman had a snobbish contempt, amusingly expressed, for Metroland and for Neasden especially. At the end of the talk, I took questions from the audience, although one was more of a furious comment: 'I think Betjeman was the ultimate Nimby. Metroland gave ordinary people a proper home with a garden. It's ridiculous to sneer at it.' But the documentary is a lament for the 'mild Home Counties acres' that Metroland supplanted.)

As I've said, in 1987 Sheffield was the place where my dreams of a legal career died. I was seeking to confirm my place in the middle class when the working class of the city were having a hard time. Sheffield, governed by David Blunkett and the Socialist Republic of South Yorkshire, was on the frontline of the North–South fight. At the Orgreave coking plant in 1984, the NUM had fought (against the police and the government) and lost the decisive battle of the Miners' Strike. J. D. Taylor sought out the Orgreave battleground for his book of 2016, *Island Story*. 'Today there is no Orgreave, no monument. The luxury housing complex where the plant once stood has been rebranded as Waverley.'

Meanwhile, the steel industry was also contracting, generating high unemployment in Sheffield, but unlike coal-mining the steel industry did not disappear, and so again the picture is nuanced. The unemployment arose partly from new, less labour-intensive methods of manufacture. While Sheffield now produces less raw steel (to use an unscientific term for a very scientific business) than formerly, it makes as many specialist steel products from advanced refinements of steel as ever.

I can't remember the location of the fatal interview, but I think it was in or near Paradise Square – a Georgian square, somewhat tilted – that takes its place amid the incredible architectural jumble of central Sheffield. I'd stayed over in Sheffield the night before, in a large black stone house in Broomhill owned by a friend of Dad's. I remember that I approached the barristers' chambers on a bus, and was amazed at the cheapness of the fare, which embodied the spirit of the Socialist Republic. The driver called me 'love' in an entirely un-homosexual way, and when I was back in Sheffield in 2021 (see below) an enormous man smoking a vaping device in a multi-storey car park also called me 'love' when I asked him for directions – so it must be a Sheffield thing, although I associate the Northern 'love' as an appellation between men with Manchester. In 1989 I interviewed Anthony Burgess, who grew up in Manchester. I spoke to him by phone; I was in London, working for the *Daily Mail*, he a tax exile in Monaco. ('You probably think I look out at the sea; in fact, I work facing the peeling back wall of a hotel.') At the end of the interview, he said, 'And what about you? How old are you?'

'Twenty-seven.'

'Oh, you've got it all before you, love.'

My other remembrance of Sheffield is of walking around

a public park, somewhat dazed in the aftermath of my experience at the chambers. Amid the usual municipal decorations – duck ponds, flower beds, neat lawns – there was an outcrop of rock, which two men, joined by a rope, were climbing. I had the idea that the proximity of the Peak District had bred a race of mountaineers. In subsequent years, I might look for the reassuring word 'Sheffield' on a knife if feeling displaced at a London dinner party. The word – the guarantee of quality – is more likely to be on the knife than the fork or spoon, which are called 'holloware' in acknowledgement of their relative unimportance compared to the blade, and the blade itself is more important than the handle of the blade, which is called the tang. I will give an instance of my own involvement with Sheffield cutlery.

As a boy visiting Scarborough, I would always visit a gift shop in Newborough called Wherritt's, after the family who have owned it since 1845. Wherritt's was, and is, a cleverly stocked treasure trove with a lightbox sign in the window, illuminated even on the sunniest day and reading, 'PLEASE WALK AROUND'. In Wherritt's I would seek a souvenir of my day in Scarborough, but it wasn't enough to buy a teaspoon bearing the Scarborough crest. It had to be something that would somehow alter my life in such a way that I could say, 'Ah, yes, this all dates from a trip to Scarborough.' An alarm clock might fit the bill, a pretty little red one with luminous hands, the colour of a greenfly's wings. 'Ever since I bought it that day in Scarborough', I would imagine telling a future biographer, 'I've got up at five o'clock in the morning to do three hours of writing.' Or I might seek out sunglasses, preferably 'polarised' in order to suddenly become a cool person. Wherritt's also sold – and sells – a huge variety of penknives, and the right one of these would turn me into a resourceful figure, at home in the wilds, the kind of person who cuts an apple before eating it, or whittles things while thinking of something else. All the Wherritt's penknives flaunted 'Sheffield', as in 'Sheffield lock-knife', 'Sheffield pruner', 'Sheffield tackler blade'.

A couple of years ago, I interviewed Charles Turner, a 'modern cutler with the scars to prove it!' Mr Turner is Managing Director of Durham-Duplex, a Sheffield firm that manufactures machine knives and industrial blades. He is also chairman of the Sheffield Assay Office[*] and a member of the Sheffield Company of Cutlers, incorporated in 1624, whose Corinthian headquarters stand opposite the cathedral. When I spoke to Mr Turner, he had recently 'formalised and registered' the trademark 'Made in Sheffield', which I thought had been formalised and registered ages ago, given that they've been making knives in Sheffield for 800 years, but apparently not. Mr Turner, a former army officer, described the new trademark as 'an attack brand', not just for cutlery but for 'engineering and coding', and the attack was directed against imposters from around the world who had appropriated the S-word for their steel products. He emphasised the importance of Sheffield to the manly life – 'It was the knife in your belt or the scythe in your hands'; he let me know that bequests of the steel barons were behind Sheffield University, Weston Park, the Town Hall, and he scotched any idea of modern Sheffield as 'post-industrial'. He mentioned some companies: Carr's Manufacturing (who have the Harrods cutlery concession), Thimo Holdings, British Silverware, William Wright Silverware, Incomen Silverware. 'The Wimbledon Roof was made half a mile away from where I'm sitting,' Charles Turner told me. Apparently, Sheffield was also somehow responsible for the

---

[*]   To 'assay' means to assess the precious metal content of an item; there has been an assay office in Sheffield since 1773.

steelier parts of Tottenham Hotspur's new stadium.

I suggested to Charles Turner that Sheffield was unclassifiable, and semi-detached from Yorkshire.

'Are you accusing me of being a southern woofter?' he said. 'We're definitely Northerners, a bit like the Scottish Border folk – more Scottish than the Highlanders. The people have a certain reserve. They could have just made the European Cup but they wouldn't mention it.'

In summer 2021, I revisited Sheffield, and I went with my wife.

Lisa was born in Canada but has lived since age eight in London. She has little interest in Yorkshire, but she'd said she 'would quite like to see Sheffield', since she'd never been there.

I said, 'If I say "Sheffield" to you, what do you think of?'

'The Hillsborough Disaster.'

'Nothing else?'

'Not really. You've been there quite a few times, haven't you?'

'Yes, but I don't understand it.'

Since Lisa has an interest in architecture, and since it seems to me that Sheffield, like Chicago, is punctuated by outrageous architectural statements, I referred her to the chapter on Sheffield in *A Guide to the New Ruins of Great Britain* (2008), by Owen Hatherley, enfant terrible of British architecture criticism. Hatherley was born in Southampton, but he is particularly taken with some Northern places.

Anyone who comes from the industrial towns of the south – say, Southampton, Portsmouth, Reading, Slough or Luton – can't help being jealous of the sheer strangeness of their Northern equivalents; their hills, their scale,

the closeness of open country, the amount of extraordi-
narily serious, world-class architecture, the lack of 1980s
and 1990s tat.

We have seen Pevsner's verdict in *Yorkshire: West Riding*
(1954): 'Architecturally, Sheffield is a miserable disappoint-
ment.' What Hatherley likes is the municipal Modernism,
and Brutalism, essayed in Sheffield in the 1960s and 1970s,
usually commissioned by J. Lewis Womersley, Chief
Architect to Sheffield Council. Hatherley makes the case
that most of the British Brutalists were Northern ('angry
young men'), which seems logical enough, and you'd
think Northern Brutalism was the most brutal Brutalism
of all. But Hatherley contends that the Park Road flats in
Sheffield were a reaction against 'orthodox slum clearance
Modernism'. These flats, embodying the 'streets in the sky'
principle derived from Corbusier, incorporated nurseries,
pubs and shops, and had decks wide enough for electric
vehicles to make deliveries. For Hatherley, they were
'Modernism as montage, messiness and the drama of multiple levels and scales'.

He also rates the less radical Gleadless Valley Estate, which
'makes breathtaking use of the hilly landscape, resembling a
strange socialist South Yorkshire version of fifties Southern
California'.

'He writes well,' Lisa said of Hatherley as she leafed
through his book on the drive north.

'What do you think of his chapter on Sheffield?'

'I haven't read that. I'm reading his chapter on Cambridge.'

On reaching the middle of Sheffield, we got lost. I blamed
the satnav, and Lisa blamed Sheffield: 'The layout's really
confusing.'

'There's a lot of reasons for that,' I said. 'One is that the street pattern's basically medieval.' But Lisa didn't seem to hear, as she scowled down at her phone map.

At this point, we were in a dead end near the river. A police car reversed rapidly towards us, and the copper wound down his window, which was alarming, but he was laughing. 'You were brought here by satnav, right?' he said, and he gave us directions.

We eventually found a multi-storey car park that was, like most places in central Sheffield, on a steep slope. The front exit was on the first floor; the back exit was on the ninth. Having given up on the satnav, we began walking to our hotel.

Central Sheffield was not coming into focus for Lisa, with its modern buildings – often granite – sprinkled amid red-brick and stone Victoriana. 'Was it badly bombed?' she asked. In December 1940, the 'Sheffield blitz' destroyed hundreds of buildings, but the irregularity of central Sheffield arises partly from being subject, along with the poorer suburbs, to a relentless churn of slum clearance and rebuilding throughout the twentieth century. At nine o'clock on Saturday night, the roads were busy, and the traffic seemed particularly noisy. In the 1950s and 1960s, new road schemes in the centre were contradicting the ethos of high-rise flats like Park Hill and nearby Hyde Park, which were meant to distance people from cars and roads.

We asked a man for directions, and even though he was getting on, he insisted on walking to the top of some steps with us to better provide them. 'The people are nice,' said Lisa, when he'd gone. Our hotel stood near the handsome Italianate Town Hall (1890s). Also adjacent were two 'gardens': first, the Winter Gardens, which looks like a modern version of a Victorian railway station that's been infested with jungle; second, the Peace Gardens, which, despite accommodating some unpeaceable drunks, did not lose their strange dignity, imparted by well-kept lawn and stone water features resembling giant scallop shells. The refurbishment of the Peace Gardens, and the creation of the Winter Gardens, were part of a project of the late 1990s labelled 'Heart of the City'. They are well regarded and Grade 1 listed, but for Owen Hatherley, Sheffield lost its nerve in the late twentieth century. He speaks darkly of 'the dubious ministrations of regeneration' and 'Pseudomodern Blairboxes'.

We checked in, then continued our walk in more relaxed mode. It was dark now, but with scudding, moonlit clouds Atkinson Grimshaw would have appreciated, and it was sometimes hard to distinguish between these and the surrounding hills. Heading downhill, towards the river, we passed Castle House, an impressive granite block that once housed a Co-Op and is now the National Videogame Museum. 'Interesting fenestration,' said Lisa. We came to a hoarding that spoke of 'Castle Market'. 'Owen Hatherley likes this,' said Lisa (who'd read his Sheffield chapter by now). 'But where is it?' There was only the hoarding which, perversely, celebrated with photographs and text a complex knocked down in 2015. The Castle Market was 'shops in the sky'. In his book, Hatherley had urged its urgent listing to prevent demolition, writing that it 'recreates the teeming strangeness of an old market in a fearlessly modern form'. Looking at the photographs, Lisa said, 'Nice ribbon walling ... It's a shame this has gone.'

As we walked back to the hotel, the Park Hill flats came into view (they're seldom out of view for long). They are currently being refurbished by Urban Splash, who have inserted coloured panels to relieve the greyness; the electric lights within added further colours to the grid, so the flats

were like a towering cliff face painted by Mondrian ... or
rather a *series* of variously angled cliff faces, and the flats
did seem to flow, like a trailing banner across the night
sky. Oddly, Lisa had no opinion about the flats: 'They're
all right.'

I couldn't sleep that night, so I got up at five and had a
walk around town. In the Peace Gardens a couple of stoned
young men hailed me. 'Have a good night, mate!' In the
light of dawn, the surrounding hills were in clear view, and
they made Sheffield seem small, because they were so big,
and even greener than I had envisaged, being usually tree-
covered. It's a relief to see the hills in the morning; you are
seeing Sheffield in its true context. In his novel, *The Year of
the Runaways*, Sunjeev Sahota evoked night-time in Sheffield
through the eyes of Avtar, a young illegal immigrant.

> The shabby restaurants were all closed, the pound shops
> shuttered. He liked this road in the day, a place of business
> and exchange, a road that seemed to carry on into the
> hills. Tonight, though, there was only a scrappy silence,
> and the city at his back, the countryside glowering ahead.

I walked to Holly Street, in the middle of town, to see
what had become of the National Union of Mineworkers'
headquarters, built in the early 1980s, when Arthur
Scargill – under siege, as it were – had decamped from
London to the more hospitable territory of the Socialist
Republic. The building is postmodern, I suppose. Hatherley
calls it 'small but tautly powerful'. It now houses a Turtle
Bay restaurant and a Pitcher & Piano pub, but some of it
is vacant and for sale: 'Leisure, retail and office space with
superb roof terrace'.

I walked along a pedestrianised shopping street called

the Moor. A series of benches were inscribed with lists of
Sheffield-made products: scalpels, bridges, nuclear reactors,
nose-studs, pipelines, Thames Barrier. I passed two women
who were unlocking the doors of a branch of Iceland,
and here was a conjunction reminiscent of the fact that
the famous (or notorious) Meadowhall shopping mall had
been built on the site of a steelworks. At the far end of the
Moor loomed council offices but, this being Sheffield, they
loomed dreamlike – a great, red-brick pyramid with the top
sliced off. (This, the Moorfoot Building, was built for the
DHSS in 1981.)

I headed towards the railway station, which took me
into the 'Cultural Industries Quarter'. ('New Labour Nu
language', chunters Hatherley.) According to a 'masterplan'
of 2000, Sheffield was to be divided, somewhat un-
mathematically, into eleven quarters. The scheme faltered,
and when – a couple of years back – I asked the barmaid
in the Roebuck pub where the Cultural Industries Quarter
was, she didn't know, even though it turned out the pub was
actually within the Quarter. The focus of it used to be four
silvery teapot-looking things built in 1999 as the National
Centre for Popular Music. They are now offices for Sheffield
Hallam University, a former poly that is being expanded,
and forms the main cultural industry of the quarter. Thanks
to Sheffield Hallam and the original Sheffield University,
the city has a student population of 60,000. On hoardings
and signs all around the Cultural Industries Quarter was
the slogan (a quote from the *Sunday Times*): 'The Northern
capital of cool', although if my notes are correct this also
appears as 'The capital of Northern cool'.

I was approaching the Park Hill flats, walking through
gardens heady with flower smells. There was nobody about,
but only because it was too early in the morning. The sense

I had was of happy occupation, and general well-being, certainly no graffiti or litter. I own a DVD called *Made in Sheffield: The Birth of Electronic Pop*, and the cover shows a man throwing an electric guitar from a high balcony of these flats. Sheffield pop was provocative and doctrinaire even before punk, and one of its themes was a rejection of guitars, which seems illogical to me, synthesisers being more expensive, less manoeuvrable and less biodegradable than guitars; they also, I suggest, don't sound as good. 'It's tempting to directly link the sound of the city's electronic music with what was once the constant sonic accompaniment of Sheffield's heavy industry,' writes Karl Whitney in *Hit Factory*. 'The thump of a hammer from a steel mill or the roar of a furnace served as an audible reminder of the machinery that underpinned the everyday existence of the city.' In their debut gig in May 1975, Cabaret Voltaire used a recording of a steam hammer as percussion. Another local influence – the Brutalist architecture – might have accounted for another characteristic of the Sheffield pop. Whitney points out that the film of Anthony Burgess's novel *A Clockwork Orange* involved 'dystopian scenes filmed in the starkly contemporary Brutalist housing of the new London suburb of Thamesmead'. The Sheffield groups Heaven 17 and Clock DVA derived their names from that film, and the Human League named an early EP *The Dignity of Labour* after a mural in *A Clockwork Orange*. Listening to their robotic-yet-peevish hit of 1981, 'Don't You Want Me', which I did more often than I would have liked, I would never have guessed at the strangeness of lead singer and song writer (and sometime Sheffield hospital porter), Phil Oakey. It went far beyond his asymmetrical haircut.

In 1979, The Human League released a single called 'Being Boiled', which is about sericulture – silkworm breeding – and sounds like distorted Morse code. Here is Whitney's account of the half-spoken B-side, 'Circus of Death': 'the Steve McGarrett character from TV show *Hawaii Five-O* arrives at Heathrow Airport to attempt to solve the particularly bizarre case of a murderous circus run by a clown who draws his power from a drug called "dominion".' Sheffield pop musicians continued their forward hurtle long after I stopped hanging about in discos wishing that 'Don't You Want Me' would be displaced by something a bit more organic, like Michael Jackson or the Rolling Stones. But with Sheffield, there are always exceptions to the rule, and I prefer the less future-oriented Sheffield pop: the slick white soul of ABC, or the mellow Fifties-style crooning of Richard Hawley, whose relaxedness suggests to Whitney 'a time before punk rock or synths or Thatcher, when the factories were open and everyone knew everyone'.

Walking back towards the hotel I saw, on the fringes of the Cultural Industries Quarter, signs of the older industry: scruffy red-brick shacks, derelict or semi-derelict. One building had been pebble-dashed and painted off-white, and I think it was still in use. A faded sign read 'Millers, Shapers, Lathes, Drills', and there was a confusing brass name plaque: 'MG Tools, incorporating J. Haworth and R. Birch, and A. Wright and Son Ltd'. If you researched the entire history of that building, you might find some sort of key to Sheffield.

I returned to the hotel. It was just gone six, and breakfast wasn't yet being served, but the man at the reception made me a coffee, which was fairly typical Sheffield behaviour, I had come to think.

A few hours later, Lisa and I were in the vicinity of City Hall (an entertainment venue, not to be confused with the Town Hall) when she stopped to photograph a litter bin that looked like either a parrot or a vertical dolphin. 'This is amazing,' she said. 'It's made of copper – must have cost an absolute fortune. This is such a weird town.' I asked what she meant. 'They've spent a lot of money on some great architecture, but the road layout in the centre's such a mess.' She seemed obsessed with the road layout, perhaps because she has little experience of the car-focused planning that blighted so many Northern towns in the 1960s and 1970s. We entered the modest cathedral, formerly a parish church, and surely one of the most messed-about-with ecclesiastical buildings in the world, but Lisa liked it.

We walked up the hill to the university campus (the original one). Sheffield University, I had read in the *Financial Times*, is 'the top UK higher education institution for engineering research . . . home of the Advanced Manufacturing Research Centre, where academics work alongside more than 100 industrial partners to create new products and make processes more efficient.' Lisa was taking a lot of photographs. I asked why. 'I like it up here,' she said, 'away from the cars.'

The university has many excellent buildings, from Victorian to post-modern. The skyscraping Arts Tower of 1966 is the architectural highlight. It struck me as resembling a great marching robot. Owen Hatherley writes that the Arts Tower, by Gollins Melvin, is 'sleeker and sharper than their similar attempts at Miesian Americana in the capital'. English Heritage loves it as well. Adjacent to the Tower, and connected to it by a walkway, is the elegant Western Library, with its cool marble and expensive hardwoods. In 2019 I spent a happy couple of days in the Western Library, researching a novel in the National Fairground Archive, but there was a new decoration on some pillars in the lobby: a quote from *Kes*, Billy speaking about the hawk: 'It's fierce, an' it's wild, and it's not bothered about anybody.' This was then translated into Chinese on another pillar, and I found the display ingratiating, not to say sinister.

We took a tram back downhill to town, a rollicking thrill-ride, and the highlight of my own visit. (I do like it that Sheffield trams have conductors.) A café in the Cultural Industries Quarter had been recommended to us. It was called Howst, and the very carnivorous Lisa ordered a steak and salad. She'd already begun eating the steak (which she pronounced 'superb') when the waitress asked if she'd like a steak knife. I urged her to go for this, because I wanted to read 'Made in Sheffield' on the blade, but when the waitress handed it over, she said, apologetically, 'I'm afraid it's made in Japan.' So Sheffield had got away from me again.

There is a postscript to this trip. Towards the end of that summer, I overheard Lisa talking to a friend on the phone. 'The most interesting thing we did this summer,' she said, 'was go to Sheffield.' It was, admittedly, a fairly uneventful, locked-down summer for us, as for everyone. On the other hand, in the middle of it we had also managed to go away to Paris.

The Former Ironopolis: Middlesbrough

Descending into Middlesbrough from the Yorkshire Moors, you see a spread-out, somehow dilute-looking town: intermittent streets of red-brick terraces, car parks, parades of anonymous shops and some tower blocks — although it's hard to say why Middlesbrough bothered with that sort of concentrated accommodation, since it seems so content to sprawl.

The slight haziness of a mediocre summer's day was being added to by steaming chimneys in the town fringes, including some cooling towers belonging (I later found out) to a chemical works. In the nineteenth century, the streets of Middlesbrough — North Middlesbrough, especially — were a grid, as in Leeds, but successive redevelopment, with a contribution from heavy wartime bombing, has ensured that few of these 'industrial barracks' remain. I parked in the middle of town where the grey, Gothic town hall stood amid less characterful modern buildings, and more car parks. The town hall clock wearily chimed three as I walked east, heading for the Tees, passing banners in the streets declaring that Middlesbrough was 'Moving Forward'.

Middlesbrough is seven miles along the Tees from the North Sea, and the Tees meets the sea at a sort of non-place called South Gare, where stand coastal retaining walls made of ironstone slag, a lifeboat station and a lighthouse. But that junction was the key to Middlesbrough's rise in the second half of the nineteenth century, together with the ironstone in the Eston Hills to the south, and the coal around Durham to the north.

In a novel, I tried to evoke Middlesbrough in 1909, when its riverbank was still the 'Ironopolis'. In those days, blast furnaces were made of brick, and the best way I could think of describing them was as resembling railway tunnels set on end, with gantries along the top, along which ironstone tubs ran. Men worked at the hearths set into the bottoms of the furnaces, and even on the coldest days they worked naked from the waist up. There would come periodic groaning roars from the furnaces that turned the sky red. The ground was intersected by a tangle of railway lines and rivulets of molten iron, and these were among the many ways in which a stranger wandering onto that infernal territory could end up dead.

My description was based on historical research, but I had also visited the banks of the Tees one winter's afternoon in 2006, aiming for the surviving redbrick clocktower that I thought had been in the middle of the iron-making district. In fact, I was a little out: that district was a mile or so upstream. All around the clocktower – with clock poignantly stopped – was a field of ash. There was a black mountain of old car tyres, and a square of black water, the abandoned Middlesbrough Dock. The Riverside Stadium had been erected nearby ten years before; it resembled a forgotten-about ship in a dry dock, and it was hard to imagine it full of fans. The Riverside replaced the cosier-sounding former home of Middlesbrough FC, Ayresome Park, whose hollowed field fitted snugly into the housing grid. In 2006, Middlesbrough seemed to have turned its back on the river, as though not wanting to contemplate the scene of its former eminence.

Fifteen years later, a cautious rapprochement seemed to be underway in the district newly defined as Middlehaven (a name very redolent of PR). The Riverside Stadium had been joined by the enormous Middlesbrough College, a further education college, which is also somewhat ship-like, but in a more uplifting way than the football ground, by virtue of its graceful lines and steel casing. The tyres had gone, replaced in 2010 by a sculpture created in steel wires by Anish Kapoor that resembles a giant fishing keep net or windsock. It's called Temenos, which means 'land cut off and assigned as a sanctuary or holy area'.

The clocktower looked cleaner than before, but the three-faceted clock still wasn't working (the side facing the river was left blank in case workmen on the waterside should 'clock watch'), and the square of water was still unclaimed, although possibly a little less black than before. To the west lay a complex resembling a giant chemistry set, so I think it was another chemical works, of which there are several in Middlesbrough. I thought I remembered it from last time. Aside from the drivers of dusty lorries that periodically rattled by along the riverside road, there were few people in sight. I eventually spotted a man in a high-vis jacket supervising an area of apparent nothingness. As I walked up to him, he looked evasively sidelong, obviously hoping I wouldn't address him; but I did. 'Is that a chemical works?' I wondered.

'Sorry, not sure,' he said.

A student was approaching from the direction of the

college. I walked up to her and said, 'Excuse me, is that a chemical works?'

'Ah,' she said, smiling. 'You've got me there. It *looks* like a chemical works, doesn't it?'

'Mind if I ask you another question?' I said.

'Go for it,' she said, in that pleasantly lilting Middlesbrough accent that's almost Geordie.

'What county do you consider Middlesbrough to be in?'

It could have been construed as a patronising question, but with the laid-back amiability that characterises Middlesbrough to an even greater extent than most Northern towns, she responded gamely, 'Teesside? Or maybe Cleveland?'

In fact, having been in Cleveland between 1974 and 1996, Middlesbrough is back in Yorkshire – at least in the sense of being a unitary district in the ceremonial county of North Yorkshire, which is surely good enough for Yorkshireness, since that's exactly what York is.

I began walking along the river. On both the Middlesbrough side and on the north side were some anonymous, boxy buildings, with empty spaces in-between. I came to a sort of compound full of cars that seemed to have been (a) scrapped and (b) burnt out. I walked up to a man who was painting a wall.

'Is that a chemical works over there?'

'I'm pretty sure it is, yes.'

'What are *these* places?' I said, indicating the boxy buildings.

'I think mainly warehouses.'

'And what's *this*?' I said, indicated the building whose wall he was painting.

'An engineering firm – makes equipment for plastic injection moulding.'

It was a relief to come across some definite activity, even if I didn't understand the nature of that activity. The man said, 'Have you had a look along the river?' and, still holding his paint brush, he crossed the road with me, and we walked to a small garden or 'viewing area'. He waved in the general direction of the college. 'That's been important for the area; and we *were* going to get a snow dome, but that's been knocked on the head.' At the water's edge was a railing with some wilting flowers tied to it. 'Somebody threw themselves in,' the man said, and I managed to resist the obvious response: 'I can see why.' To one side of us on the water was a police launch. On the other side, a rotting wooden jetty led to a rotting wooden boat. Beyond the police launch was the Middlesbrough Transporter Bridge, which looks like two blue cranes reaching across the river from either bank with the tips of their jibs touching. Actually, the Transporter Bridge is one unit, by which a platform or gondola (with vehicles or people on it) is transferred from one bank to the other. The gondola dangles down from the 'jibs', which are very high to allow big boats or ships to pass below. The scale of the bridge, which opened in 1911, has made it a symbol of Middlesbrough. In 1919, it carried five million people, mainly iron and steel workers; for the past couple of years, it has not been in use.

'Most of the stuff's up-river,' said the man, and certainly there came great reverberating clangs from that direction. I asked whether that 'stuff' included any iron- or steelmaking.

'In Middlesbrough itself?' he said. 'I don't think so. That all went thirty or forty years ago.'

I asked the man whether he considered that Middlesbrough really was 'moving forward' (and by now we'd walked back to the wall, where he'd resumed his painting)?

'Oh, yes, definitely. Things are looking better than they have for years.'

From where I stood, with the static Transporter Bridge on one side, the burnt-out cars on the other and rain beginning to fall, it didn't look like it.

On the walk back to town I crossed a typically unfathomable field of rough grass and dandelions. Four teenagers were making a film. I walked over to them, and they explained that they were making a film to promote the Media Studies course at Middlesbrough College, where they were all students. I asked if they thought Middlesbrough was 'moving forward'.

'Course not,' one of them said. 'That's all propaganda.' They were all making university applications. One of them was eyeing Manchester, another Leeds. I asked what county they considered Middlesbrough to be in. Cue some shrugging of shoulders. One said, 'Cleveland', but it seemed fitting that the one hoping to go to Leeds University replied, 'I'd definitely say Yorkshire.'

I asked whether they found a sort of anti-glamour in Middlesbrough, such as young people found in the Sheffield of the 1980s, for instance. Heads were shaken. 'Nah,' said one of them. 'Middlesbrough doesn't work in that way.'

I drove away east, heading towards Redcar along the A66, passing the interminable Teesside Steelworks, which is both interminable and dead. The last surviving blast furnace is cold, and the whole site awaits demolition. Signs also indicated Wilton International, which stands on the site of the old ICI chemical works. I wondered whether it, like its predecessor, could be seen twinkling by nocturnal walkers on the North York Moors.

When I returned home, I had a Zoom chat with Dr Tosh Warwick, a historian of Middlesbrough who runs a heritage consultancy and is the author of *Central Middlesbrough*

Through Time, among other books. 'Until ten years ago', he said, 'the town *had* turned its back on the river, as if there was no longer any fondness for it, compared to, say the 1930s when people competed in swimming races on it.'

'But surely,' I objected, 'it was even dirtier back then?'

'Well, yes,' said Dr Warwick.

Today, according to Dr Warwick, the picture is different, despite what those students thought: 'Middlesbrough is being quite extensively regenerated.' He spoke of a big new manufacturing park, TeesAMP, which will accommodate the UK's first hydrogen transport centre; of a 'River Tees Rediscovered' project and a 'plan for a huge housing development' on the riverside. 'Middlesbrough is definitely on the up. There's been a shift change, a change in psyche.' Levelling-up money is coming through from the Johnson government, and Dr Warwick, with apologies for cynicism, suggested it's been useful in this respect that Middlesbrough – as part of Tees Valley – has a Metro Mayor who is a political independent, rather than Labour as you might expect. 'People talk about post-industrial, but Middlesbrough is still industrial. It's chemicals, engineering, transportation and digital industries.' When he mentioned a 'massive new chemical contract' for the Wilton International site, I asked if that still twinkled like ICI, when viewed from the Moors.

'I believe so, yes.'

True, the Middlesbrough Dock is gone, but there is Teesport, located downriver of the town; and although no iron or steel is made in Middlesbrough today, there is still a brass foundry.

As for the Yorkshire question, 'We haven't really been in Yorkshire since 1974,' said Dr Warwick, 'and we were never defined by a Yorkshire identity. The old ironmasters spoke of Teesside, and the coal came from Durham. It's only people over fifty-five that are bothered about the Yorkshire question.'

Well, that was me 'told', as they say in Yorkshire. At the time of writing, I'm fifty-eight; Dr Warwick is thirty-seven.

Beck Hole

A few weeks after speaking to Dr Warwick of Middlesbrough, I was back in Yorkshire – for a weekend jaunt and to take some photographs. I went first to York, where heavy traffic alerted me that this was a race day, which surprised me, since this was a Sunday. In my boyhood, horse racing wasn't allowed on Sundays, and this innovation, as it seemed to me (even though Sunday racing has been legal for thirty years), brought out the Sabbatarian in me, much though I love York races.

I parked on the edge of town and walked over the Knavesmire towards the course. It was a beautiful day; everyone was dressed up. The women walking towards the course kept stopping to smooth their skirts or adjust their hats. Some wore pumps, carrying their high-heeled shoes. As they neared the course, they stopped to swap shoes, putting the pumps in their handbags. As they approached the turnstiles you could see them walking in a different way, and not just on account of the heels. It was showtime. But not for me; I didn't go through the turnstiles. As I looked over the railings at the crowd, I speculated that I would have known a few people in there, but not many, and the number would be down again next year, and the year after that.

I went up to South Bank, the district of terraced houses that overlooks the racecourse, and I walked along to the house where I was born. There was a new front gate, and I knew this was a recent addition, since I'm afraid I have fallen into the habit of regularly checking out the property. The new gate wasn't as good as the old gate, which had been made by the brother of Dad's best friend. It was not as solid-looking; it incorporated unnecessary decorative embellishments and it was the wrong colour – green instead of red. It seemed a less Yorkshire sort of gate to me.

I was in a particularly retrospective mood. The remark of Dr Tosh Warwick about how young people in Middlesbrough aren't bothered about questions of Yorkshire identity had rankled with me, to the extent that I had been seeking to rebut it in my head ever since I spoke to him. In the first place, I told myself, Middlesbrough was a special case in Yorkshire terms, being on the brink of somewhere else. Then I fished out an email sent to me a few months beforehand from my brother-in-law, Peter, who runs a PR firm. In 2015, Peter had attended a Guardian Masterclass about publicity generation, given by someone from the news and entertainment website, Buzzfeed. 'Anything to do with regional identity is really popular,' the Buzzfeed man had said, citing a piece on Buzzfeed written called '57 Reasons Why Living in Yorkshire Ruins Your Life'. The title had been ironic, in that the reasons included things like 'Because the Hepworth Gallery in Wakefield is itself a work of art' and 'Because Yorkshire gets even more beautiful when it snows'. The piece – accompanied by scenic photographs – had gone viral in Yorkshire, and presumably not just among the Yorkshire elderly. Further reassurance had come a few weeks after I spoke to Dr Warwick in the form of a BBC News story of September 2021 headlined 'Why Scotland and Yorkshire are TV's Top UK Destinations.' The answer, apparently, is 'a yearning for stunning scenery, traditional lifestyles and down to earth personalities', a need, the article suggested, increased by Covid-related anxieties. Hence the success of all those television documentaries like *Yorkshire Firefighters*, *Jay's Yorkshire Workshop*, *The Yorkshire Vet*, *Our Yorkshire Farm* and *The Yorkshire Jobcentre*. I had watched only one of these programmes – and that for three minutes by accident – and their success doesn't alter my view that the voices of Yorkshire and the North are not so much heard in British culture as they were fifty years ago. But again: I'm sure the Yorkshireness of these programmes appeals across a range of ages.

I drove away from York before the start of the first race. I was heading in my default or reflex direction (the way I would go if ever on the run from the police, for example): to the coast via Pickering and the North York Moors. The Moors were particularly beautiful in late afternoon: green, gold and purple tones – a few very white clouds like floating sheep. And I always love driving over the Moors on the A159, which is like a switchback or Scalextric track, although of course I'm always mindful of the actual sheep. I turned left, taking the road for the sunken village of Beck Hole, one of my Yorkshire idylls. The final descent to Beck Hole was closed because of some works going on, so I parked on a verge and walked the last mile and a half, past woods and stony meadows. On the way down, you pass a colonial-looking house with foreign-looking trees in the garden: an idyll within an idyll. I saw a pretty, crimson moth on the top of a grey drystone wall, which struck me as a very Yorkshire conjunction of the fanciful and the utilitarian, and I was reminded that the ships used by Captain Cook on his voyages of exploration were nothing fancier than Whitby colliers.

In Beck Hole, that perfect little pub, the Birch Hall Inn,

was closed because of Covid, but it would apparently be opening soon, according to a sign on the window. The Murk Esk river flowed past the sleeping pub. Two women had lifted up their long white skirts to paddle in its greenish waters. 'Bloody 'ell, it's cold!' one of them called out to the other, as if she'd only just noticed, and here again was the Yorkshire conjunction, because you wouldn't have expected those words to come from the mouth of this small, well-dressed, Edwardian-looking woman.

Beck Hole is primarily a village green, with a few stone cottages pushed towards the edges, as though present on sufferance. One of them has a sign on its front saying, 'This is not the front door. The front door is around the back.' Now there, I thought, is a good instance of the daft, dreamy version of the Yorkshire tone. I began to hear the sound of a steam train – it would be the last one of the day on the North York Moors Railway. I couldn't see the train, the line being both higher than the village, and behind hills, but so vivid was the sound that I didn't need to. The train was putting on that 'performance in the landscape' Andrew Scott, chairman of the railway, had described to me, even though it was out of sight.

Halfway up the hill back to my car, I sat down on a bench. A farmer was coming up the hill, driving a mud-spattered buggy and towing a trailer on which sat a typically shrewd-looking border collie. The farmer nodded and smiled at me. Well, as John Shuttleworth says, 'It's nice up North.' About five minutes later, the farmer was coming back *down* the hill, and he nodded and smiled at me again. Now, in London that wouldn't have happened. Two strangers might nod to each other on a quiet road or footpath, but in London if you meet for a second time soon after, you're exempt from nodding again.

Walking back up to the car, I asked myself why I was noting these instances of Yorkshireness, and, as I rejoined the A169 to head back to London via Pickering and York, the answers came quickly. I was noticing Yorkshire things because, however important Yorkshire is or is not to the young people of the county, it's important to me. And it might be that any young person in Middlesbrough who doesn't think about Yorkshire very much just now might come to do so if they leave Yorkshire, as I did, especially if they move to London, because London is very different from Yorkshire. I'm sure that people who live in Yorkshire all the time don't go around noticing instances of Yorkshireness; it's the habit of an exile.

As the goldenness of the Moors increased, and the A169 seemed to become suddenly deserted except for myself, I became rather romantically interested in the idea that I was an exile. I wander through Yorkshire like a ghost, or perhaps like somebody trying to verify that what they remember really occurred in a real place and wasn't all a dream.

I began this book by fretting that, since I no longer lived in Yorkshire, I was not qualified to write it. I conclude with the thought that I would never have written it had I *not* left.

Quotation Permission and Acknowledgements

I am grateful to the following for providing quotation permissions: Granta, for some quotes from my article for *Granta 89: The Factory* (2005); the *Financial Times* for the quote from my article, 'Home Truths', which first appeared in the *Financial Times Magazine* on 2 June 2006 (© The Financial Times Limited 2006. All rights reserved); Short Books for the quote from my book, *Ghoul Britannia*; Mike Parker for the quote from his book, *The Wild Rover*, as amended for his 'Map Addict' blog of 1 August 2015; the *New Statesman* for permission to reprint my column about the Dales that appeared in the issue of 27 May 2002. The photograph of the author and his father at the National Railway Museum was taken by Dom McPhee for a *Guardian* article on 26th August 2006. (Don McPhee, *Guardian*, eyevine.) All other photographs are taken, or owned, by the author.

I would like to thank my editor at Corsair, James Gurbutt, for commissioning this book, even though he's from Essex, and Graham Coster for copy-editing it, even though he's from Croydon. I am also indebted to Stephen Chalke; Peter Freedman; Barry Forshaw; Dr David Fowler, ex of York; Eddie Lawler of Scarborough; Brenda Martin of York; Sue Martin of Knaresborough; John McGoldrick of the Leeds Industrial Museum; Jude Secombe, ex of Hull; Colin Speakman of the Yorkshire Society; Charles Turner of Sheffield; Malcolm and Edna Walker of York, and Paul Walker, ex of York; Dr Tosh Warwick of Middlesbrough; Paul Windust.

I first developed some of the themes in this book while writing a series of five talks about Yorkshire (first broadcast in January 2019) for the BBC Radio Three slot, 'The Essay'.

Bibliography of Quoted Sources

Simon Armitage, *All Points North*, Penguin, 2009

Rob Bagchi and Paul Rogerson, *The Unforgiven: The Story of Don Revie's Leeds United*, Aurum, updated, 2014

Paul Barker, *Hebden Bridge: a Sense of Belonging*, Frances Lincoln, 2012

Stan Barstow, *A Kind of Loving*, Michael Joseph, 1960

Stan Barstow, *The Watchers on the Shore*, Michael Joseph, 1966

Alan Bennett, *Writing Home*, Faber, 1994

Alan Bennett, *Untold Stories*, Faber and Profile, 2005

Alan Bennett, *Keeping on Keeping On*, Faber and Profile, 2016

Derek Birley, *A Social History of English Cricket*, Aurum, 1999

Michael Bradford, *The Fight for Yorkshire*, Hutton Press, 1988

John Braine, *Room at the Top*, Eyre & Spottiswoode, 1957

Anne Brontë, *Agnes Grey*, Thomas Cautley Newby, 1847

Charlotte Brontë, *Jane Eyre*, Thomas Cautley Newby, 1847

Emily Brontë, *Wuthering Heights*, Thomas Cautley Newby, 1847

A. S. Byatt, *Possession*, Chatto and Windus, 1990

Angela Carter, *Nothing Sacred: Selected Writings*, Virago, 1982

Stephen Chalke, *Summer's Crown: the Story of Cricket's County Championship*, Fairfield Books, 2015

Paul Chrystal, *Confectionery in Yorkshire Through Time*, Amberley Publishing, 2012

Paul Chrystal, *York in the 1970s*, Amberley Publishing, 2016

Anthony Clavane, *Moving the Goalposts: A Yorkshire Tragedy*, Riverrun, 2016

Ron Cooke, *Why York is Special*, York Civic Trust, 2006

Lettice Cooper, *National Provincial*, Gollancz, 1938

Peter Davidson, *The Idea of North*, Reaktion, 2005

Dan Davies, *In Plain Sight: The Life and Lies of Jimmy Savile*, Quercus, 2014

A. A. Dhand, *Streets of Darkness*, Bantam Press, 2016

Douglas Dunn (editor), *A Rumoured City: New Poets from Hull*, Bloodaxe, 1982

Antonia Evans (editor), *The York Book*, Blue Bridge, 2002

Michel Faber, *The Hundred and Ninety-Nine Steps*, Canongate, 2010

Graham Fellows, *Two Margarines and Other Domestic Dilemmas: John Shuttleworth's Guide to Everyday Life*, Omnibus Press, 2020

Elizabeth Gaskell, *The Life of Charlotte Brontë*, Smith, Elder and Co., 1857

A. B. Granville, *The Spas of England: Northern Spas*, Henry Colburn, 1841

Owen Hatherley, *A Guide to the New Ruins of Great Britain*, Verso, 2008

Roy Hattersley, *A Yorkshire Boyhood*, Chatto & Windus, 1983

Roy Hattersley, *Goodbye to Yorkshire*, Pan Books, 1991

Hannah Hauxwell (with Barry Cockroft), *Innocent Abroad: The Travels of Miss Hannah Hauxwell*, Century, 1991

Hannah Hauxwell (with Barry Cockroft), *Hannah's North Country*, Ted Smart, 1993

James Herriot, *If Only They Could Talk*, Michael Joseph, 1970

John Heywood, *Beside the Seaside: a History of Yorkshire's Seaside Resorts*, Pen and Sword, 2017

Barry Hines, *A Kestrel for a Knave*, 1968

Richard Hoggart, *The Uses of Literacy: Aspects of Working-Class Life*, Penguin, 1957

Winifred Holtby, *South Riding*, Collins & Co., 1936

Gordon Home, *Yorkshire Dales and Fells*, A & C Black, 1906

Glyn Hughes, *Glyn Hughes' Yorkshire: Millstone Grit Revisited*, Hogarth Press, 1985

Ian Jack (editor), *Granta 89: The Factory*, Grove Press, 2005

Max Jaffa, *A Life on the Fiddle*, Hodder & Stoughton, 1991

Sam Jordison and Dan Kieran (editors), *The Idler Book of Crap Towns: the 50 Worst Places to Live in the UK*, Boxtree, 2003

David Joy (editor), *The Dalesman: A Celebration of Fifty Years*, Pelham Books, 1989

Marion Keighley, *Whitby Writers: Writers of Whitby and District 1867–1949*, Horne and Son, 1957

Philip Larkin, *Collected Poems*, Faber, 2003

Tom Laughton, *Pavilions by the Sea*, Quality Book Club, 1977

S. M. Lubbcock, *The Child in the Crystal*, Jonathan Cape, 1939

Stuart Maconie, *Pies and Prejudice: In Search of the North*, Ebury, 2008

Andrew Martin, *Ghoul Britannia*, Short Books, 2009

Andrew Martin, *Seats of London: A Field Guide to London Transport Moquette Patterns*, Safe Haven, 2019

Andrew Martin, *Steam Trains Today: Journeys Along Britain's Heritage Railways*, Profile, 2021

Lucasta Miller, *The Brontë Myth*, Vintage, 2002

Richard Morris, *Yorkshire: A Lyrical History of England's Greatest County*, Weidenfeld & Nicolson, 2018

John Morrison, *View From the Bridge*, Pennine Pens, 1998

Andrew Motion, *Philip Larkin: a Writer's Life*, Faber, 1993

Charles Nevin, *Lancashire, Where Women Die of Love*, Mainstream, 2004

George Orwell, *The Road to Wigan Pier*, Gollancz, 1936

Mike Parker, *The Wild Rover: A Blistering Journey Along Britain's Footpaths*, Collins, 2012

F. R. Pearson, *Charlotte Brontë on the East Yorkshire Coast*, East Yorkshire Local History Society, 1957

Lynn F. Pearson, *People's Palaces: Britain's Seaside Pleasure Buildings*, Joyland Books, 1991

Bryan Perrett, *A Sense of Style: A Brief History of the Grand Hotel, Scarborough*, Bryan Perrett, 1991

Walter Pickles, *Our Grimy Heritage*, Centaur Press, 1971

Sylvia Plath, *Selected Poems*, Faber, 1985

Michael Pocock, *York*, Dalesman Books, 1971

Ella Pontefract and Maria Hartley, *Yorkshire Tour*, J. M. Dent & Sons, 1939

J. B. Priestley, *English Journey*, William Heinemann, 1934

J. B. Priestley, *Bright Day*, William Heinemann, 1946

Stuart Rayner, *The War of the White Roses: Cricket's Civil War 1968–1986*, Pitch Publishing, 2016

Herbert Read (editor), *Writers on Themselves*, (including 'The Rock' by Ted Hughes), BBC Books, 1964

Sunjeev Sahota, *The Year of the Runaways*, Picador, 2016

Michael T. Saler, *The Avant-Garde in Interwar England: Medieval Modernism and the London Underground*, Oxford University Press, 1999

Harry J. Scott, *Portrait of Yorkshire*, Robert Hale, 1965

Alan Sillitoe, *The Loneliness of the Long-Distance Runner*, W. H. Allen, 1959

Jack Simmons and Gordon Biddle (editors), *The Oxford Companion to British Railway History*, Oxford University Press, 1997

Osbert Sitwell, *Triple Fugue*, Grant Richards, 1924

Colin Speakman, *Walk! A Celebration of Striding Out*, Great Northern Books, 2011

Fleur and Colin Speakman, *The Yorkshire Wolds, A Journey of Discovery*, Gritstone Publishing, 2017

Bram Stoker, *Dracula*, Archibald Constable and Company, 1897

David Storey, *This Sporting Life*, Longman's, 1960

J. D. Taylor, *Island Story: Journeys Through Unfamiliar Britain*, Repeater Books, 2016

Laura Thompson, *Agatha Christie, An English Mystery*, Headline, 2007

Jonathan Tulloch, *Larkinland*, Seren, 2017

Andrew Vine, *Yorkshire Coast Path*, Safe Haven, 2019

Philip Waller, *Town, City and Nation: England 1850–1914*, Oxford University Press, 1983

Leo Walmsley, *Three Fevers*, Jonathan Cape, 1932

Keith Waterhouse, *Billy Liar*, Michael Joseph, 1959

Keith Waterhouse, *City Lights*, Hodder & Stoughton, 1994

Karl Whitney, *Hit Factory: A Journey Through the Industrial Cities of British Pop*, Orion, 2019

Nicholas Whittaker, *Sweet Talk: The Secret History of Confectionery*, Victor Gollancz, 1998

Walter Wilkinson, *Puppets in Yorkshire*, Geoffrey Bles, 1931

Recommended Reading
(Books I've not quoted from, but which are instructive about Yorkshire)

Simon Armitage, *Paper Aeroplane: Selected Poems 1989–2014*, Faber & Faber, 2014

J. L. Carr, *A Month in the Country*, Harvester Press, 1980

Lettice Cooper, *National Provincial*, Gollancz, 1938

Margaret Drabble, *The Radiant Way*, Penguin, 1987

Douglas Dunn (editor), *A Rumoured City: New Poets From Hull*, Bloodaxe Books Ltd, 1982

Philip Hensher, *The Northern Clemency*, HarperCollins, 2008

Susan Hill, *A Change for the Better*, Penguin, 1969

Ted Hughes, *New Selected Poems 1957–1994*, Faber & Faber, 1995

Arnold Kellett, *The Yorkshire Dictionary of Dialect, Tradition and Folklore*, Smith Settle, 1994

Ian McMillan, *Neither Nowt Nor Summat: The Meaning of Yorkshire*, Ebury, 2014

Harland Miller, *Slow Down Arthur, Stick to Thirty*, Fourth Estate, 2001

Hugh Murray, *A Directory of York Pubs 1455–2003*, Voyager Publications, 2003

David Peace, *The Damned United,* Faber & Faber, 2007
J. B. Priestley, *The Good Companions*, William Heinemann, 1929